ASPEN PUBLISHERS

S0-BBV-435

PROPERTY

5TH EDITION

NEIL C. BLOND
YORAM CHEN
JOHN MARAFINO

Wolters Kluwer
Law & Business

AUSTIN   BOSTON   CHICAGO   NEW YORK   THE NETHERLANDS

To contact Customer Care, e-mail customer.care@aspenpublishers.com, call 1-800-234-1660, fax 1-800-901-9075, or mail correspondence to:

Aspen Publishers
Attn: Order Department
PO Box 990
Frederick, MD 21705

Printed in the United States of America.
1 2 3 4 5 6 7 8 9 0

ISBN 978-0-7355-8617-8

About Wolters Kluwer Law & Business

Wolters Kluwer Law & Business is a leading provider of research information and workflow solutions in key specialty areas. The strengths of the individual brands of Aspen Publishers, CCH, Kluwer Law International and Loislaw are aligned within Wolters Kluwer Law & Business to provide comprehensive, in-depth solutions and expert-authored content for the legal, professional and education markets.

CCH was founded in 1913 and has served more than four generations of business professionals and their clients. The CCH products in the Wolters Kluwer Law & Business group are highly regarded electronic and print resources for legal, securities, antitrust and trade regulation, government contracting, banking, pension, payroll, employment and labor, and healthcare reimbursement and compliance professionals.

Aspen Publishers is a leading information provider for attorneys, business professionals and law students. Written by preeminent authorities, Aspen products offer analytical and practical information in a range of specialty practice areas from securities law and intellectual property to mergers and acquisitions and pension/benefits. Aspen's trusted legal education resources provide professors and students with high-quality, up-to-date and effective resources for successful instruction and study in all areas of the law.

Kluwer Law International supplies the global business community with comprehensive English-language international legal information. Legal practitioners, corporate counsel and business executives around the world rely on the Kluwer Law International journals, loose-leafs, books and electronic products for authoritative information in many areas of international legal practice.

Loislaw is a premier provider of digitized legal content to small law firm practitioners of various specializations. Loislaw provides attorneys with the ability to quickly and efficiently find the necessary legal information they need, when and where they need it, by facilitating access to primary law as well as state-specific law, records, forms and treatises.

Wolters Kluwer Law & Business, a unit of Wolters Kluwer, is headquartered in New York and Riverwoods, Illinois. Wolters Kluwer is a leading multinational publisher and information services company.

Law school is very different from your previous educational experiences. In the past, course material was presented in a straightforward manner both in lectures and texts. You did well by memorizing and regurgitating. In law school, your fat casebooks are stuffed with material, most of which will be useless when finals arrive. Your professors ask a lot of questions, but don't seem to be teaching you either the law or how to think. Sifting through voluminous material seeking out the important concepts is a hard, time-consuming chore. We've done that job for you. This book will help you study effectively. We hope to teach you the law and how to think.

Preparing for Class

Most students start their first year by reading and briefing all their cases. They spend too much time copying unimportant details. After finals they realize they wasted time on facts that were useless on the exam.

Case Clips

Case Clips help you focus on what your professor wants you to get out of your cases. Facts, Issues, and Rules are carefully and succinctly stated. Left out are details irrelevant to what you need to learn from the case. In general, we skip procedural matters in lower courts. We don't care which party is the appellant or petitioner because the trivia is not relevant to the law. Case Clips should be read before you read the actual case. You will have a good idea what to look for in the case, and appreciate the significance of what you are reading. Inevitably you will not have time to read all your cases before class. Case Clips allow you to prepare for class in about five minutes. You will be able to follow the discussion and listen without fear of being called on.

"Should I read all the cases even if they aren't from my casebook?"

Yes, if you feel you have the time. Most major cases from other texts will be covered at least as a note case in your book. The principles of these cases are universal and the fact patterns should help your understanding. The Case Clips are written in a way that should provide a tremendous amount of understanding in a relatively short period of time.

EasyFlow™ Charts

A very common complaint among law students is that they "can't put it all together." When you are reading 400 pages a week it is difficult to

remember how the last case relates to the first and how November's read-
ings relate to September's. It's hard to understand the relationship between
different torts topics when you have read cases for three or four other
classes in between. Our EasyFlow™ Charts will help you put the whole
course together. They are designed to help you memorize fundamentals.
They reinforce your learning by showing you the material from another
perspective.

Outlines

More than 100 lawyers and law students were interviewed as part of the
development of this series. Most complained that their casebooks did not
teach them the law and were far too voluminous to be useful before an
exam. They also told us that the commercial outlines they purchased were
excellent when used as hornbooks to explain the law, but were too wordy
and redundant to be effective during the weeks before finals. Few students
can read four 500-page outlines during the last month of classes. It is
virtually impossible to memorize that much material and even harder to
decide what is important. Almost every student interviewed said he or she
studied from homemade outlines. We've written the outline you should
use to study.

"But writing my own outline will be a learning experience."

True, but unfortunately many students spend so much time outlining
they don't leave time to learn and memorize. Many students told us they
spent six weeks outlining, and only one day studying before each final!

Mnemonics

Most law students spend too much time reading, and not enough time
memorizing. Mnemonics are included to help you organize your essays
and spot issues. They highlight what is important and which areas deserve
your time.

CONTENTS

EASYFLOW™ CHARTS

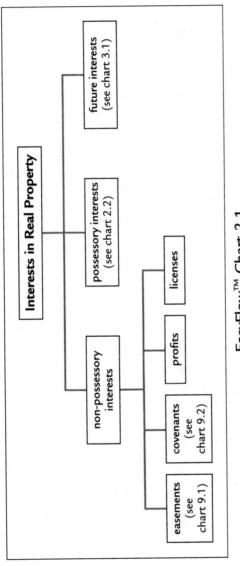

EasyFlow™ Chart 2.1

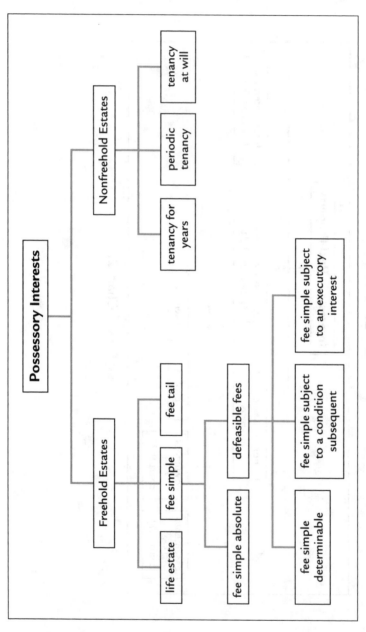

EasyFlow™ Chart 2.2

Freehold Estates

ESTATES	FEE SIMPLE ABSOLUTE	FEE SIMPLE DETERMINABLE	FEE SIMPLE SUBJECT TO A CONDITION SUBSEQUENT	FEE SIMPLE SUBJECT TO AN EXECUTORY INTEREST	FEE TAIL	LIFE ESTATE
EXAMPLES OF CREATION	"to A," "to A and his heirs"	"so long as," "until," "while"	"but if used for"	"so long as," "until," "while"	"to A and the heirs of A's body"	"to A for life"
DURATION	indefinite	until condition is broken	until condition is broken and grantor re-enters	until specified event occurs	indefinite, passed to heirs	until death of the measuring life
MODERN APPLICABILITY	created without specific language	wording must be explicit	wording must be explicit	wording must be explicit	abolished	effective
ALIENABILITY	freely alienable	freely alienable subject to the condition	freely alienable subject to the condition	freely alienable subject to the condition	none	grantee may transfer his rights, but property reverts to grantor at grantee's death
FUTURE INTEREST IN:		grantor	grantor	third party		grantor or third party

EasyFlow™ Chart 2.3

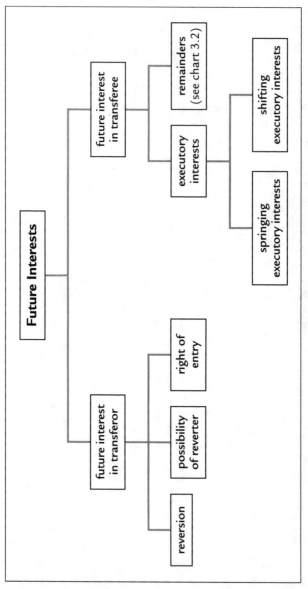

EasyFlow™ Chart 3.1

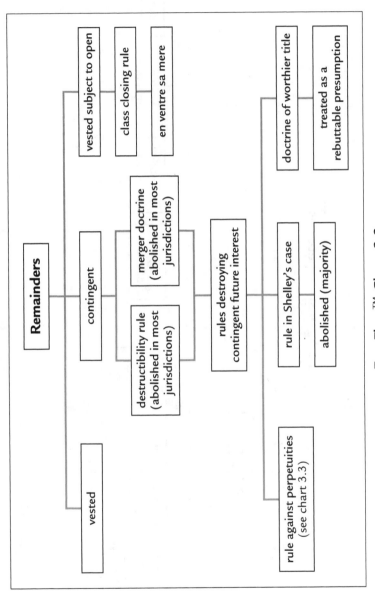

EasyFlow™ Chart 3.2

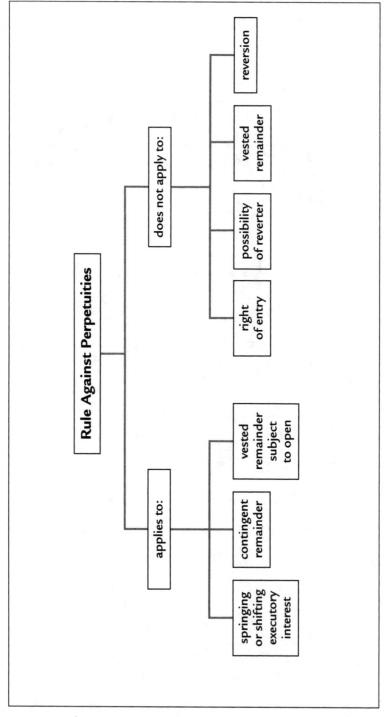

EasyFlow™ Chart 3.3

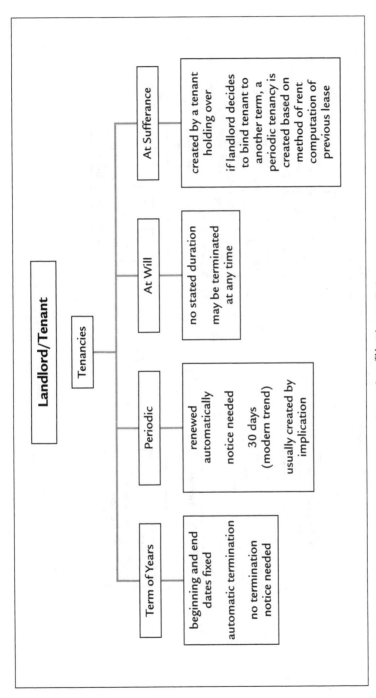

EasyFlow™ Chart 5.1

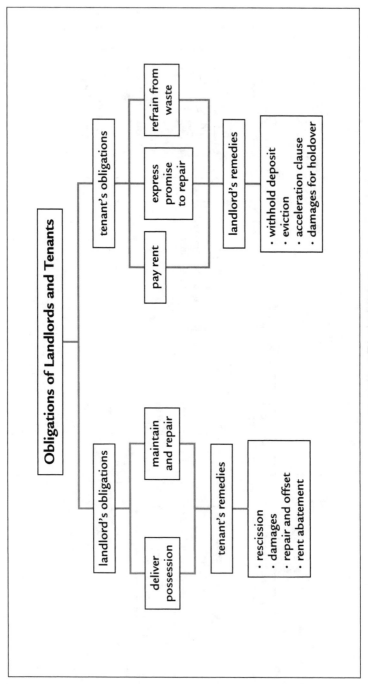

EasyFlow™ Chart 5.2

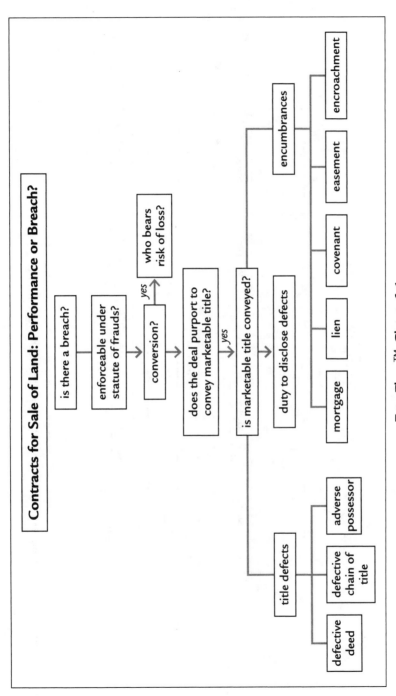

Contracts for Sale of Land: Performance or Breach?

is there a breach?

enforceable under statute of frauds?

conversion?

yes → who bears risk of loss?

does the deal purport to convey marketable title?

yes → is marketable title conveyed?

title defects
- defective deed
- defective chain of title
- adverse possessor

duty to disclose defects

encumbrances
- mortgage
- lien
- covenant
- easement
- encroachment

EasyFlow™ Chart 6.1

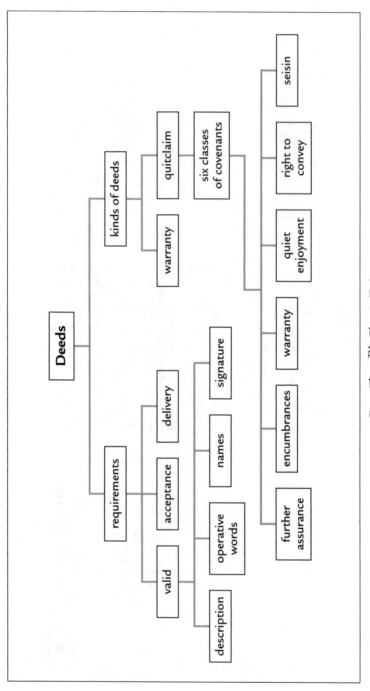

EasyFlow™ Chart 7.1

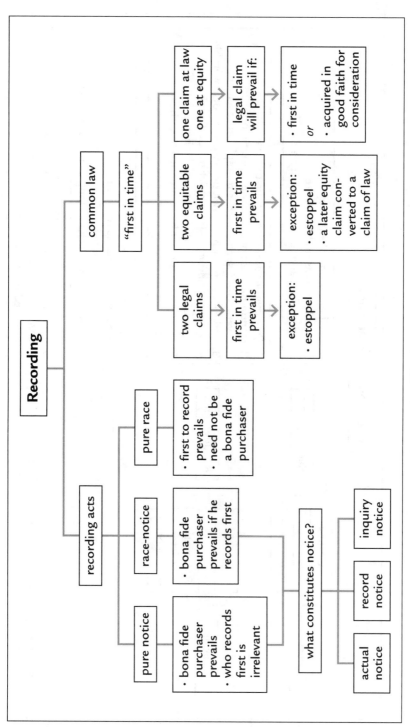

EasyFlow™ Chart 7.2

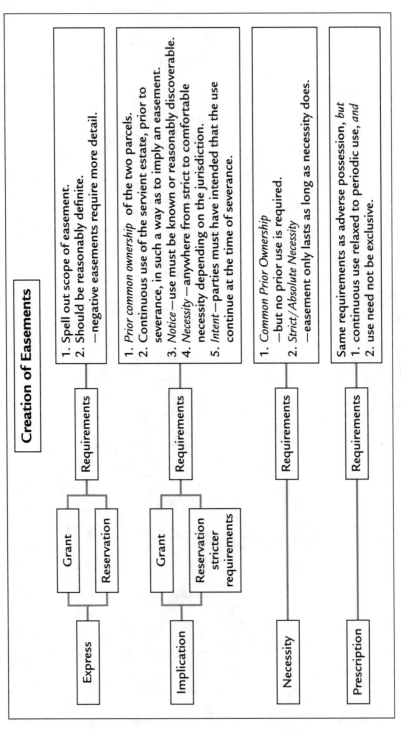

Creation of Easements

Express → Requirements → **Grant** / **Reservation**

1. Spell out scope of easement.
2. Should be reasonably definite.
   — negative easements require more detail.

Implication → Requirements → **Grant** / **Reservation stricter requirements**

1. *Prior common ownership* of the two parcels.
2. Continuous use of the servient estate, prior to severance, in such a way as to imply an easement.
3. *Notice* — use must be known or reasonably discoverable.
4. *Necessity* — anywhere from strict to comfortable necessity depending on the jurisdiction.
5. *Intent* — parties must have intended that the use continue at the time of severance.

Necessity → Requirements

1. *Common Prior Ownership*
   — but no prior use is required.
2. *Strict/Absolute Necessity*
   — easement only lasts as long as necessity does.

Prescription → Requirements

Same requirements as adverse possession, *but*
1. continuous use relaxed to periodic use, *and*
2. use need not be exclusive.

EasyFlow™ Chart 9.1

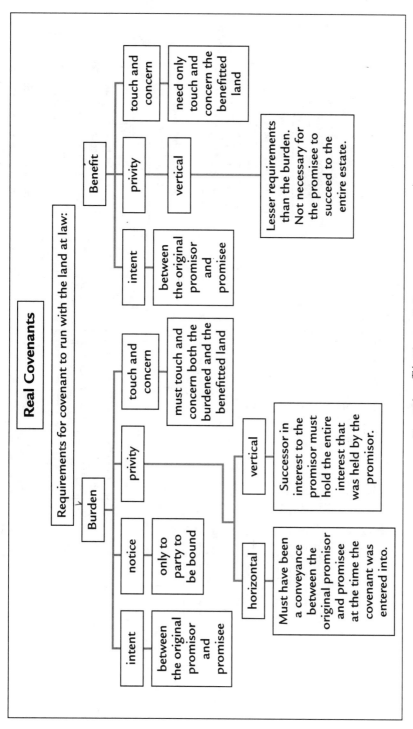

EasyFlow™ Chart 9.2

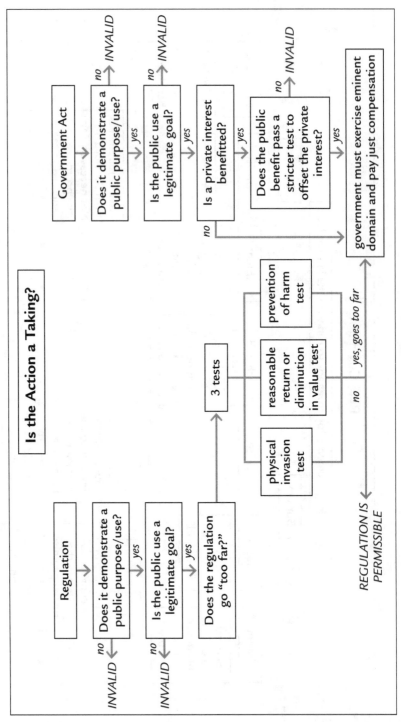

EasyFlow™ Chart 10.1

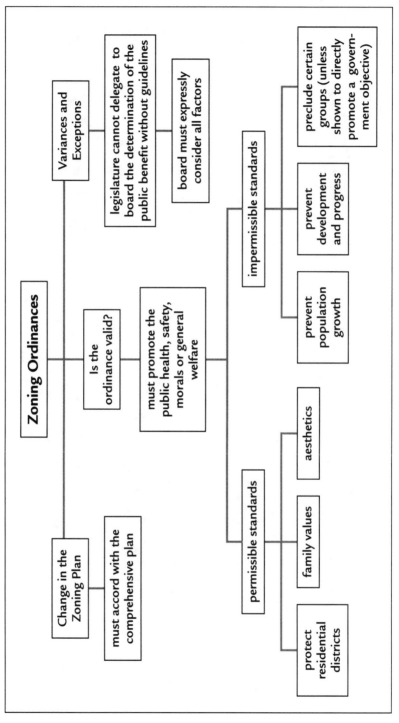

Zoning Ordinances

Is the ordinance valid?

Change in the Zoning Plan
- must accord with the comprehensive plan

must promote the public health, safety, morals or general welfare

permissible standards
- protect residential districts
- family values
- aesthetics

impermissible standards
- prevent population growth
- prevent development and progress
- preclude certain groups (unless shown to directly promote a government objective)

Variances and Exceptions
- legislature cannot delegate to board the determination of the public benefit without guidelines
- board must expressly consider all factors

EasyFlow™ Chart 10.2

Rights in Personal Property

I. CAPTURE

A. An individual obtains a property right, possession, and ownership, in a wild animal by "so trapping, wounding or ensnaring so as to deprive it of its natural liberty."
   1. Actual physical possession is not necessary for capture.
   2. Mortal wounding or trapping a wild animal constitutes capture provided the hunter pursues the wounded/trapped animal.
   3. However, mere pursuit of a wild animal does not create a property right.
B. A property owner has the exclusive right to reduce wild animals to possession while the animal is on his or her land. Thus, if a trespasser captures an animal on the land of another, the landowner can bring an action for the return of the animal (replevin) or for its value (conversion) against the interloper.
C. The owner of a captured animal loses his or her property right in the animal if the animal escapes and returns to its natural state.
D. However, the captor retains a property right in a tamed or domesticated animal that escapes if it has the propensity to return.
E. Animals that are not indigenous to the area are excluded from the law of capture, because a potential captor should be on notice that another has a property right in the exotic animal.

II. LOST, MISLAID, AND ABANDONED PROPERTY AND TREASURE TROVE

A. Property is regarded as **lost** when a person in possession of a chattel involuntarily and accidentally parts with possession.
B. Property is regarded as **mislaid** when the person in possession of a chattel intentionally places the chattel in a particular place, but

does not retrieve it. The assumption is that the individual has "forgotten" about the property.

C. Property is regarded as **abandoned** when the person in possession of a chattel intentionally and voluntarily relinquishes both ownership and possession.

D. Unclaimed gold, silver, currency, etc. intentionally concealed or buried by an unknown owner is classified as **treasure trove**.

E. Regardless of the characterization of the property in A through D above, a finder has a right to possession of a found chattel. That right, however, may be subject to those of others depending on the characterization of the property.

F. A finder of lost property has a right against all other possessors except the rightful owner and prior possessors who may have lost the property. According a finder a right in found property subject to the paramount right in the rightful owner encourages honesty and the return of the property to the person who likely values it most highly: the rightful owner. Finders are keepers unless a prior possessor or rightful owner is not located.

G. There is a clash of interests when property is found on the land of another, the *locus in quo*. A finder's right to a lost chattel found when the finder was on another's property with consent (express or implied) is generally superior to that of the property's owner.

   1. If one finds a chattel on private premises open to the public (e.g., the public area of a shop), the finder's possessory rights are superior to all except the rightful owner.

   2. If a chattel is found in a private portion of a landowner's premises, the landowner (not the finder) acquires a possessory right to the chattel.

   3. Trespassers are generally not accorded the right of a finder unless the trespass is technical and not undertaken in bad faith, that is, either to commit a crime or look for lost objects. As against trespassers, the law regards an owner of the locus as in constructive possession of all property on the land.

H. The law generally does not accord a finder a priority over the owner of the *locus* in cases in which property is regarded as mislaid. The owner of the property where a mislaid chattel is found acquires a possessory right to the chattel that is superior to all but the rightful owner.

I. The finder of abandoned property is usually accorded similar rights as the finder of lost property.

J. In the rare cases in which property is regarded as treasure trove, rights are generally accorded to the owner of the *locus*. In Britain, treasure trove belongs to the Crown.

K. Thus, how the court classifies the property — lost, mislaid, abandoned, or treasure trove — determines whether the superior property right is in the finder or the owner of the locus.

L. The holder of found property is treated like a bailee. The possessor must exercise due care toward a lost or mislaid chattel in his custody. If he or she knows, or can reasonably ascertain, a rightful owner's identity, the law creates a duty to do so. A breach of this duty is grounds for a charge of larceny and an action for conversion.

M. Every jurisdiction has a statute of limitations prescribing the period during which the rightful owner must bring suit to recover possession of a lost or mislaid chattel. (See Adverse Possession of Real Property, Chapter 2, below.) Modern courts tend to depart from the rule applying adverse possession to chattels and apply the *discovery rule*, which dictates that a rightful owner's cause of action accrues when he knew, or reasonably should have known through the exercise of due diligence the location or the identity of the possessor.

N. Statutory reform has had an impact in the law of finders, but the changes are by no means uniform amongst the jurisdictions. Most jurisdictions have enacted statutes which create an obligation in the finder of a lost chattel to turn it over to the proper authorities. If the chattel is unclaimed after a certain amount of time, the finder is accorded the rights of a rightful owner.

III. BAILMENTS

A. Definition
   A bailment is a temporary transfer of the right to possess property from the owner (bailor) to the bailee.
   1. A contract is not essential to creating a bailment.
   2. To constitute a bailment, the bailee must:
      a. have physical control of the property;
      b. intend to assume custody of the property; and
      c. consent to the bailment.
   3. Even if the bailee lacks an intent to assume custody of property, a constructive or involuntary bailment may arise. Thus, a finder or proprietor of a business establishment is a bailee of an umbrella left behind at his or her establishment.

B. Bailee's Rights and Duties
   1. A bailee has a right to possession superior to all, except the rightful owner or possessors who hand over the property to the bailee. The bailee can maintain a suit against third parties interfering with his possession.
   2. Absent a contrary agreement, a bailee has no right to use the bailed goods. Any intentional unauthorized use resulting in loss

makes the bailee absolutely liable. Incidental use essential to the performance of the bailee's duty is permitted.

3. The bailee must redeliver the property to the bailor at the termination of the bailment. A bailee is strictly liable for mis-delivery of the bailed property. Constructive bailees are liable only for negligent mis-delivery. If the bailee either refuses to return the property or departs without authorization from the terms of the bailment, strict liability attaches.

4. If a bailee's use of the bailed property harms a third party, the bailee (not the bailor) is liable due to his possession and control of the property.

5. Although not an insurer, the bailee owes a duty of care regarding the treatment of the bailed property. The standard of care turns on who is benefited by the bailment.

   a. If the bailment solely benefits the bailor, the bailee is liable only if he is grossly negligent.

   b. If the bailment is mutually beneficial, the bailee must exercise ordinary due care.

   c. If the bailment solely benefits the bailee, the bailee must exercise extraordinary care.

IV. GIFTS

A. A gift is a gratuitous transfer of property. It can transpire *inter vivos* from a living person or testamentary upon the death of a person.

B. Valid gifts require:

   1. Donative intent.

   2. Delivery — the physical transfer of the gift — or its constructive delivery — a manifestation by the owner to transfer of property that cannot easily be handed over.

C. Gifts are absolute and unconditional transfers, although the *gift causa mortis* is an exception, where the owner makes the gift on her deathbed and in contemplation of death, but recovers.

V. CREATION

A. The Constitution (Article 1, sec. 7, cl. 7) accords powers to the Congress to "promote the progress of science and the useful arts by securing for limited times to authors and inventors the exclusive right to their writings and discoveries."

B. Congress has adopted numerous statutes governing copyright of literary, musical, graphical, and architectural works. In general, the author has the right to exclusive use for 70 years after the death of the author.

1. After the period has expired, the property enters the public domain.
2. During the period of copyright protection, others may comment on, criticize, or otherwise use the work for the purposes of teaching, research, or scholarship, under the "fair use" doctrine.
3. The expression of ideas and not ideas themselves may be the subject of copyright.
4. Only works that contain a "creative spark" may be protected.

C. New and useful inventions are subject to patent protection.
1. The inventor must apply to the patent office, which will determine the novelty and the utility of the invention. Protection normally lasts for 17 years, after which time the process or device enters the public domain.
2. Ideas may not be copyrighted, though products and processes may be protected.

D. Trademark law protects names or images that individuals or businesses use to identify their products. Federal law allows trademarks to be registered, and its holder may prevent others from using the name or mark. The thrust of trademark law is to avoid consumer confusion.

E. A right of publicity is accorded by state common law in some jurisdictions to those individuals who commercially exploit their name and likeness. Others cannot use their "name and likeness" without permission.

F. Although dealing with land, the doctrine of "discovery" bears some relation to "creation" of intellectual property. The classic case of *Johnson v. McIntosh* considers whether Europeans could receive rights in property by transfer from Native Americans. The Supreme Court recognized that while they may have had occupancy of the land, they did not have ownership. Ownership in American land could be derived only from Europeans who held grants from the Crown, whose ownership right was derived from first discovery.

CASE CLIPS

I. Capture

Pierson v. Post (1805)

Facts: The plaintiff, Lodowick Post, brought an action against Pierson for killing a fox that Post himself was pursuing and about to capture.
Issue: What acts are required to acquire ownership of a wild animal?
Rule: Mere pursuit of a wild animal confers no property right to the animal. The pursuer must deprive the animal of its natural liberty by wounding, ensnaring, or otherwise subjecting it to his control.

Keeble v. Hickeringill (1707)

Facts: The plaintiff owned a pond to which he attracted ducks with decoys so as to kill and bring them to market. By discharging guns nearby, the defendant purposefully scared the fowl away.
Issue: Does an action for damages lie against one who purposely scares away wild animals that another has induced to come to his property so as to capture for market?
Rule: An action lies in all cases in which a violent or malicious act is done to a person's occupation, profession, or way of getting a livelihood.
Note: This rule is inconsistent with the rule announced in *Pierson v. Post* (above) and no longer represents valid law.

Young v. Hichens (1844)

Facts: Young had placed a net almost completely around a shoal of fish when Hichens interfered with the operation and captured the fish for himself. Young brought a suit for trespass.
Issue: Can one acquire a property interest in a wild animal without reducing it to possession?
Rule: Until a party takes actual possession of a wild animal, he has no property interest in it.

Ghen v. Rich (1881)

Facts: The plaintiff (libelant) brought suit to recover the market value of a whale that his ship had harpooned. The defendant (respondent) had purchased the whale from a third party that found it washed up on the beach. According to the local custom of the Massachusetts coastal whaling trade, one who harpooned a whale acquired an ownership interest in it, vis-à-vis any finder of the dead whale. Unique markings were used on the harpoons of each whaling vessel for identification purposes.

Issue: Is it possible to acquire a property right in a wild animal without actually reducing it to possession and control?

Rule: Where one undertakes the only act of appropriation that is possible in the nature of the case, and otherwise does all that is possible to make the animal his own, he acquires a property right in the wild animal.

Glave v. Michigan Terminix Co. (1987)

Facts: Peggy Glave alleged that the defendants' act of chasing away pigeons from certain city buildings caused the birds to flock to her property and thereby caused her to contract an infection.

Issue: Under what circumstances can a defendant be held responsible for the actions of ferae naturae (wild animals)?

Rule: Individuals can be held liable for the actions of wild animals only if they have asserted dominion over them in the form of taming or confinement, and have not later relinquished this control.

Hammonds v. Central Kentucky Natural Gas Co. (1934)

Facts: After legally extracting gas from a natural underground field, the defendant refilled it with gas brought in from other fields. A small portion of the field was located under the plaintiff's land, and she brought an action for trespass, charging that the gas was placed there without her knowledge or permission.

Issue: How does the migratory nature of oil and gas affect the property rights associated with their extraction?

Rule: Generally, oil and gas do not belong to anyone until captured and reduced to possession, and only the owner of the property directly under which these resources lie has the right to extract them. However, by analogy to wild animals, if the oil or gas is captured and then escapes or is released, all ownership interest is destroyed.

II. Finders

Armory v. Delamirie (1722)

Facts: The plaintiff found a jewel and brought it to a jeweler for appraisal. The jeweler's apprentice removed the stones from the jewel, and the plaintiff brought an action for money damages.

Issue: What is the nature of the title held by the finder of a chattel?

Rule: The finder of a lost chattel has superior title in the chattel as against everyone but the rightful owner.

Bridges v. Hawkesworth (1851)

Facts: Bridges found bank notes lying on the floor of the defendant's shop, which he requested the defendant hold until the rightful owner claimed them. Three years later, the defendant refused to return the still-unclaimed notes to Bridges.

Issue: When a chattel is found in the public area of a shop, does the shop owner or the finder acquire a property right in it?

Rule: Because not intentionally left behind, a chattel lost in a public shop is not within the shop owner's custody. Consequently, the finder of an article lost in a public shop is entitled to possession of it as against all parties except the true owner.

South Staffordshire Water Co. v. Sharman (1896)

Facts: The defendant found two rings on the property of the plaintiff while in the process of cleaning out the plaintiff's pool. The plaintiff brought suit to regain possession of the rings.

Issue: Does the finder of lost property or the owner of the land on which it is found acquire a right to possess the property?

Rule: The owner of the land on which the lost property is found acquires a superior possessory interest to that of the finder if the owner exercises actual control over the locus in quo (the land) and the things on it.

Hannah v. Peel (1945)

Facts: The plaintiff found a brooch in a house owned by the defendant but never occupied by him.

Issue: Does the finder of a lost chattel have a superior claim to possess the chattel than the owner of the freehold on which it was found?

Rule: Where the owner of the freehold was never physically in possession of the premises, the finder of a chattel lost on the freehold has a superior claim to the chattel.

McAvoy v. Medina (1866)

Facts: The plaintiff, a customer in the defendant's barbershop, found a pocketbook accidentally left behind by one of the defendant's prior patrons.

Issue: Does the lost-mislaid distinction play a part in determining ownership of a chattel found by one person on premises owned by another?

Rule: In a case in which the court finds that the chattel has been mislaid (inadvertently forgotten), the owner of the premises is awarded possession. However, property that is lost goes to the finder.

Schley v. Couch (1955)

Facts: The plaintiff found money buried in a glass jar on Schley's property.

Issue: In jurisdictions not recognizing the treasure trove doctrine, does the finder of buried money or the owner of the property on which it is found acquire a possessory right in the money?

Rule: Money found embedded in soil under circumstances repelling the idea that it was involuntarily parted with through inadvertence constitutes a mislaid chattel to which the owner of the property acquires a possessory interest, good against all but the true owner. However, when it appears that the true owner involuntarily parted with it through inadvertence, it is lost property and may be retained by the finder as against all but the true owner.

Goddard v. Winchell (1892)

Facts: Goddard claimed ownership of a meteorite that was found by a third party on Goddard's property and subsequently sold to the defendant without Goddard's knowledge.

Issue: Are natural deposits embedded in the soil considered lost or abandoned and thus the property of the finder?

Rule: Natural deposits on property become a part of the realty and are not lost or abandoned. Hence, they belong to the realty's owner.

Anderson v. Gouldberg (1892)

Facts: The plaintiffs wrongly removed timber from land that did not belong to them and brought it to a mill. The owner of the mill promptly appropriated the timber for himself.

Issue: Is bare possession of property, although obtained through improper means, a sufficient interest to enable the wrongdoer to maintain an action of replevin against another wrongdoer who subsequently takes the property from him?

Rule: One who has acquired possession of property, whether by finding, bailment, or even by tort, has a right to retain possession as against a wrongdoer who is a stranger to the property.

Ganter v. Kapiloff (1986)

Facts: The Kapiloff brothers owned valuable stamps and did not realize that they had lost them until they saw the stamps being advertised in a publication. The stamps were found by Ganter, with whom they had no relation. The Kapiloffs brought an action for replevin to obtain the return of the stamps.

Issue: Does the finder of lost property acquire absolute ownership of it?
Rule: The finder of lost property has a superior right to the property as against everyone *but* the true owner.

Favorite v. Miller (1978)

Facts: Miller found a piece of a 200-year-old statue of King George III buried on the plaintiff's property. He unearthed and removed the artifact without the plaintiff's permission and contracted to sell it to the Museum of the City of New York. Upon learning of the discovery, the plaintiff brought suit to regain possession of the valuable find.
Issue: May the finder of lost property retain possession of it, even if it was found by trespassing on another's land?
Rule: The finder of lost property on the land of another does not acquire a possessory interest in the property if it was buried in the ground or discovered by trespass. In these two instances, the owner of the land is entitled to possession of the property.

III. Bailments

Parking Management, Inc. v. Gilder (1975)

Facts: Gilder's car was vandalized while parked in the defendant's garage.
Issue: Does a commercial parking lot operator have an implied duty of reasonable care to protect a patron's car?
Rule: Where a patron reasonably expects that reasonable care will be exercised to prevent tampering with his car, an implied duty of reasonable care by the lot operator to protect the auto from theft or malicious mischief is created.

Shamrock Hilton Hotel v. Caranas (1972)

Facts: The Caranases, guests at the defendant hotel, lost a purse containing $13,000 in jewelry in the hotel dining room. A hotel employee found it and gave it to a superior, who mistakenly gave it to a stranger. The Caranases filed suit for negligent misdelivery of the purse.
Issue: To establish a bailment, must the bailor knowingly intend to entrust the property to the bailee?
Rule: A constructive bailment arises if it is apparent that the loser of the property was aware of the circumstances and would have expected the person finding the property to have kept it safely for its subsequent return to him.

Porter v. Wertz (1979)

Facts: Porter, the plaintiff, entrusted a Maurice Utrillo painting to Harold Von Maker (a con artist), hoping that the latter would buy the painting. Acting in concert with one Peter Wertz, a delicatessen employee, Von Maker sold the painting to an art dealer, Feigen, who subsequently sold it to Brenner. Ultimately the painting wound up in Venezuela, and Porter brought suit against all of the above-named actors.

Issue 1: May a rightful owner be statutorily estopped from recovering his stolen property from a subsequent purchaser for value based on UCC §2-403?

Rule 1: An owner will not be statutorily estopped from asserting his title against a person who is not "a buyer in the ordinary course of business," defined in UCC §1-201 as "a person who in good faith and without knowledge that the sale to him is in violation of the ownership rights or security interest of a third party in the goods buys in ordinary course from a person in the business of selling goods of that kind."

Issue 2: May an owner be equitably estopped from asserting his title against a bona fide purchaser for value?

Rule 2: If an owner invests another with the usual evidence of title or an apparent authority to dispose of his property, he will not be allowed to make a claim against an innocent purchaser dealing on the faith of such apparent ownership.

Peet v. Roth Hotel Co. (1934)

Facts: The Roth Hotel Co. lost a ring left with it by the plaintiff for delivery to a third party. The plaintiff sued to recover the value of the ring.

Issue 1: For there to be a valid bailment, must the bailor divulge the value of the property left with the bailee?

Rule 1: Even if he erroneously underestimates its value, a bailee is liable for the value of the property entrusted to his care when the identity of the property and all its attributes, except its value, are known to him.

Issue 2: Must a bailee exercise a degree of care commensurate to the hazard?

Rule 2: A bailee must exercise the degree of care that an ordinarily prudent person would have exercised in the same or similar circumstances.

Allen v. Hyatt Regency-Nashville Hotel (1984)

Facts: Allen parked his car in the defendant's garage, which had only one exit and was guarded by an attendant. He was not required to surrender his keys. The car was stolen, and Allen brought suit against the owners of the garage.

Issue: Is a commercial parking garage liable to a customer for the theft of a vehicle if it has only one exit and has attendants monitoring the exit?

Rule: A bailment is created when an owner leaves his vehicle in the custody of a parking garage with limited access, and where the patron must present a ticket to an attendant on leaving the premises. On proof of nondelivery, the patron is entitled to plead a presumption of negligence.

Cowen v. Pressprich (1922)

Facts: The plaintiffs delivered the wrong bond to the defendants. In an attempt to return it, the defendants handed it to a messenger who they mistakenly believed was employed by the plaintiffs. Consequently, the negotiable bond was lost and never recovered. The plaintiffs brought suit to obtain the return of the bond.

Issue: Is a constructive bailee absolutely liable for the goods in his possession?

Rule: When a constructive bailee exercises any dominion over the bailed goods, his duty to deliver the bailed goods to the proper person is absolute. Hence, he is absolutely liable for the value of misdelivered goods.

Dissent: An implied contract of bailment with its consequent obligations arises only where a person in possession of the property of another does some act that is inconsistent with the view that he does not accept the possession that has been thrust upon him.

Note: On appeal, this case was reversed and the dissent's position adopted.

The *Winkfield* (1901)

Facts: The British Postmaster General sued the owners of the *Winkfield*, which collided with and sank another ship that was laden with mail and parcels. In his capacity as the bailee of the mailed materials, the Postmaster General was not liable to the multiple bailors under British law.

Issue: May a wrongdoer defend against a claim brought by a bailee on the ground that the bailee himself is not liable to the bailors, and therefore the bailors themselves are the only ones with standing to bring the suit?

Rule: As between a bailee and a third party, possession gives the bailee title. Consequently, the stranger cannot defend against the bailee's claim for damage to the bailed property by showing that title was in the bailor.

IV. Gifts

In Re Cohn (1919)

Facts: Leopold Cohn made a gift to his wife of certain stock certificates, which he did not have in his physical possession. The gift was evidenced by an unambiguous writing, which was also witnessed by several individuals. Several days later, he died without having the opportunity to make actual delivery of the stock certificates to his wife.

Issue: Is an inter vivos gift valid without actual delivery of the thing given?

Rule: When a gift is evidenced by an instrument of gift executed and delivered to the donee and the circumstances surrounding the making of the gift afford a reasonable and satisfactory excuse for not making actual delivery of the object constituting the gift, a constructive or symbolic delivery is sufficient to establish the legal validity of the gift.

Gruen v. Gruen (1986)

Facts: Victor Gruen (decedent) made an inter vivos gift of a painting but reserved a life estate. His son, the recipient of the gift, brought suit against his stepmother for possession of the painting.

Issue: Is an inter vivos gift valid when the donor has reserved a life estate in the chattel and the donee never had physical possession before the donor's death?

Rule: As long as the evidence establishes an intent to make a present and irrevocable transfer of title or the right of ownership, there is a present transfer of some interest and the gift is effective immediately.

Foster v. Reiss (1955)

Facts: Just prior to her death, Ethel Reiss wrote a note to her husband expressing her desire that he receive some of her personalty on her death. She did not actually deliver the personalty to him. The plaintiffs in the case were the representatives of the deceased's estate.

Issue: To be a valid gift causa mortis, must the thing given be actually delivered?

Rule: To be a valid gift causa mortis, the delivery of the thing must be such as is actual, unequivocal, and complete during the lifetime of the donor, wholly divesting the donor of the possession, dominion, and control thereof.

Note: This case represents a minority position.

Scherer v. Hyland (1977)

Facts: Before committing suicide, Ms. Wagner (the plaintiff's cohabitor) endorsed a blank check, wrote a note expressing her desire to leave it to the plaintiff, and left it where the plaintiff would be sure to find it. The defendant, Hyland, was the administrator of her estate.

Issue: Absent actual delivery, when is constructive delivery sufficient to support a gift causa mortis?

Rule: Where there is unequivocal evidence of the donor's intent to presently transfer the subject matter of the gift to the donee, and the donor did all that she could or thought necessary to do to effect such a transfer, constructive delivery is sufficient to support a gift causa mortis.

V. Creation

Johnson v. McIntosh (S. Ct. 1823)

Facts: The plaintiff, who purchased land from a Native American tribe, brought an ejectment action against the defendant who acquired the same land by a grant from the United States.

Issue: Is a title to real property conveyed by Native American tribes recognized by courts of the United States?

Rule: (Marshall, C.J.) A title conveyed by a Native American tribe cannot be valid unless it was granted to the tribe by the U.S. Government.

Wetherbee v. Green (1871)

Facts: Wetherbee cut the plaintiff's timber without his consent and made hoops from it. The plaintiff brought an action in replevin to regain possession of his improved property.

Issue: Does one who has taken the property of another and significantly increased its value gain title to the property if it was taken in good faith and in reliance on a supposed right, without intention to commit wrong?

Rule: When one takes another's property in good faith and adds value to it that is wholly disproportionate to the original material's value, he gains title to the property. The remedy of the owner of the original materials is to recover damages for unintentional trespass.

Cheney Brothers v. Doris Silk Corp. (1929)

Facts: Doris Silk copied one of Cheney Brothers' popular designs and then undercut plaintiff's price.

Issue: May a party duplicate another party's property?

Rule: In the absence of a right or statute stating otherwise, an individual's property is limited to the chattels that embody his invention. Others may imitate these at their pleasure.

White v. Samsung (1992)

Facts: Vanna White sued Samsung for using in an advertisement without her permission a robot dressed in a blond wig and an evening dress on a set that resembles "Wheel of Fortune" and in front of the gameboard.

Issue: Was her right to publicity infringed by the advertisement's use of her name and likeness?

Rule: Even though her acual name or an image of her was not used, the fact that a viewer would associate the advertisement with her was sufficient to constitute an appropriation of her name and likeness.

International News Service v. Associated Press (S. Ct. 1918)

Facts: Associated Press sought to enjoin the International News Service from selling news taken from its publications.

Issue: May a news organization be restrained from appropriating news published by a competing organization for the purpose of selling it to its own clients?

Rule: (Pitney, J.) Generally, published news materials are not regarded as property and may be used for any purpose whatsoever by the general public. However, between competing professional organizations, published news materials are quasi-property. Therefore, a competitor must postpone distributing or reproducing news it gathers from another news organization's publications, but only to the extent necessary to prevent that competitor from reaping the benefit of the other news organization's efforts and expenditures.

Smith v. Chanel, Inc. (1968)

Facts: A perfume company claimed in an advertisement that its product was the equivalent of the more expensive Chanel No. 5.

Issue: May a party advertise its product as comparable to another when the original party put great effort and expense into its product's creation?

Rule: If a product is unpatented, a party has the right to copy it. The public interest in a competitive market is maintained in part through the ability of a marketer to identify the copied article by its tradename.

Moore v. The Regents of the University of California (1990)

Facts: Dr. Golde removed plaintiff's spleen and other bodily tissues after learning that the cells were unusually useful to his genetic research. A cell wall was then developed by Golde and his colleagues that was licensed for commercial development.

Issue: Does an individual have a sufficient legal interest in his own bodily tissues following their removal from his body?

Rule: An individual does not retain an ownership interest in his cells when they are removed for medical research. Such an individual is without an action for conversion, which is a tort that protects against interference with possession and ownership interests in personal property. However, a physician who is seeking a patient's consent for a medical procedure must disclose all facts relevant to that consent, including personal interests unrelated to the patient's health that may affect his medical judgment.

CHAPTER 2

Adverse Possession

I. REAL PROPERTY

A. Operation of Adverse Possession

The titleholder of land must commence an action to eject an individual who enters into possession of his or her land (the occupier) within a statutorily prescribed period that varies by jurisdiction and the circumstances of possession. Provided certain other elements are satisfied, a titleholder after the statute of limitations has run loses the right to bring an action to eject the occupier. Through his possession, the occupier has greater right in the land than do others; and if the titleholder's action is barred, the possessor has a greater right in the property than all others. The possessor may then bring an action to quiet title. She then becomes the titleholder of record.

B. Elements of Adverse Possession

For adverse possession to be perfected, the occupier must be in actual possession open and notorious, continuous, exclusive, and adverse for the statutory period.

1. Actual Possession

The occupier must enter on the land and undertake acts consistent with the character of the land. For example, if land is in an agricultural area, the occupier must exploit it as a titleholder would use farm or ranch land. If residential, the occupier should live on the land or otherwise exploit it consistent with the way in which titleholder uses residential land. If undeveloped, the occupier must exploit it in its natural state or improve it.

2. Open and Notorious

Possession is "open and notorious" when its use is not concealed. The occupier must actually use a reasonable percentage of the claimed land in a manner as typical owners of similar land would exploit it, and this use is sufficient to put the true owner on notice of his or her occupation.

3. Continuous

The occupier must "continuously" occupy the land throughout the statutory period, in a manner consistent with the normal uses of similar land. Although intermittent occupancy is insufficient, an occupier need not be on the land every day of every year during the statutory period (e.g., if the land is normally used only in the summer, seasonal possession suffices to satisfy this requirement).

4. Adverse

Possession is "adverse" or "hostile" when the occupier exploits the land without the titleholder's consent and in a manner inconsistent with his rights. Jurisdictions define "adversity" according to three distinct formulations:

   a. Under the so-called Maine rule, the occupier must claim the right to hold the land regardless of the right of the titleholder. It is often said that the occupier must subjectively know that the land is owned by another.

   b. Under the so-called Connecticut rule, the occupier's entry and continued use is presumed adverse; his or her subjective knowledge of ownership is not relevant.

   c. Under the good faith rule, the occupier must have a bona fide belief that he has title to the land through a defective deed or a misrepresentation by another about right in the land.

5. Statutory Period

An adverse possessor must remain in possession for a statutorily prescribed period, which differs by jurisdiction, usually from 5 to 20 years depending on the nature of the land, claim, and circumstances.

C. Constructive Possession Doctrine

One actually possessing under "color of title" (i.e., the possessor holds a defective deed) a portion of a large, unitary tract of land may gain title by adverse possession to the whole tract as described in the defective document, even if she never actually possessed or used the entire tract. The portion actually possessed must be in reasonable proportion to the whole, such that it is sufficient to put the true owner or community on notice.

D. Concurrently Held Land

To gain title by adverse possession to concurrently held land, the adverse possessor must oust his cotenant.

E. Tacking

When possession is continuous, and the parties are in privity (i.e., a blood relation, oral or written transfer, will, or intestacy), the time in possession of successive adverse possessors may be added together to fulfill the statutory period.

F. Tolling the statute of limitations
   1. Disabilities
      If at the time of an adverse possessor's entry onto the land the titleholder is disabled, the statute of limitations is tolled for the duration of the disability.
      a. Most jurisdictions recognize insanity, infancy, and imprisonment as disabilities.
      b. Disabilities may not be tacked.
   2. Future Interests
      a. If at the time of the adverse possessor's entry onto the land another holds a future interest in the land, the statute of limitations is tolled until the future interest becomes possessory.
      b. However, if the future interest is created after the adverse possessor enters the land, the statute of limitations runs against the future interest holder before such interest becomes possessory.
G. The adverse possession doctrine does not apply to land owned by the federal government. Many states have statutes exempting state land, and lands given, granted, or held for public, charitable, or religious uses.
H. Rights of an Adverse Possessor
   1. An adverse possessor may convey his possessory right to property.
   2. In conflicts between adverse possessors of the same land, a first possessor's right to the land is generally superior to the rights of subsequent possessors.
   3. An adverse possessor may bring trespass and ejectment actions against third parties.

II. PERSONAL PROPERTY

A. Personal property may be acquired by adverse possession.
B. Personal property, such as art, need not be openly displayed in a claim by a possessor.
C. Three different rules have been established to determine when the statute of limitations begins to run:
   1. Discovery Rule: At the time when the owner actually discovered the location of the property, or when a reasonably diligent owner would have discovered it.
   2. Conversion Rule: When the property was taken from the possession of the owner.
   3. Demand Rule: On demand by the owner for its return.

CASE CLIPS

I. Real Property

Tapscott v. Cobbs (1854)

Facts: Having been in prior possession, Cobbs, who did not have legal title, brought an ejectment action against Tapscott who, without title, took possession of the land.

Issue: May an action for ejectment be maintained on the force of mere prior possession?

Rule: A peaceable prior possessor may maintain ejectment as against all the world except the rightful titleholder.

Van Valkenburgh v. Lutz (1952)

Facts: The defendant, Lutz, claimed title by adverse possession to a lot that was purchased by the plaintiffs. He built a *dwelling* on the lot, cultivated a large portion of it, and used the property as his own for over 25 years.

Issue: What facts need to be established to satisfy the "actual" and "hostile and under claim of right" requirements of acquiring title by adverse possession?

Rule: The requirement of "actual" possession is satisfied when the adverse possessor improves, cultivates, or encloses the premises to such an extent that he generally appears to be the rightful owner. The "hostile and under claim of right" requirement is met if the adverse possessor knows that he is not the rightful owner of the property but claims it as his own anyway.

Note: The remaining requirements for acquiring title by adverse possession involve proof that the occupancy is "exclusive," "open and notorious," and "continuous" for the period of time required under the applicable statute of limitations.

Jarvis v. Gillespie (1991)

Facts: Possessor brings an action to quiet title alleging that he openly, notoriously, continuously, exclusively, and adversely occupied an undeveloped tract of land owned by the town for the period of the statute of limitations, land that subsequently was transferred by the Town to a private party.

Issue 1: Was the sporadic use of the tract by the defendant sufficient to perfect adverse possession?

Rule 1: Regular, unconcealed use of the land was regarded as open and notorious, because the use made was similar to that which a titleholder would make, and sufficient to put a reasonably vigilant titleholder on notice that his property interest was infringed by the possessor.

Issue 2: Was ownership by the town within the statutory exclusion for lands "given, granted, sequestered, or appropriated to a public . . . use"?
Rule 2: Land not presently used by the town is not within the ambit of the exclusion unless the town has some intended use.

State v. Shack (1971)

Facts: Pursuant to federal statutes mandating legal and other aid for migrant workers, the defendants, Tejeras and Shack, entered a farmer's land to see certain workers. The farmer executed a complaint alleging violation of the state trespass statute.
Issue: Do landowners have an absolute right to exclude others from their property?
Rule: Real property rights are not absolute. Hence, private or public necessity may justify entry on the lands of another.

Monroe v. Rawlings (1951)

Facts: Monroe brought an ejectment action against Rawlings who entered on the land, paid taxes on it, built and used a hunting lodge, and otherwise exercised dominion over it for the statutory period.
Issue: To establish title by adverse possession, must one live on the land or improve it, fence it off, or otherwise attempt to exclude others?
Rule: To establish title by adverse possession, it is sufficient if the acts of ownership are of such a character as to openly and publicly indicate an assumed control or use that is consistent with the character of the premises in question.

Peters v. Juneau-Douglas Girl Scout Council (1974)

Facts: The defendants held title to a piece of beachfront property, but Peters used the property continuously and openly for over 40 years. During this period, people other than Peters occasionally made use of the land. Peters brought suit to establish his title to the property.
Issue: Will a claim of title by adverse possession be defeated because parties other than the adverse possessor also made use of the property?
Rule: To satisfy the "exclusivity" element of the adverse possession doctrine the possessor must hold the land only for himself, as his own, and not for another.

Mannillo v. Gorski (1969)

Facts: Mannillo's and Gorski's lots shared a boundary. Unknowingly, when making improvements on his house, Gorski encroached on

Mannillo's lot by 15 inches. Mannillo filed a trespass action. In defense, Gorski claimed title by adverse possession.

Issue: To establish title by adverse possession, must the possession be accompanied by an intention to invade the property rights of another?

Rule: Any entry and possession for the required time that is exclusive, continuous, uninterrupted, visible, and notorious, even though under mistaken claim of title, is sufficient to support a claim of title by adverse possession.

Porter v. Posey (1979)

Facts: The Porters purchased land, part of which was acquired by adverse possession by the grantor, but their deed did not describe the adversely acquired portion of the property. However, the same land was in the deed by which the Poseys acquired their adjacent property. The dispute led the Porters to bring suit to establish their right to the parcel in question.

Issue: May title to property acquired by adverse possession be transferred by a deed that did not contain a description of that property?

Rule: Title to property acquired by adverse possession may be transferred without a written conveyance where the title owner intends to transfer the property and the transferee takes possession of that property.

Taffinder v. Thomas (1977)

Facts: The Taffinders claimed ownership by adverse possession of land that they used for eight years, but their period of usage fell two years short of the statutorily prescribed period for acquiring title by adverse possession. However, the Taffinders proposed to tack their period of possession onto that of a tenant of their grantor, who had been occupying his leased premises for more than the statutory period.

Issue: May title be acquired through adverse possession by tacking a tenant's occupation onto that of the grantees to comply with the statute of limitations?

Rule: Where the area in question is either expressly or impliedly within the terms of a lease, prescriptive rights can be established through a tenant.

Hardy v. Burroughs (1930)

Facts: The plaintiff mistakenly built a house on Burroughs' land and brought suit to recover the value of the improvements.

Issue: May one who mistakenly improves another's land recover the value of the improvements?

Rule: One who improves another's land in good faith and is evicted by the true owner may sue in equity for the value of the improvements.

Gillespie v. Dew (1827)

Facts: Duncan Dew removed timber from land to which the plaintiff had title, although he was never in possession of it. The plaintiff brought an action for trespass.
Issue: To maintain a trespass action, must the title holder be in actual possession of his land?
Rule: Where there is no adverse possession, the titleholder of realty has constructive possession and may maintain a trespass action.

Ewing v. Burnet (S. Ct. 1837)

Facts: Through a common grantor, both the plaintiff and the defendant had title to the same unimproved lot, although the plaintiff's grant was earlier in time. The defendant, however, publicly exercised dominion and control over it for the statutory period. The plaintiff brought an action of ejectment.
Issue: Must an adverse claimant actually possess, cultivate, fence, or otherwise improve land to sustain a claim of adverse possession?
Rule: (Baldwin, J.) When property is so situated as not to admit of any permanent useful improvement, a claim of adverse possession is sustainable on evidence of public acts of ownership such as would be exercised by an owner over property being claimed as his own.

Brumagim v. Bradshaw (1870)

Facts: The plaintiff's predecessor in interest repaired a wall on the neck of a 1,000-acre peninsula and used it for pasturage. Bradshaw entered on the land and the plaintiff sought ejectment.
Issue: To sustain a claim of adverse possession, must the claimant use a reasonable percentage of the claimed land?
Rule: Where the enclosure consists wholly or partially of natural barriers, the acts of dominion and ownership that establish actual possession must reasonably correspond to the size of the tract and its condition and appropriate use, and the acts must be such as usually accompany the ownership of land similarly situated.

Mendonca v. Cities Service Oil Co. (1968)

Facts: The Cities Service Oil Co. built a fence on its property 24 feet from the common boundary of its own and the plaintiff's lots. Except for a three-week period, during which a contractor working for the Oil Co. stored material on the disputed strip and tore down and replaced the fence, the plaintiff used the strip for the statutory period without the objection of the City Services Oil Co. The plaintiff brought suit to enjoin the defendant from entering on the strip and to recover damages for trespass.

Issue: Will a brief re-entry by the owner defeat the "continuity of possession" element needed to establish adverse possession?

Rule: An adverse claimant must prove all the elements of adverse possession and a brief re-entry by the owner, even if not for the purpose of regaining possession, interrupts, and thereby defeats, the continuous possession element.

United States v. Stubbs (1985)

Facts: The United States sued Stubbs to quiet title to a tract of land that it claimed to have acquired either through a valid conveyance or by adverse possession.

Issue: Does the doctrine of adverse possession apply to the U.S. Government?

Rule: The United States can acquire title by adverse possession in the same way as a private individual. However, a person cannot acquire land by adverse possession against the government.

Lasalle County Carbon Coal Co. v. Sanitary District (1913)

Facts: Lasalle County Carbon Coal Co. took possession of land to which it did not have title. The land was later damaged by floods caused by the defendant. Five years later, Lasalle's adverse possession ripened into title, and it brought suit to recover for permanent damage to the land.

Issue: Can one recover damages for permanent injury to his land if the cause of action accrued before he gained title through adverse possession?

Rule: An owner may not rely on title by adverse possession to recover damages for injury to realty unless his possession had ripened into title before the cause of action accrued.

Illinois & St. Louis Railroad & Coal Co. v. Cobb (1879)

Facts: Cobb adversely possessed certain land that, before the ripening of this possession into title, the defendant entered and damaged. Cobb brought a trespass action seeking damages.

Issue: May a trespasser escape liability for damage to a freehold by showing that the party in possession of the property has no title to it?

Rule: A trespasser who is not claiming title to the property may not escape liability for damage to the freehold because the possessor of the estate does not have a valid title. Therefore, a recovery against a wrongdoer is not limited to the possessory interest of the party in possession, but is determined by the full amount of the damage done to the freehold.

Chapin v. Freeland (1886)

Facts: The plaintiff purchased a chattel from a vendor who became the owner of it by adverse possession. Freeland, the original owner of the chattel, used self-help and simply took the chattel from the plaintiff.

Issue: Does the running of the statute of limitations for bringing suit to recover personalty bar the owner from using self-help to recover the personalty from a subsequent purchaser?

Rule: A purchaser from one against whom the remedy is already barred by the running of the statute of limitations is entitled to stand in as good a position as his vendor. Thus, the original owner may not use self-help to recover the chattel from the vendee.

O'Keeffe v. Snyder (1980)

Facts: In 1946, three of Georgia O'Keeffe's paintings were stolen from a gallery, but she took no formal action to recover them. In 1976, she instituted suit against the defendant, the owner of an art gallery who was then in possession of the paintings.

Issue: When does the statute of limitations begin to run on an action for replevin of chattels?

Rule: Under the discovery rule the statute of limitations on an action for replevin begins to run when the owner knows or reasonably should know of her cause of action and the identity of the possessor of the chattel.

CHAPTER 3

Estates in Land

I. FEUDALISM AND TENURE

During the Middle Ages, land was held in a variety of distinct tenures. The central feature of feudalism was the relationship of lord and vassal. All land was owned in the first instance by the sovereign, who then granted it to his "tenants-in-chief" in return for stipulated military service. The tenant-in-chief was the King's vassal. He might grant part of his estate to others in turn for military service, largely to help defray his own obligation. These mesne tenants might do the same, hiving off a swathe of land he held to other tenants. Eventually land might be transferred to unfree peasants called villeins, who worked the land in return for services performed on the lord's land. This process of subinfeudation resulted in the formation of a feudal pyramid, with the King at the top and the peasants at the base. In between were successive layers of mesne lords, who were vassals to those above them and lords to those below. Another frequent metaphor for landholding in the Middle Ages was that each lord and vassal had a place on the feudal ladder, bound to each other by the duties and privileges of lordship.

A. Tenure

Each rung on this feudal ladder created a particular set of rights and obligations called "tenure." There were a variety of different tenures.

B. Feudal Tenures and Services

1. Free Tenures

These tenures involved services that were defined and fixed as to quantity and manner of performance. By the latter part of the twelfth century, a tenant who held a free tenure could sue anyone who disturbed his possession in the King's court. There were four principal types of free tenures, differentiated by the nature of services the vassal had to render in return for possession of the land.

    a. Military Tenure: Tenure by Knight Service
       This was the most common type of tenure. The vassal was
       required to provide his lord with a previously agreed-on quota
       of knights for the king's military. Personal service morphed into
       a monetary contribution (scutage), which allowed the Crown to
       employ a professionally trained mercenary army.
    b. Serjeanty Tenure
       The serjeanty tenant had to perform a personal service, which
       was definite as to time and often localized to a specific place.
       Types of services that were performed included working in the
       King's or a lord's household (e.g., cook, chamberlain, butler,
       etc.), or supplying the lord with specific goods and military
       service by the tenant/vassal himself. As the practice of hiring
       servants became widespread, serjeanty tenants paid rent
       instead of performing services.
    c. Religious Tenure (Frankalmoign)
       These tenures were granted to churches or other religious
       bodies or officials in return for the performance of religious
       services.
    d. Economic Tenure (Socage)
       Tenants in socage tenure were required to perform specified
       agricultural work on the lord's land or to supply a fixed
       amount of agricultural produce. Sometimes the tenant had
       to pay a fixed monetary sum, either nominal or substantial,
       instead of giving crops.
  2. Unfree Tenures: Villeinage
    Each lord kept possession of some of his land, apart from the
    land he granted to others. The lord used villeins (serfs) who lived
    on manorial property in exchange for working it. The villein,
    unlike a slave, had the rights of a free man against all persons
    except his lord. A serf land was often held in unfree tenure. His
    home and plot of land could be arbitrarily taken by his lord,
    but only subject to the "custom of the manor." The amount of
    services that the serf had to render might or might not be fixed
    and could vary according to his lord's wishes. The serf could
    enforce his rights only in his lord's court. The arbitrary nature of
    unfree tenures gradually disappeared as serfs were granted a
    greater degree of freedom, particularly after the Black Death
    made it more difficult for lords to bear down heavily on their
    villeins.
C. Feudal Incidents
  A lord was also entitled to the incidents of tenure. These obligations
  were created by the feudal relationship (i.e., lord–vassal) and existed

regardless of the specific terms of the tenure agreement. There were five principal incidents:

1. Homage and Fealty

   Homage was a feudal ceremony in which an unarmed tenant knelt before his lord and pledged loyalty. Fealty was the oath that the tenant swore.

2. Aids

   A tenant was obligated to financially assist his lord in some situations.

3. Liabilities at Death of Tenant

   a. Relief and Primer Seisin

      At the death of a tenant, his heir had to pay a relief for the right to take over the land. If the tenant was by socage tenure, relief was equal to one year's rent. At the death of a tenant-in-chief (i.e., one who was a direct tenant to the King), the King was entitled to primer seisin (i.e., first possession) of all of the tenant's lands and the accompanying reliefs.

   b. Wardship and Marriage

      If a military or grand serjeanty tenant died leaving a male heir under age 21 or a female under age 14, the lord was entitled to the rents and profits from the land until the male heir reached majority or the female heir either married or reached age 16. The lord was entitled to arrange a marriage for the male heir and pocket the profit. Socage tenure was not subject to these incidents.

4. Escheat

   If a tenant died without heirs the land returned to the lord.

D. Statute Quia Emptores (1290)

   Two ways in which land was transferred during the Middle Ages were subinfeudation and substitution. Subinfeudation was the process by which a tenant transferred lands in his possession to others, who became his tenants. He was entitled to both services and incidents from his tenants. He could also modify the incidents (i.e., lower them). Substitution involved the transfer of all of a tenant's interests in the land to another party who took the place of the original tenant. Thus, the original tenant was removed from the chain of ownership and received neither services nor incidents. The new tenant was directly responsible to the former tenant's lord. The Statute Quia Emptores was enacted to permit free alienation of land by substitution only. It forbade subinfeudation and relieved tenants from a previously existing fine that was levied every time they transferred land. Thus, it permitted greater alienability of land and preserved valuable incidents for the lords.

II. THE SYSTEM OF ESTATES

A. Although the incidences of tenure described above are of little modern practical value, they generated the common-law estates, which have contemporary relevance. An estate in land is an interest that (a) is possessory or may become possessory (unlike easements, covenants, rents, and other land interests) and (b) has ownership measured in terms of duration of possession. (Rest. §9).

B. A key factor in classifying the various types of estates is the length of time during which the grantee (i.e., one receiving possession) is entitled to possess the land. Duration can vary from the life of an individual (i.e., a life estate), to infinity (i.e., fee simple absolute). Because a right in land can endure forever, but alas, no individual will, the owner of fee simple absolute can limit both present possessory interests and future interests, those interests in which the right to come into possession may occur in the future.

C. Estates thus differ with regard to the time at which they become possessory. The holder of a presently possessory estate is entitled to immediate possession of the land. Future interests, discussed in the following chapter, become possessory only at the expiration of a prior estate or upon the occurrence of a specified event.

D. Words of Purchase and Limitation

Because an estate has two components (i.e., possession and duration), every conveyance of an estate must indicate who is to receive possession and the length of time that possession will last. Thus, the words of every grant are divided into two groups:

1. Words of *purchase* designate the grantee.
2. Words of *limitation* designate the quantum of interest transferred. Example: In the grant "To B for life," "To B" are words of purchase, indicating that B is the grantee; "for life" are words of limitation, defining the interest granted, a life estate.

E. Present Possessory Freehold Interest

Another distinction between estates, although mainly historical, involved the concept of seisin, the highest level of ownership at common law. To be "seized" of land meant to occupy it under claim of having a freehold estate in it (non-freehold estates are discussed under Landlord-Tenant). The following are the various types of freehold estates.

1. Fee Simple Absolute

a. Creation

A grant "To A," "To A and his heirs," or "To A in fee simple." Today, there is a presumption in favor of fee simple conveyances. Thus, a vague or uncertain grant is construed as a fee simple absolute if possible. In the past, a grant "To A until the end of time" created a life interest in A, while in modern law it is regarded as a grant in fee simple absolute.

b. Duration

A fee simple absolute can potentially last forever. In terms of duration, is the greatest estate.

c. Alienability

A fee simple absolute is freely alienable. If no conveyance was made during the grantee's life, the estate passes to his devisees if he has made a will, if not then the estate will descend to his heirs as specified in a jurisdiction's intestacy statutes. In default of heirs, the estate escheats (i.e., goes to the state).

2. Defeasible Fees — Fee Simple Determinable

a. Creation

A grant "To A and his heirs, so long as they use the land for specified purposes only" creates this estate. Critical words are "so long as," "until," and "while."

b. Duration

A fee simple determinable is also of potentially infinite duration, as long as the condition is not violated (e.g., alcohol is not served on the premises). The grantor retains a future interest called a "possibility of reverter." If the condition is broken, the estate automatically terminates and possession reverts to the grantor.

c. Alienability/Transferability

A fee simple determinable is freely alienable. The new owner also holds subject to the condition, and possession may revert to the original grantor when the condition is violated. If no inter vivos transfer is made, the estate on the death of the grantee passes to his devisees, or if he dies without a will (or the will does not bequeath the interest) then it descends to his intestate takers heirs specified by state law. In default of heirs, the estate escheats. As to the future retained interest, the possibility of reverter, it passes to the grantor's devisees, or to his interstate heirs. In default thereof, the interest escheats. Most jurisdictions permit the transfer of the "possibility of reverter."

d. Public Policy

Courts are hostile to the fee simple determinable because a forfeiture occurs if the condition is broken. If the wording of the grant is not explicit or is open to other interpretations, courts will be reluctant to construe a clause as creating a fee simple determinable (or prefer to interpret the interest as a fee simple subject to a condition subsequent).

3. Fee Simple Subject to a Condition Subsequent
   a. Creation
      A grant "To A and his heirs, but if the land is used for other than specified purposes, G or his heirs shall have the right to enter and declare the estate forfeited" creates a fee simple subject to a condition subsequent. The grantor has retained a "right of entry."
   b. Duration
      The grantee keeps possession until the grantor enters and terminates the estate if and when the condition is broken. Unlike a fee simple determinable, violation of the condition does not lead to automatic forfeiture of the property. The grantor must enter and terminate. If the condition is not broken, or if the grantor decides not to terminate, the estate can last forever. By keeping the right to enter and the power to terminate the estate, the grantor has not conveyed all of his interests in the land.
   c. Alienability/Transferability
      The estate is freely alienable, but always subject to the condition. If no *inter vivos* transfer is made, then devisees or heirs are entitled to possession. Escheat is also possible should the grantor die intestate and without heirs. As to the future retained interest, the "right of entry" passes to the grantor's devisees, or to his interstate heirs. In default thereof, the interest escheats. Most jurisdictions permit the transfer of the "possibility of reverter."
   d. Public Policy
      Courts are generally hostile to this type of estate and will construe the condition as a restrictive covenant, if possible, to avoid a forfeiture. The grantor must specifically and expressly retain his right of entry and power of termination (see future interests) because they will not be assumed absent clear language.
4. Fee Simple Subject to an Executory Interest (Defeasible Fee)
   This type of fee simple is like an ordinary fee simple determinable or one subject to a condition subsequent, except that if the condition is broken the estate goes to a third party and not the grantor.
   Example: G grants to "A and his heirs, but if the land is used to sell alcohol then to B and his heirs," or ". . . B and her heirs shall have the right to enter and declare the estate forfeited," or ". . . , but if A has no sons then to B and his heirs."
5. Life Estate
   a. Creation
      A grants "To A for life."
      Note: At common law, any grant that was intended to create a fee simple absolute but failed to use the specific words "To A and his heirs" was deemed to create a life estate.

b. Duration
  i. Grantee's Lifetime
     A life estate lasts until the death of the grantee, whereupon possession of the land reverts to the grantor or his heirs. Thus, the grantor has only transferred possession of his land for the grantee's life. The estate can terminate before the grantee's death if he *renounces* it.
  ii. An Estate *Per Autre Vie*
     This is a life estate in which duration is measured by the life of a third party. Sometimes a grant will state "To B, for A's life." A life estate *per autre vie* is created because the life that is used to measure the duration of possession is not that of the party actually in possession. Possession terminates only at the death of the measuring life. If the party in possession (i.e., B) dies first, the estate goes to his heirs, devisees, purchasers, or even by escheat, until the death of the measuring life. Likewise, in a grant "To A for life," if A transfers her interest to B, it is also an estate *per autre vie:* B has an estate for the life of A.
c. Alienability
   The grantee is free to make inter vivos transfers, but possession of the land by the third party terminates at the death of the original grantee. Obviously this type of estate is not inheritable by the grantee's heirs.
d. Defeasible Life Estate
   As with a fee simple, a life estate can be conditioned on a certain event, the occurrence of which will entitle the grantor either to automatic reversion or to enter and reclaim possession.
e. Duties and Powers of a Life Tenant
   A life tenant has certain obligations to his remaindermen (i.e., those who will take possession after the tenant's death). These obligations include the following:
   i. Not to commit waste (i.e., an act which constitutes an unreasonable impairment of the future value of the property, e.g., cutting down trees or demolishing a building);
   ii. To undertake reasonable repairs (does not include rebuilding structures destroyed by natural causes);
   iii. To pay interest charges on the mortgage (does not have to repay principal). Obligation is limited to value of income received from the land; and
   iv. To pay property taxes on estate.
   The life tenant is entitled to all rents and profits from the estate.

6. Fee Tail
    a. Creation
       A grant "To A and the heirs of A's body" created this estate at
       common law. The purpose of this type of grant was to keep
       ownership of land within a family.
       Note: This grant is different from "To A and his heirs."
    b. Duration
       At common law, the grantee received an estate for his life,
       which passed to his first heir at his death. The heir also held
       for life and then it passed to his heir, and so on.
    c. Alienability
       At common law, the grantee could not transfer an interest in
       the estate that exceeded his lifetime. At the grantee's death, the
       only persons who could take the estate were his lineal heirs. If
       he had no lineal heirs, the estate would revert to the grantor
       and his heirs.
    d. Modern View
       Most states have abolished the fee tail or greatly modified its
       effect. Some courts treat such a grant as creating an ordinary
       fee simple absolute. Others construe it as a fee simple
       conditional, so that a grantee has a fee simple conditioned
       on having *issue* (i.e., children). Once the grantee has a child,
       he acquires a freely alienable fee simple. Still another approach
       has been to allow the fee tail to exist for one generation only.

CASE CLIPS

I. The System of Estates
White v. Brown (1977)

Facts: The decedent devised her house to Evelyn White "to live in and not to be sold." White filed an action to obtain a construction of the will to determine whether the house was conveyed in fee simple or as a life estate.
Issue: When interpreting an ambiguous will, is a construction that conveys the whole estate preferred over a partial conveyance?
Rule: Where a will is ambiguous, a construction that conveys the entire estate is preferred if it is reasonable and consistent with the general scope and provisions of the will.

Lewis v. Searles (1970)

Facts: The plaintiff received all of the decedent's property subject to a condition that if she were to marry, the property would be divided evenly between her and two other relatives of the decedent.
Issue: Is a will provision that reduces a devise in the event of the beneficiary's marriage always contrary to public policy?
Rule: If the provision is incorporated in the will for legitimate purposes, and is not intended to restrict marriage unreasonably or maliciously, it will not be voided on public policy grounds.

Mahrenholz v. County Board of School Trustees (1981)

Facts: The grantor conveyed land that was "to be used for school purposes only; otherwise to revert to grantor." The land was not used as directed.
Issue: Does the granting clause create a fee simple determinable or a fee simple subject to a condition subsequent?
Rule: The difference between a fee simple determinable and a fee simple subject to a condition subsequent is solely a matter of judicial interpretation of the words of a grant. Generally, a grant of exclusive use, followed by an express provision for reverter when that use ceases, will be interpreted as creating a fee simple determinable.

Mountain Brow Lodge No. 82, Independent Order of Odd Fellows v. Toscano (1968)

Facts: The Toscanos deeded land to the plaintiff, a non-profit corporation, on condition that if any or all of the land was sold or transferred, or if the plaintiff failed to use the land, it would revert to the grantor. The plaintiff brought an action to quiet title.

Issue: May a grantor restrict the use of land?
Rule: A restriction on the "use" of land does not constitute a restraint on alienation and is not void as against public policy.

Oldfield v. Stoeco Homes, Inc. (1958)

Facts: The plaintiffs deeded land to Stoeco Homes, Inc. with the condition that the land be filled and graded within one year.
Issue: Does a durational requirement create a fee simple determinable or a fee simple subject to condition subsequent?
Rule: Absent an intent that time is of the essence, courts will construe durational requirements as creating a fee simple subject to condition subsequent.

Roberts v. Rhodes (1982)

Facts: Without reversion or other language of limitation, grantor deeded land conditioned on its being used for school purposes. When no longer so used, Roberts, the successor in interest to the original grantor, claimed title to the land by reversion.
Issue: Does a statement of purpose, without more, limit a grant?
Rule: When the grantee accepts and uses for a reasonable time land on which a use condition is imposed, and the deed does not contain language limiting the grant, a fee simple, not a determinable fee, is conveyed.

The City of Klamath Falls v. Bell (1971)

Facts: A corporation granted land to the City to be used as a library. The deed provided that if not so used, title should pass to the descendants of the corporation's shareholders. Subsequently, the City ceased using the land as a library. The City filed an action against the shareholders' descendants for declaratory judgment.
Issue: Does a grantor who alienates his possibility of reverter destroy it?
Rule: An attempt by a grantor to transfer his possibility of reverter does not destroy his interest.

Harrison v. Marcus (1985)

Facts: Irving K. Taylor conveyed in trust two parcels of land for the exclusive use of a Boy Scout Troop. The terms of the conveyance specifically stated that if the parcels were no longer used for this purpose the trustees were to convey the land back to the grantor or his heirs or their assigns. The Boy Scout Troop disbanded and its successor in interest, as well as the trustees, brought suit to quiet title to the parcels.

Issue: Do the words "so long as" used in the conveyance necessarily indicate that the trustees held title in fee simple determinable, or is there a possibility that they held title in fee simple absolute despite the phrasing of the document?

Rule: Generally, the words "so long as" are interpreted as creating a fee simple determinable, but the particular terms of a conveyance cannot stand on their own and must be interpreted in light of the general purposes of the instrument as a whole.

Wood v. Board of County Commissioners of Fremont County (1988)

Facts: The Woods conveyed land to the defendant "for the purpose of constructing and maintaining" a memorial hospital. The land was used for a hospital for 35 years before the hospital's location changed. The Woods filed suit to regain possession of the land.

Issue: Does a conveyance "for the purpose of constructing and maintaining a hospital" create either a fee simple determinable or a fee simple subject to a condition subsequent?

Rule: Unless the deed clearly states either that the property will automatically revert if the purpose is not fulfilled or that grantor intended to create discretionary power to terminate the estate, neither a fee simple determinable nor a fee simple subject to condition subsequent is created.

Stoller v. Doyle (1913)

Facts: Lawrence Doyle first conveyed a fee to Frank Doyle with a contingent interest in the wife and children of the grantee and a reversion in the grantor. Later, Lawrence executed a new deed purporting to remove all restrictions of the first grant. Frank Doyle subsequently conveyed the land to Stoller. Stoller sued to quiet title.

Issue: Did the first grant create a contingent remainder subject to destruction or an executory interest not subject to destruction?

Rule: An interest following a fee held by one other than the grantee or grantor is an executory interest not subject to destruction.

Martin v. City of Seattle (1986)

Facts: When the city of Seattle bought a parcel of land from the plaintiff's predecessor in title, the deed contained a condition requiring the city to acquire the land necessary for the grantor to build a boathouse. A breach of the condition allowed the grantor or the successors to reenter and forfeit the grant. The original grantor did not hold the city to its promise, but the grantor's successor asked the defendant to acquire the land for the boat-house nearly 80 years later. The defendant refused.

Issue: Will the passage of time, without more, extinguish the grantor's right to exercise a condition subsequent in a deed, and if so, does the state's failure to perform amount to an unconstitutional taking?

Rule: The passage of time does not prevent a landowner from exercising the right to a condition subsequent, and the state's failure to perform is a restriction of the use of the land amounting to an unconstitutional taking.

Johnson v. City of Wheat Ridge (1975)

Facts: Paul Johnson, the plaintiff, claimed title when grantee failed to satisfy a condition of the conveyance.

Issue: May a right of reentry be time-barred?

Rule: A condition subsequent is subject to the statute of limitations, which begins to run when the stated event occurs.

Leeco Gas & Oil Co. v. County of Nueces (1957)

Facts: The defendant gave 50 acres of land to Nueces County, so long as the land would be used as a public park. Subsequently, the county began condemnation proceedings against the defendant's reversionary interest.

Issue: May the state condemn a possibility of reverter on land given to the state and pay mere nominal damages to the owner of the reversionary interest?

Rule: When a governmental entity is the grantee in a gift deed in which the grantor retains a reversionary interest, if the same governmental entity condemns the reversionary interest, it must pay as compensation the amount by which the value of the unrestricted fee exceeds the value of the restricted fee: not merely nominal damages.

Moore v. Phillips (1981)

Facts: The remaindermen of the life tenant's estate sued for damages resulting from the life tenant's neglect of the property.

Issue: Will a mere delay in instituting suit for waste result in dismissal of the claim?

Rule: The affirmative defense of laches will not succeed because of delay unless the delay resulted in a disadvantage to another party.

Brokaw v. Fairchild (1929)

Facts: Brokaw, a life tenant, sought to demolish a mansion and erect an apartment building in its place.

Issue: May a life tenant exercise rights of ownership over an estate?
Rule: Although a life tenant may make reasonable use of an estate and improve its value, he cannot so change the inheritance as to preclude its transfer to the remaindermen or reversioners.

Melms v. Pabst Brewing Co. (1899)

Facts: Pabst Brewing Co., held a life estate in a quarter-acre plot of land. It destroyed the building situated thereon and graded the land down to street level, thereby increasing the value of the property. The reversioners of the estate brought an action for damages for destruction of the building.
Issue: Is a life tenant always guilty of waste when he alters property in such a way that the identity of the property is changed?
Rule: In the absence of any express or implied contract to use the property for a specified purpose, or to return it in the same condition in which it was received, a radical and permanent change in surrounding conditions is always an important consideration when deciding whether a change in the identity of the property implemented by a life tenant constitutes waste.

Baker v. Weedon (1972)

Facts: A life tenant's income from the decedent's property provided insufficient support. She petitioned the court for judicial sale of the property and investment of the proceeds.
Issue: May a court of equity order property sold when future interests are affected?
Rule: Necessity must be demonstrated for a court of equity to order a sale of property in which there are future interests. The court will consider whether a sale is necessary for the best interest of all the parties.

Cole v. Steinlauf (1957)

Facts: Steinlauf contracted with Cole to sell land and convey a "marketable title." Subsequently, Cole refused to close the transaction and sued for return of his deposit because, he said, the title was not clear.
Issue: Is a title marketable when there is doubt as to the validity of a prior grantor's deed?
Rule: When there is enough doubt in the chain of title to make the plaintiff believe that he risks a future title contest, the title is not marketable.

Caccamo v. Banning (1950)

Facts: The decedent willed property to the plaintiff. The will stated that she forfeit the land if she should die without issue. The plaintiff contracted to sell the land to Banning. Banning breached, arguing that the title was not marketable due to the restriction.

Issue: Do the words "should die without leaving lawful issue of her body" give rise to a definite or indefinite failure of issue construction?

Rule: Absent a contrary expression of a decedent's intent, an indefinite failure of issue construction obtains, and a fee tail estate will be created.

Note: This case represents a minority view.

In Re O'Connor's Estate (1934)

Facts: The estate of John O'Connor escheated to the state of Nebraska for want of heirs.

Issue: When real estate escheats, is the state liable for the payment of an inheritance tax?

Rule: Because escheated real estate reverts to the state, and the inheritance tax is applicable to property acquired by a right of succession only, no inheritance tax is due on escheated realty.

CHAPTER 4

Future Interests

I. INTRODUCTION

Chapter 3 considered estates that are possessory, estates in which the holder was entitled to immediate possession. This chapter outlines the various future interests, property rights that presently exist, but are not currently possessory yet may become possessory sometime in the future.

II. RETAINED FUTURE INTERESTS — FUTURE INTERESTS IN THE TRANSFEROR

A transferor who conveys (or wills) his property to another can retain part of his interest. Remember that ownership is measured by the duration of possession. Thus, if a person holding a fee simple absolute (i.e., infinite duration) transfers an estate of shorter duration (e.g., fee simple determinable, life estate, etc.), possession reverts to the transferor at the expiration of that estate. There are three types of future interests that a transferor can retain.

A. Reversion

A reversion in the transferor is retained if he transfers an estate of a shorter duration than the one he holds. At the expiration of the shorter estate, this future interest becomes possessory, and the property reverts to the transferor.

Example: B, who has a fee simple absolute, transfers a life estate to C. C has a present possessory interest, a life estate. At C's death, the life estate terminates and possession of the land reverts to B. A transferor does not have to expressly reserve this future interest. It is assumed in the grant.

1. Extinguishment

A reversion may not become possessory. This will occur if the condition that must transpire for the reversion to take effect cannot be met. For example, O grants "To B for life, then to

C, if she outlives B." B has a present possessory life estate that terminates at her death. Two things can happen at B's death: If C is dead, then possession reverts to O, because there are no other takers; but if C is alive, she takes possession in fee simple absolute and the reversion is extinguished.

  2. Alienability

  A reversion is freely alienable (*inter vivos*), devisable or heritable (there is also a possibility of escheat). However, the new holder of the reversion also runs the risk that it will not become possessory.

B. Possibility of Reverter

  A possibility of reverter is a retained future interest held by a transferor of a fee simple determinable only. Thus, a grant "To A for so long as no alcohol is sold on the property" creates a possibility of reverter in the grantor.

  1. Duration

  The possibility of reverter runs with the fee simple determinable that was conveyed. It is a future interest that only becomes possessory, if at all, when the condition is broken. It entitles the grantor to automatic repossession of the property.

  Note: A grantee who stays in possession after the condition is broken is considered to be in adverse possession.

  2. Alienability

  This future interest is freely alienable and inheritable (majority rule).

  3. Public Policy

  Courts are generally hostile to possibilities of reverter, because they cause forfeiture and encumber the free use and transfer of land. Unless the language is completely unambiguous, courts will construe the restrictions as only a suggestion or a covenant.

C. Right of Entry

  A right of entry is the retained future interest in the transferor of a fee simple subject to a condition subsequent, where the transferor expressly reserves the right to reenter the land and reclaim possession when the condition stipulated is broken.

  Example: "To A, but if the land is used to sell alcohol, Grantor or his heirs shall have the right to enter and declare the estate forfeit."

  1. Duration

  The right of entry runs with the land and can be asserted against any subsequent grantee of the original transferee. It becomes possessory only if the condition is broken. However, to take possession of the land, grantor must actually enter and declare the prior possessor's claim void. A grantor who fails to enter within a reasonable time is later barred by laches.

2. Alienability

This future interest is devisable and inheritable but jurisdictions are divided as to whether they can be transferred *inter vivos*.

3. Public Policy

Rights of entry are not favored by courts, and unless expressly reserved will not be allowed. If at all possible, courts will try to construe the grant otherwise (i.e., restrictive covenant). However, a court will usually construe a defeasible fee as a fee simple subject to a condition subsequent rather than as a fee simple determinable to avoid the uncertainty of title that occurs with automatic termination rather than optional.

D. Legislation

Rights of entry and possibilities of reverter are presently limited by statute. States have taken the following approaches:

1. Some limit the permissible duration of these interests.
2. Some require the holders of these interests to rerecord them periodically.
3. Some allow only equitable remedies such as injunction, but do not permit forfeiture.
4. Some adopt the approach taken in (3) above, but hold that the restrictive covenant is unenforceable if neighborhood conditions sufficiently change.

III. TRANSFERRED FUTURE INTERESTS

A grantor may also limit future interest in a transferee. This occurs if the transfer is made to several sequential transferees or if the transferor places some condition to delay possession (e.g., "To A when he graduates"). There are two types of future interests that a transferee can have.

A. Remainders

A remainder is a future interest that becomes possessory upon the natural expiration of a simultaneously created estate (usually a life estate).

Example: "To A for life, remainder to B," A has a life estate and B has a remainder in fee simple, which becomes possessory when A dies. Remember that a remainder always follows a life estate.

1. There are two types of remainders.

   a. Vested

   A vested remainder is one that becomes possessory at the termination of the prior life estate and is subject to no other condition precedent. It is limited to a certain person to take effect upon an event that is certain to occur.

Example: "To A for life, remainder to B." B has a vested remainder in fee simple, which becomes possessory at A's death. The transferee's future interest becomes possessory when the prior "supporting" estate naturally terminates: When A dies. B is a certain person, and there are no conditions that she must satisfy to come into possession. There is no requirement built into B's interest that B must outlive A. If B is dead at A's death, possession goes to his transferees, devisees, heirs, or even by escheat. A vested remainder can be lost only if it is subject to a condition subsequent (see executory interests).

  b. Contingent

A contingent remainder is one that is limited to take effect to persons who are not ascertained and/or takes effect on the event that is not certain to occur. It usually follows a life estate, becomes possessory only at the termination of that life estate and the fulfillment of some other condition precedent.

   i. Example: "To A for life, then to B's children." B has no children at the time of the grant. The taker of the future interest is not yet ascertained; nor may he or she ever be. Likewise, a remainder may be contingent as to event. "To A for life, then to B if she outlives A." In both of these cases it is not enough for A to die (i.e., B must either have children or outlive A) for the estate to become possessory. A reversion in the grantor is automatically created by the conveyance of a contingent remainder because of the possibility that the contingency will not be met (e.g., B does not have children; B predeceases A). If the condition is not met, the remainder is "destroyed." If the condition is met, the remainder vests and the grantor's reversion does not take effect.

   ii. Example: More than one contingency. "To A for life, then to the heirs of B," and B has no children yet. (Heirs are those persons to whom an estate will pass by intestate succession.) Here there are two contingencies. The heirs must be born, and they also must survive B to become his heirs. (Note that this contingent remainder vests or fails at the death of B.)

  c. Vested or Contingent?

Whether a remainder is vested or contingent is often a difficult question, and frequently depends on technical distinctions. A few rules do exist to facilitate this determination.

i. Grammatical Construction.

If the condition is contained in the clause that creates the interest, then the interest will be interpreted as a contingent remainder. If the condition is stated in a clause separate from that which creates the interest, then it will be construed as a vested remainder subject to divestment — the condition is regarded as subsequent. If the condition occurs, it will defeat the remainder — the holder will not take possession; but if it does not, it will take effect in possession on the termination of the supporting estate.

ii. Reversion.

A contingent remainder creates a reversion in the grantor. A vested remainder subject to divestment may create an executory interest in a third party.

Example: "To A for life, remainder to B, but if B dies before A then to C." B has a vested remainder in fee simple subject to total divestment by a condition subsequent. C has an executory interest. "To A for life, remainder to B if B survives A." B has a contingent remainder. B's interest is subject to a condition precedent. The remainder is vested in the grantor until the condition is satisfied.

2. The Destructibility Rule

This rule applies only to contingent remainders. At common law, a contingent remainder was automatically extinguished at the time the prior estate expired if it was not vested by then.

Example: "To A for life, then to B's children." B has no children at A's death (i.e., expiration of prior estate — the remainder is still contingent), the remainder was destroyed under the destructibility rule and possession reverted to the grantor.

a. Merger Doctrine

Contingent remainders could be destroyed through merger, a common-law legal doctrine. The doctrine provides that when successive vested estates are held by the same person the interests combine; the lesser estate mergers with the greater.

Example: "To A for life, remainder to A and his heirs." (i.e., A has a life estate and also a remainder in fee simple absolute). A's life estate is merged into his remainder and A has one estate in fee simple absolute. If another estate intervenes between the two estates, merger does not occur if the intervening estate is vested. But, if it is contingent, merger occurs and the intervening estate is destroyed. Contingent remainders were not viewed as an estate by common law standards.

Example: C grants "To B for life, then to A if he marries." C then conveys his reversion to B before A gets married. B has a life estate and a reversion in fee simple; A has a contingent remainder in fee simple. B's interests merge into a fee simple, destroying A's contingent remainder.

b. Modern View

Most jurisdictions today have abolished the destructibility rule. Remainders that are still contingent are not destroyed at the expiration of the prior life estate. Instead, the original grantor is allowed to retake possession (i.e., reversion) subject to the remainder. Thus, in a grant "To A for life, then to B's children" possession reverts back the grantor until B has children, at which time the remainder vests and becomes possessory and the grantor's reversion terminates. If B dies without having children, the remainder is destroyed; the estate can never vest. Merger as a common law legal doctrine, has also been abolished in most states.

3. Open

This is a remainder that is granted to a group of persons.

Example: "To A for life, then to the children of B" may be completely contingent (e.g., B has no children yet), or it may be vested subject to open (e.g., some members of the class of grantees are living, but the class is still open to further additions if B has more children). The significance of a vested remainder being "open" is that the living class members hold a vested remainder that is subject to partial divestment (additional remainder interests will decrease the proportional share each holder of the vested remainder interest) if members are added to the class.

a. Class Closing Rule

If a remainder is vested subject to open, the class will close at the time when the supporting estate terminates, and the remainder interest becomes possessory. Additional individuals who are thereafter coming in to being are excluded from receiving a share.

Example: "To A for life, then to B's children." B has two children. B later has another child, then A dies. At A's death, his life estate is terminated and the vested remainder of B's children becomes possessory. B's three children can move to close the class, so that if B has more children at a future date, they will not receive a share of the estate. But, if no class members are alive at the time the estate becomes possessory, the class must stay open and includes all children born after that time.

b. *En Ventre Sa Mere*

An exception to the class closing rule is that children "conceived before but born after" the estate becomes possessory are deemed to be alive at the time of possession. Generally, any child born within nine months of the time that an estate becomes possessory is considered to be a life in being at the time possession was taken.

4. Alternative Contingent Remainders

These are future interests created where occurrence or nonoccurrence of the same condition lead to opposite results.

Example: O grants "To A for life, remainder to B if B survives A; if she does not to C." B has a contingent remainder in fee simple subject to the condition that he outlives A. C also has a contingent remainder in fee simple subject to the condition that B dies before A (i.e., both remainders are contingent until either A or B dies). Arguably one or the other contingency must happen: A will survive B, or she will not. If she does, she takes; if she does not, C takes. However, what if A and B die simultaneously? The estate reverts to the grantor.

5. A Life Estate in Remainder

A life estate may be granted in a remainder.

Example: "To A for life, then to B for life." A has a presently possessory life estate and B has a life estate in remainder. B's life estate is treated as vested despite the implied condition of surviving the previous owner. The life estate in remainder can be contingent (e.g., "To A for life, then to B's children for life") if B has no children at the time of the grant.

6. Alienability

Vested remainders are freely transferable by *inter vivos* transfer, will, intestate succession, etc. Contingent remainders are also freely transferable in most states, although at common law, they could not be conveyed *inter vivos*.

B. Executory Interests

An executory interest is the second type of future interest that a transferee can hold. Unlike a remainder, an executory interest always follows and cuts short a fee simple.

Example: "To A and his heirs, but if A dies without issue, to B and his heirs." A has a present possessory fee simple subject to divestment by B's shifting executory interest. There are two types of executory interests, springing and shifting.

1. Springing Executory Interest

A springing executory interest is one that limits a fee simple in the grantor.

Example: G grants "to A and his heirs, when A is 25." A is 22. Or, "To B for life, and one day later to C." In the first case, G has given a fee simple to A that will begin in the future. A has a springing executory interest in fee simple (i.e., that he reaches 25).

G has a present possessory fee simple subject to total divestment by A's springing executory interest. In the second example, B has a present possessory life estate. However, C does not take possession when it terminates (he must wait a day). The estate reverts to G for the one day gap, and then C takes possession, cutting short G's "fee simple subject to a springing executory interest in C."

2. Shifting Executory Interest

A shifting executory interest is one that limits a fee simple held by a previous grantee.

Example: G grants "To A and his heirs, but if A has no issue, then to B and his heirs," A has a present possessory fee simple subject to total divestment by B's shifting executory interest. Notice that this time B's interest cuts short that of another grantee.

3. Duration

Executory interests last as long as the conditions that morph them into possessory estates may occur. Once the condition precedent cannot be met, they are extinguished. In the example above, if A has children, B's shifting executory interest is extinguished. (Note that A's children receive nothing because "and his heirs" are only words of limitation; once A has a child, A acquires a fee simple absolute.) **Note:** Executory interests are *not* subject to destructibility or merger.

4. Alienability

Executory interests are freely transferable, devisable, and inheritable. There is also a possibility of escheat.

5. Common Law

All executory interests were prohibited at common law, but this is not the case today.

IV. RULES FURTHERING MARKETABILITY BY DESTROYING CONTINGENT FUTURE INTERESTS

A. The Rule in Shelley's Case

If a conveyance creates a life estate in a grantee and a remainder in fee simple in the heirs of the grantee, a remainder that would otherwise be contingent) the words "heirs of grantee" are treated as words of limitation and the grantee takes a fee simple absolute.

1. Example: "To A for life, remainder to the heirs of A," or "to the children of A." In both cases the Rule in Shelley's Case will regard the estate of A as a present possessory fee simple absolute, and his children/heirs therefore have no interest.

2. Modern View

This rule is abolished in most jurisdictions. In the example above, A gets a life estate and his heirs have a contingent remainder in fee simple absolute.

B. The Doctrine of Worthier Title

If a grantor creates a life estate in the grantee and then grants the remainder in fee simple to the grantor's heirs, the remainder is construed as a reversion in fee simple absolute in the grantor.

1. Example: G grants "to A for life, remainder to G's heirs." A has a presently possessory life estate and G has a reversion in fee simple absolute, G's heirs do not have any interest. This rule is only applied to *inter vivos* transfers.

2. Modern view

Most states treat "Worthier Title" as a presumption only, which is rebuttable by evidence of the grantor's actual intent. Some states have abolished the doctrine.

C. The Rule Against Perpetuities

The rule states, "no interest is good unless it must vest if at all no later than 21 years after the death of all lives in being." The basic thrust of the rule is that the contingencies that make a remainder a contingent or an interest an executory interest happen no later than 21 years after the death of all "lives in being." The rule does not mean that a remainder has to vest or that an executory interest has to become possessory within the measuring period (21 years). They must either fail or succeed within that time, so that their effect will be known with certainty.

1. Interests subject to the rule:

a. Springing and shifting executory interests;

b. Contingent remainders; and

c. Vested remainders subject to open — as long as the class of grantees is still open, the rule applies.

2. Interests that are NOT subject to the rule:

a. Reversions;

b. Rights of entry;

c. Possibilities of reverter; and

d. Vested remainders.

3. Effect

The rule goes into effect at the time the interest is created. For a will, that means at the death of the grantor; for a deed it is the time of transfer. The rule operates as follows: If it is possible to create a scenario, no matter how improbable, under which one of the future interests subject to the rule will neither succeed nor fail within the measuring period, then that interest is invalid and eliminated from the grant. The analysis is done at the time of the grantor's death or at the time of the grant.

Infectious invalidity — If cutting out a piece of the grant will defeat the purpose of the entire grant, the court will strike down the entire grant, not just the specific part.

4. Life in Being

A "life in being" is any party, living at the time the transfer was made, who has a causal effect on when and whether the future interests will vest or become possessory. Lives in being are usually named expressly in the grant, although they don't have to be. There is no requirement that they must receive an interest.

  a. Example: O grants "To A for life, remainder to A's children for life, remainder to A's grandchildren living at death of A's last child." Lives in being are A, any of his children who are alive at the time of transfer, and any of his grandchildren who are alive at that time.

  Rationale: A has a causal effect because he can have more children, which affects the vesting of the secondary life estate. His children have a causal effect because their very existence affects vesting and they affect the class of grandchildren. Finally, the very existence of the grandchildren affects the vesting of their future interest.

  b. Example: O grants "To my children for life, remainder to their grandchildren." Lives in being are O, any of his children living at the time the grant was made, and any of O's grandchildren and his children's grandchildren living at the time of transfer.

  Rationale: O has a causal effect because he can have more children. O's children have an effect both on the vesting of their life estate and on having more children of their own. Their children (O's grandchildren) have a direct effect on the size of the class of grandchildren. (Note that O's grandchildren are neither named nor have any interest). Finally, the children's grandchildren have an effect on the vesting of their future interest.

5. Time

The perpetuities period runs for 21 years after the death of the last life in being. Gestation periods (i.e., 9 months) are added.

6. Procedure

To determine whether a future interest violates the rule, go through the following steps:

  a. Identify all interests created in the grant, will, etc.

  b. Identify all "lives in being."

  c. Add 9 months to permit a gestation period.

d. Add a "nonlife in being" who is a potential taker or the source of a taker.

e. Kill off all "lives in being."

f. Will the future interests definitely vest or fail to vest within 21 years?

g. If there is uncertainty, the void provision is struck and possession reverts to the preceding estate or to the grantor.

h. Example: O grants "To A for life, remainder to A's children for life, remainder to his grandchildren at the death of A's last child," where A has two sons and a grandchild at the time of transfer.

Step 1

A has a present possessory life estate (not subject to the rule); A's sons have a vested remainder in a life estate, which is subject to open (and to the rule); A's grandchildren have a vested remainder subject to open (and to the rule).

Step 2

A, A's sons, and A's grandchildren living at the time of transfer are all "lives in being."

Step 3

If A has another child within nine months, that child will also be a life in being.

Step 4

A could have a son two years after the grant is made. Although the child affects the vesting of his life estate with his brothers and has a causal effect on the class of grandchildren, he was not alive at the time of transfer.

Step 5

A, his two sons, and his grandchild (living at the time of the grant) might all die in a plane crash a year later, so that only the third son remains alive.

Step 6

The surviving son's life estate becomes possessory on the death of A, and the class is also closed by that event, so that his estate does not violate the rule. However, he could live for longer than 21 years, or he could die sooner. Thus there is no guarantee that the grandchildren's remainder in fee simple will close (remember that it is vested already) or not within 21 years. The remainder violates the rule and is struck out. Possession reverts to O, or his heirs, after the surviving son dies.

i. Example: O grants "To A for life, remainder to A's widow for life, then to A's children alive at the death of A's widow." A has two sons at the time of transfer; A is married to Z.

Step 1

A has a present possessory life estate (not subject to the rule); A's children have a vested remainder in a life estate, which is subject to open (and to the rule). A's widow has a contingent remainder. Do you see why? Z may die, and A may remarry, and die before Z2.

Step 2

A and A's sons living at the time of transfer are all "lives in being."

Step 3

If A has another child within nine months, that child will also be a life in being.

Step 4

A could have a son two years after the grant is made.

Step 5

A, his two sons, and his grandchild (living at the time of the grant) might all die in a plane crash a year later, so that only the third son remains alive.

Step 6

Z might die and A might marry Z2, a person not in being at the time of the grant. The surviving son's reminder vests and then becomes possessory at the death of Z2, who could live for longer than 21 years after A and the children alive at the grant die. The remainder to A's children violates the rule and is struck out. Possession reverts to O, or his heirs, after the surviving son dies.

j. Example: O grants "To A and her heirs after the closing of my estate.

Step 1

A has a spring executory interest, which will vest when O's estate is closed.

Step 2

A's sons and grandchildren living at the time of transfer are all "lives in being."

Step 3

The so-called slothful executor could fail to offer the will for probate.

Step 4

A's heir, A the VIII, a great-great-grandson, unborn at the time of the grant, could offer the will for probate in 2100 more than 21 years after a life in being at the time of the grant.

7. Charity-to-Charity Exception

Transfers from one charity to another are not subject to the rule, even if they violate it.

8. Statutory Remedies

The harsh effects of the Rule Against Perpetuities have led most jurisdictions to modify it in one of three ways:

a. "Wait-and-See" Statutes

Instead of making an immediate decision as to whether or not a future interest violates the rule, "wait and see" if it ends up violating the rule. Thus, the court will strike out an interest only if, 21 years after the death of the last life in being, the interest actually did not succeed or fail.

b. *Cy-pres* Statutes

Instead of striking out the invalid provision, courts try to reform the grant to achieve the grantor's intent as nearly as possible without violating the rule. The process, however, is done at the time the grant is made.

c. *Cy-pres* and "Wait-and-See" Statutes

Some jurisdictions have combined both, so that courts will "wait and see" until a problem actually arises and will then reform the grant if possible.

V. RULE AGAINST RESTRAINTS ON ALIENATION

Courts will invalidate some restrictions placed on the alienation of land in the grant as a matter of public policy.

A. Three Types of Restrictions

1. Disability

A grant states that any transfers made by the grantee are of no force or effect.

2. Forfeiture

A grant states that the grantee forfeits the land if he makes a transfer.

3. Promissory

A grant has a covenant forbidding alienation. Remedy is either injunction or damages for breach of contract.

B. Effect of Rule

The type of estate that was conveyed influences the effect of the rule.

1. Fee Simple

If a fee simple was conveyed, all restrictions on alienation are unenforceable.

2. Life Estate

Disabling restraints (that life tenant cannot alienate) will not be enforced, but others may be enforced.

3. Leaseholds

Forfeiture and promissory restraints are enforceable. Disabling restraints are also likely to be enforced by most courts.

CASE CLIPS

I. Retained Future Interests — Future Interests in the Transferor/III. Transferred Future Interests

Kost v. Foster (1950)

Facts: A deed drawn by his parents gave Kost a life tenancy with the remainder in his children. One child was bankrupt. Local law allowed the trustee in bankruptcy to sell vested but not contingent remainders. The trustee sold the bankrupt son's remainder. The parties disputed whether the remainder was vested or contingent.

Issue: How should a court determine whether a remainder is vested or contingent?

Rule: Whether a remainder is vested or contingent depends on the grammatical structure employed. If the condition is contained in the clause that creates the interest, then the interest will be interpreted as a contingent remainder. If the condition is stated in a clause separate from that which creates the interest, then it will be construed as a vested remainder subject to a condition subsequent.

Abo Petroleum Corp. v. Amstutz (1979)

Facts: The Amstutzes conveyed a life estate to their children, with contingent remainders in their grandchildren, the defendants. The parents retained a reversionary interest. Later, the parents purported to convey the same property in fee simple absolute to their children. The children subsequently attempted to convey fee simple interests to the predecessors of the Abo Petroleum Corporation (plaintiff). The defendants argued that the first deed gave their parents only life estates.

Issue: Under the doctrine of destructibility of contingent remainders, when a grantor conveys land and creates a contingent remainder in a third party, but reserves a reversionary interest in himself, will that remainder be destroyed by a subsequent conveyance in fee simple by the same grantor to the same grantee?

Rule: The doctrine of destructibility of contingent remainders is obsolete. Therefore, a conveyance of property in fee simple will not destroy contingent remainders that have been created previously.

Stoller v. Doyle (1913)

Facts: Lawrence Doyle first conveyed a fee to Frank Doyle with a contingent interest in the wife and children of the grantee and a reversion in the grantor. Later, Lawrence executed a new deed purporting to remove all restrictions of the first grant. Frank Doyle subsequently conveyed the land to Stoller. Stoller sued to quiet title.

Issue: Did the first grant create a contingent remainder subject to destruction or an executory interest not subject to destruction?

Rule: An interest following a fee held by one other than the grantee or grantor is an executory interest not subject to destruction.

II. Rules Furthering Marketability by Destroying Contingent Future Interests

Sybert v. Sybert (1953)

Facts: The testator, J.H. Sybert, bequeathed a life estate to his son, Fred Sybert (the defendant's husband), "to vest in fee simple in the heirs of his body." The son died intestate without issue. The life tenant's brothers (plaintiffs) contended that they should inherit the testator's reversion. The defendant contended that the Rule in Shelley's Case converted the heir's contingent remainder into a fee simple in her husband.

Issue: Is the Rule in Shelley's Case applicable to Testator's devise?

Rule: Unless language qualifying the words "heirs of his body" establishes that a testator did not intend the words to be used in their technical sense, the Rule in Shelly's case will apply.

City Bank & Trust Co. v. Morrissey (1983)

Facts: A testamentary trust gave the trustee discretion to distribute it in kind or after a cash conversion to the beneficiary's heirs at law following the beneficiary's death. The defendant contended that the trustee's power to convert the assets resulted in creating two estates of unequal kind, realty and personalty, and that, therefore, the Rule in Shelley's Case is inapplicable.

Issue 1: Does the discretionary power of a trustee to distribute assets in kind or in cash effect an equitable conversion triggering the Rule in Shelley's Case?

Rule 1: To effect an equitable conversion, the trustee must be mandated to convert the assets.

Issue 2: To trigger the Rule in Shelley's Case, must estates be of equal quality?

Rule 2: There are three requisites for the application of the Rule in Shelly's Case: (1) a freehold estate must be granted to the ancestor; (2) a remainder must be limited to his heirs, general or special; and (3) the two estates, freehold and remainder, must both be of the same quality, either legal or equitable.

Braswell v. Braswell (1954)

Facts: James Braswell conveyed land to his son, Nathaniel Braswell, "during his natural life . . . and if said (son) should die leaving no lawful heir . . . then the land herein conveyed shall revert back to the grantor or to his lawful heirs." Nathaniel died without issue, devising all his real property to Charles Braswell. Charles was not a lawful heir of James Braswell. Charles brought suit against the lawful heirs of James Braswell for partition.

Issue: Will a remainder left to a grantor's heirs become a reversion in the grantor under the Doctrine of Worthier Title?

Rule: The Doctrine of Worthier Title, a rule of construction, creates a presumption in favor of reversions, which may be rebutted by indication of the grantor's contrary intent gathered from the instrument as a whole.

Estate of Annie I. Kern (1979)

Facts: The testator devised all her property to her only son, Ralph, who predeceased her. Pursuant to Iowa's antilapse statute, the collateral heirs of the testator's deceased husband claim the property should have been divided among Ralph's heirs. The testator's collateral heirs contend that the Doctrine of Worthier Title compelled the division of her property entirely among them alone.

Issue: Is the testamentary branch of the Worthier Title Doctrine operative in an antilapse statute context?

Rule: The Worthier Title Doctrine is prospectively abrogated in antilapse situations.

Jee v. Audley (1787)

Facts: Audley willed that in default of issue by Mary Hall, the estate should pass to the daughters of John and Elizabeth Jee.

Issue 1: When does a failure of issue of an individual occur?

Rule 1: A failure of issue occurs when an individual is dead and all of the individual's descendants are dead.

Issue 2: At what age does the law recognize that a person can no longer have children?

Rule 2: Every individual is presumed to be capable of having offspring at any time before the individual's death.

Issue 3: Can a will contain a limitation that upon failure of issue of a certain living individual, an estate passes to the offspring of a third party?

Rule 3: Limitations on personal estates are void unless they necessarily vest within 21 years of a life in being when the interest was created. Any person alive at the testator's death may be employed as a measure of "lives in being."

Broadway Nat'l Bank v. Adams (1882)

Facts: The creditor sued an income beneficiary in an attempt to attach the trust income. The grantor had expressly provided that the income shall remain "free from the interference or control of his creditors."

Issue: May the founder of a trust attach to the trust a condition that the income from it cannot be alienated?

Rule: A person may create a trust in favor of a beneficiary, and provide that it shall not be alienated by him, nor be seized by his creditors in advance of its payments to him.

Connecticut Bank and Trust Company v. Brody (1978)

Facts: Testator's will devised successive life estates in trust for his children and grandchildren with the corpus to be divided equally per capita among his great-grandchildren. At his death, he was survived by children and grandchildren; after his death, 12 great-grandchildren were born.

Issue: Does the remainder interest in the great-grandchildren vest after the period of the rule against perpetuities?

Rule: The court applies the rule. Subsequent to the testator's death, his child could have a child. All those living at the time of the grant could die. The after-born grandchild lives for an additional 50 years. The gift vests in his child more than 21 years after a life in being at the time of the grant.

Brown v. Independent Baptist Church of Woburn (1950)

Facts: The defendant held a determinable fee that might last indefinitely.

Issue: Can the Rule Against Perpetuities prevent a possibility of reverter from passing through a will's residuary clause?

Rule: The Rule Against Perpetuities does not apply to reversionary interests such as possibility of reverter.

Central Delaware County Auth. v. Greyhound Corp. (1991)

Facts: Two parcels of land had been conveyed to Central Delaware. Both deeds contained a fee simple interest subject to a restrictive covenant, giving the grantor or its successor the right to repurchase the land if the Authority ceased to use it for public purposes.

Issue: Does a deed restriction which states that a grantor or its successor may repurchase a property after the tract has ceased to be used for its deeded purpose fall under the Rule Against Perpetuities?

Rule: Where a clause maintains that upon abandonment, payment of a certain sum of money will follow, the interest can be seen as either a repurchase option or a fee simple subject to a condition subsequent.

The distinction is important because a repurchase option is subject to the Rule Against Perpetuities, whereas a fee simple subject to a condition subsequent, being a vested interest, is not.

Note: The court held that this restriction was a repurchase option rendered void by the rule against perpetuities.

III. Rule Against Restraints on Alienation

Capitol Federal Savings & Loan Ass'n v. Smith (1957)

Facts: The owners of certain lots agreed to forbid the sale of those lots to blacks. Failure to abide by the agreement resulted in automatic divestment of ownership rights.

Issue: Are future interests subject to equal protection analysis?

Rule: A future interest arising from a racially restrictive covenant violates the Fourteenth Amendment.

CHAPTER 5

Concurrent Ownership

I. CONCURRENT OWNERSHIP

Situations arise in which two or more persons have simultaneous rights of present or future possession. There are three main types: the joint tenancy, the tenancy in common, and the tenancy by the entirety.

A. Joint Tenancy

Each joint tenant has an undivided interest in the whole of the property.

1. Right of survivorship is the primary characteristic of the joint tenancy. When one joint tenant dies, the decedent's interest is extinguished and the survivors continue to hold an undivided right in the property. The decedent's will has no impact on the property.

Note: A deceased joint tenant's creditor cannot reach the surviving joint tenant's interest.

2. Four Unities are essential to a joint tenancy at common law and in many states today.

a. Time

The interests of each joint tenant must be acquired at the same time.

b. Possession

Each joint tenant must have an equal right to possess the whole property.

c. Interest

All the joint tenants must have identical interests in the property, both as to duration and fractional share.

d. Title

All joint tenants must acquire title by the same instrument.

3. Creation of joint tenancies

At common law, there was a presumption that a cotenancy was a joint tenancy.

   a. Modern statutes now presume that a cotenancy is a tenancy in common (see below) in the absence of language that clearly indicates an intention to create a joint tenancy.

   b. Explicit language is required to create a joint tenancy (e.g., "to A and B as joint tenants with right of survivorship, and not as tenants in common").

   c. A wants to convert his fee simple into a joint tenancy with B.

      i. Common-law view

      This could not be accomplished by conveying "from A to A and B" because the requirements of unity of time and unity of title would not be satisfied. A had to transfer to a strawperson X who then transferred to A and B as joint tenants so that the unities of time and title are present.

      ii. Modern statutes allow a property owner to create a joint tenancy in himself and another party without the use of a strawperson.

4. Severance of a joint tenancy by destroying one of the unities leaves the parties as tenants in common. There are many ways to sever a joint tenancy.

   a. Lifetime (*inter vivos*) conveyance by one of the joint tenants to a third party destroys unity of title and time, because the third party received the interest by a different instrument, and at a different time than the remaining original joint tenant. The joint tenancy is severed and the third party is a tenant in common with the remaining original joint tenant.

      i. More than two original joint tenants

      A conveyance by one of the joint tenants to an outsider will result in a tenancy in common between the outsider and the remaining joint tenants, but the joint tenancy will stay intact as between the remaining original joint tenants.

      ii. Example: A, B, and C are joint tenants. C transfers his interest to X. X now holds an undivided one-third interest in the property as a tenant in common with A and B, but A and B hold the remaining two-thirds as joint tenants with the right of survivorship. If A dies, his interest is extinguished and the whole is held by B. If X dies, however, his devisees or heirs receive his interest.

   b. Lease

   Although unities of interest and possession are destroyed once a lease is granted to an outside party, some courts hold that a joint tenancy is not severed by a joint tenant's execution of a lease. There is disagreement over this issue.

c. Mortgage

There is disagreement over whether the granting of a mortgage by a joint tenant destroys the joint tenancy. It depends on the theory of mortgages to which the jurisdiction adheres.

   i. Lien theory (majority rule)

   This principle views a mortgage as a lien to secure payment and, therefore, does not consider the execution of a mortgage as a transfer of title to the mortgagee. According to this majority rule, a mortgage does not sever a joint tenancy.

   ii. Title theory (minority rule)

   This principle views the execution of a mortgage as a transfer of title from the mortgagor to the mortgagee. According to this minority rule, a mortgage does sever a joint tenancy.

d. Mutual agreement

A joint tenancy may be terminated by mutual agreement of the owners, express or implied.

e. Judicial sale

A creditor of a joint tenant can levy execution during the lifetime of the debtor and terminate the joint tenancy. If the debtor joint tenant dies before the creditor is able to secure a judicial sale, the surviving joint tenant is entitled to the property free from the claims of the creditor.

B. Tenancy in Common

Tenants in common have separate, but undivided, interests in the property.

1. No right of survivorship exists in a tenancy in common. A deceased tenant's interest will pass to his heirs or devisees.

2. To create a tenancy in common requires only one unity is required: unity of possession (i.e., each tenant is entitled to possess the whole property). Unities of interest, title, and time (discussed above) are not required. Therefore, tenants in common can obtain unequal interests by different deeds at different times.

3. A statutory or common law presumption favoring tenancies in common over joint tenancies exists in most states.

4. Heirs taking an estate are classified as tenants in common.

C. Tenancy by the Entirety

A form of concurrent ownership which can only be created in a married couple. This tenancy is recognized in less than half of the states.

1. The four unities (time, title, interest, and possession) are required just as they are for joint tenancies.

2. Presumption of tenancy by the entireties: in most states that recognize this tenancy, there is a presumption that a property grant

to a husband and wife is intended to establish a tenancy by the entirety.

Note: A man or a woman cannot transfer a partial interest to his/her spouse and create a tenancy by the entirety because unities of time and interest are absent.

3. Right of survivorship: the surviving spouse has a right of survivorship (just as the surviving joint tenant).

4. Not subject to severance: Neither spouse can terminate the tenancy and thereby defeat the other's right of survivorship by unilateral action (e.g., by inter vivos transfer or judicial partition).

5. Termination results when:

   a. There is a mutual agreement to terminate.

   b. One spouse dies.

   c. Judgment is executed against husband and wife by a joint creditor of both.

   d. There is a divorce (which leaves the parties as tenants in common).

6. Management

   At common law, the husband had exclusive right to manage marital property (see marital interest section, below). Married Women's Property Acts adopted in the late nineteenth century in most states gave the woman equal rights with her husband to manage the property.

   a. Most states hold that neither husband nor wife may sell or burden the property without the consent of the other spouse.

   b. Creditors in most states cannot encumber a debtor spouse's property while the other spouse is still living. If the debtor spouse dies first, the surviving spouse's interest supersedes the creditor's interest. Only if the debtor survives his spouse may the creditor's claim be satisfied.

7. Personal Property

   The majority rule is that a tenancy by the entirety may exist with respect to personal property.

II. RIGHTS AND RESPONSIBILITIES OF COTENANTS APPLICABLE TO THE THREE MAIN TYPES OF COTENANCIES

A. Right of Possession: Each cotenant has the right to possess the entire property (i.e., unity of possession). No cotenant has the right to exclusive possession of the premises.

B. Possession by One Cotenant: Because there is unity of possession, the cotenant in sole possession does not ordinarily have a duty to account (i.e., to pay the other cotenant one-half the rental value of the property).

1. Duty to Account If an Ouster Occurs

   If the cotenant in sole possession wrongfully excludes his cotenants from the property, an ouster occurs. The tenant in possession must pay the ousted cotenant his share of the rental value of the property.

2. Duty to Account if the Tenant in Sole Possession Depletes the Land

   If the cotenant lessens the value of the land by taking away and selling resources such as coal, timber, etc., he will have to account to his cotenant for the fair share of the revenues he received.

3. Duty to Account for Lease to a Third Party

   If one cotenant makes use of the property for his own benefit, he is not required to account for the reasonable rental value. However, if the cotenant rents the property to a third party, he must pay his cotenants their fair share of the rents collected.

C. Contribution: A cotenant may wish to receive contributions from the other cotenants for certain payments he has made to benefit the property. If the cotenant has a duty to account, he may deduct the contribution owed him before paying the other cotenants their fair share of the property's proceeds.

1. Real Estate Taxes and Mortgage Payments

   Paid to benefit the entire property for both cotenants. Contribution from other cotenants may be sought.

2. Improvements

   The cotenant that pays for improvements will almost never be compensated. However, the cotenant can receive the portion of land containing the improvements in a partition in kind or the value of the improvement in a partition by sale (see below).

3. Repairs

   If one cotenant makes repairs without the consent of the other, most courts will not enforce contribution. However, there is a trend toward allowing contribution if the repairs were necessary, especially if possession is shared by the cotenants. Adjustments for uncompensated repairs may be made before a property is partitioned (see below).

D. Partition

   Any cotenant, except a tenant by the entirety, may bring an action for the partition of property.

1. Partition in kind occurs when the property is physically divided to reflect each cotenant's proportional interest.

2. Partition by sale is executed when the property is sold and the proceeds are divided to reflect the proportional interests of the cotenants.

3. The partition will be adjusted to account for uncompensated repairs, improvements, tax payments, and rents (see section C above).

III. MARITAL PROPERTY RIGHTS: COMMON-LAW SEPARATE PROPERTY REGIMES

All legal systems have laws that have an impact on property owned by partners to a marriage, whether the property was acquired before or during marriage. The Anglo-American common law treated a married couple as a single juridical entity, and absent a prenuptial settlement, a husband controlled the property of his wife during marriage. Significant changes in a married woman's property rights status did not take place until the mid-nineteenth century.

A. Husband's Interest in Wife's Property
   1. The husband was entitled to the use of *all* the lands and personal property that his wife possessed before, or acquired during, the marriage.
      a. The husband had a right to occupy and alienate his wife's land and to collect all its rents and profits.
      b. Husband's control terminated on his death or in very rare cases of separation or divorce. The wife's land passed to her heirs, although with respect to personal property, a husband could appropriate his wife's personal property, because a wife could only make a will with the consent of her husband.
   2. Curtesy
      On the birth of a live child (survival of the child was not necessary), the husband had a life interest in his wife's land if she predeceased him. If a child was not born, the husband's right in his wife's land terminated on her death, and the land passed to her heirs.
   3. Modern View: Separate Ownership and the "Elective Share"
      a. Married Women's Property Acts were passed in the mid-nineteenth century, which allowed a woman to hold separately and to dispose of her property during the marriage and at her death.
      b. Curtesy has been abolished by statute in most states. In these states, if a wife dies intestate, her husband is considered an heir and receives a share of her property that is prescribed by statute. If she dies testate, the husband may take the bequest or elect between the will's provisions and a statutory share (normally the intestate share reserved to a surviving spouse).

B. Rights of the Wife in Husband's Property
   1. Dower
      The common law did not consider a wife to be her husband's heir and she therefore received no land on his death. To ensure that a widow was provided for, dower was developed which gave

the wife a life estate in one-third of all the lands he held at anytime during marriage. Dower rights attached to land, even if the husband sold the property or had creditors who claimed the property to settle debts owed.

   a. Requirements
     i. The land must have been owned and possessed by the husband at some point during the marriage; it need not be owned at death.
     ii. The land had to have been hereditable estates.
     iii. Unlike with respect to curtesy, there was no requirement that the wife produce a child.
     iv. Termination of right to dower occurred on legal separation, divorce, or the death of the wife.

  2. Legitimate Share of Personal Property
Local custom usually allowed widows one-third of their husbands' personal property; however, these customs eroded in the latter middle ages, and by the year 1700, wives had no claim to the personal property of their deceased husbands.

  3. Modern View: Dower Abolished and Replaced by the "Elective Share"
   a. Abolished in most states
In these states, if a husband dies intestate, his wife is considered an heir and receives a share of his property that is prescribed by statute. If he dies testate, the wife may take the bequest or elect between the will's provisions and a statutory share (normally the intestate share reserved to a surviving spouse).
   b. Retained in a few states
In these states, the wife may elect between dower and the statutory share. The principal benefit of choosing dower is that it passes free from the claims of the decedent's creditors.

IV. MARITAL PROPERTY RIGHTS: THE COMMUNITY PROPERTY SYSTEM

Eight states (Arizona, California, Idaho, Louisiana, Nevada, New Mexico, Texas, and Washington) have a system of community property. The system's basic assumption is that the husband and wife should share equally any wealth produced by the other spouse during the marriage. Thus for each dollar the husband earns, one-half belongs to the wife, and vice versa.

A. Effect
All property earned during the marriage (not that property owned before marriage or inherited during marriage) by either spouse is

community property owned jointly by husband and wife. When a marriage is dissolved or when property is sold, each is entitled to one-half of the proceeds.

B. Strong Presumption That Property Acquired or Possessed During Marriage Is Community Property
   1. Community property includes:
      a. Income from community property (even if the property is only listed in one spouse's name).
      b. Earnings by both spouses during the marriage.
   2. The presumption can be rebutted by a preponderance of the evidence proving that the property is separately owned.

C. Separate property includes:
   1. Property obtained by either spouse before marriage.
   2. Property obtained by either spouse by gift, devise, or descent.
   3. Five out of eight community property states also include income from all separate property in this category.

D. Separate property can be transformed into community property by the act of the spouse who owns the property. Neither spouse can change community property into separate property without the consent of the other.

E. Management
   1. Before 1960
      The husband had exclusive control over community property as a fiduciary. However, he could not convey real property without his wife's consent in most cases.
   2. Present
      Community property states give each spouse equal control over the property.

F. Comparison with the Common Law
   1. None of the eight states adopts the concepts of dower, curtesy, or tenancy by the entirety.
   2. Tenancies in common and joint tenancies are recognized as separate property, but cannot be simultaneously held as community property.

G. Death
   Community property is considered to be owned by each spouse in equal halves. As a result, each spouse has the power to devise half the property. If there is no will, some states grant the property to the surviving spouses; others pass the property onto the decedent's heirs.

H. Divorce
   Some states evenly divide the property upon divorce. Others require the courts to make an equitable distribution.

I. Conflict of Laws Rule

Property acquires its character at the time of procurement.

1. Personal property is classified in accordance with the law of the couple's domicile at the time of acquisition.

2. Real estate is always classified in accordance with the laws of the state where it is situated unless the party is domiciled in a state with a different marital property regime.

CASE CLIPS

In Re Estate of Michael (1966)

Facts: A deed's language failed to explicitly create a joint tenancy, although it did state that the grantees had a "right of survivorship."
Issue: Does a devise to two or more persons (not husband and wife or trustees) with a right of survivorship create, without more, a joint tenancy?
Rule: Within the four corners of the instrument, a grantor's intent to create a joint tenancy must be clearly expressed, otherwise no right of survivorship exists, and a tenancy in common, not a joint tenancy, is created.

Laura v. Christian (1975)

Facts: Laura, the plaintiff, and Christian were cotenants of property threatened with foreclosure. The plaintiff averted foreclosure by paying a lien without contribution from the defendant. The plaintiff sued to quiet title in himself. After the property's value increased, the defendant asserted that he could redeem his interest.
Issue: Does a derelict cotenant have an option to reimburse his fellow cotenants who, in order to avert foreclosure on commonly held property, paid a lien on the property without contribution?
Rule: When a cotenant pays an obligation, on common property subject to contribution, the fellow cotenants can exercise their option, within a reasonable time, to redeem or prevent loss of their interest by proportionately reimbursing the paying cotenant.

Goergen v. Maar (1956)

Facts: Goergen (defendant) was one of four cotenants, but exclusively occupied the common property, collected and retained the rent, and paid the taxes and maintenance expenses. The other cotenants sought a partition and accounting.
Issue: May cotenants not in possession of the commonly held property impose on the possessing cotenant's interest an equitable charge when the possessing cotenant retained more than his proportionate share of the rents?
Rule: Any item of rent received by a cotenant in excess of his share of the income of the property is an equitable charge against his interest, and any expenditure made by a cotenant in excess of his share of the obligation is a charge against the interests of his cotenants.

White v. Smyth (1948)

Facts: The plaintiff and defendant were tenants in common. White (plaintiff) mined the land and kept for himself all proceeds of the mining operation. The defendant sought partition by sale and division of the profits already realized in proportion to each party's interest in the property.

Issue: Must a cotenant who kept all the profits realized from the common property account to his co-owners for the profits realized from the common property?

Rule: When a co-owner of mineral property works the property and disposes of the minerals produced, he must account to his cotenants for all profits made.

Michalski v. Michalski (1958)

Facts: A husband and wife held property as tenants in common. They agreed in writing that neither would convey or mortgage their interest without the others' consent and that neither party "shall do or permit anything in respect thereto to defeat the common tenancy of said properties by said parties," A year later, they divorced. The husband (plaintiff) sought to partition some of the property by sale.

Issue: May tenants in common agree to prohibit partition of property?

Rule: Although the right of partition between cotenants is absolute, cotenants can, if they explicitly state or clearly manifest their intent, bar partition for a reasonable time. If, however, the agreement is no longer fair and equitable due to changed circumstances, a court can decline to enforce it.

Miller v. Riegler (1967)

Facts: An aunt reregistered stock in which she had sole title. The reregistered stock listed the aunt and her niece, Mary Jane Riegler, as joint tenants. On the aunt's death, Marjorie Miller, also a niece, argued that a joint tenancy was not created.

Issue: Is the common-law requirement of unity of time essential to the creation of a joint tenancy?

Rule: Where it is grantor's intent to create a joint tenancy, the absence of unity of time is not fatal. A grantor can convey her own property to herself and another as joint tenants.

Jackson v. O'Connell (1961)

Facts: Three sisters held property as joint tenants. One sister conveyed her interest to another sister, who devised her property by will to her heirs.

The heirs (plaintiffs) sued the third sister, O'Connell, to partition the real estate.

Issue: Does a conveyance by one joint tenant of real estate to another of the joint tenants destroy the joint tenancy in its entirety or merely sever the joint tenancy with respect to the undivided interest so conveyed, leaving the joint tenancy in force and effect as to the remaining interest?

Rule: Where one joint tenant conveys her interest to one of her cotenants, the cotenant grantee holds the share conveyed as a tenant in common and her original share is held with the remaining cotenants as a joint tenancy.

Palmer v. Flint (1900)

Facts: A bank (defendant) conveyed property to a married couple as "joint tenants, and not as tenants in common, to them and their assigns and to the survivors, and the heirs and assigns of the survivor forever." After a divorce, Alice Flint, the wife conveyed the premises to her ex-husband. His sister, Roxa Palmer (plaintiff), subsequently acquired the property. The defendants claimed the bank's conveyance to Flint, and her ex-husband created a joint life estate with a contingent remainder in the survivor.

Issue: Does the use of the word "heirs" in the phrase "and the heirs of the survivor forever," and in no other part of the granting or habendum clauses of a deed, preclude a severance of the property and thus create a life estate in the grantees with a contingent fee in the survivor?

Rule: If the intention of the parties to create a joint tenancy clearly expressed in a deed is in conflict with technical rules of common law in the construction of deeds, the intent takes precedence and overrides the technical rules of the common law.

Jones v. Green (1983)

Facts: Dorothy Jones (plaintiff) and James Green (defendant) purchased property together as joint tenants, each with full rights of ownership. They were unmarried. The plaintiff sued to partition the property.

Issue: May property conveyed to unmarried individuals as joint tenants and not as tenants in common be partitioned?

Rule: Real estate owned by joint tenants may not be partitioned.

People v. Nogarr (1958)

Facts: Elaine Wilson and her husband, Calvert, owned real estate as joint tenants. Before his death, Calvert executed and delivered to the State of California a mortgage on the land, without the consent of Elaine. After Calvert died, the State commenced an action to condemn the subject property. Elaine challenged that action, arguing that Calvert's conveyance was only effective as to his interest in the property.

Issue: Is a mortgage on real property executed by one of two joint tenants enforceable after the death of that joint tenant?

Rule: A mortgage is but a lien on the mortgagor's interest and it does not destroy the unity of title or possession and does not terminate the joint tenancy.

Hawthorne v. Hawthorne (1963)

Facts: A wife (plaintiff) and her husband (defendant) were tenants by the entirety. They bought a fire insurance policy. After their dwelling burned down, the wife sought an equal division of the insurance proceeds.

Issue: Must the proceeds of a fire insurance policy insuring an interest held by a wife and husband as tenants by the entirety be divided at the demand of one of the owners?

Rule: Because an insurance contract is personalty and personalty cannot be held by the entirety, insurance proceeds must be divided on the demand of one of its recipients.

D'Ercole v. D'Ercole (1976)

Facts: A wife (plaintiff) and husband (defendant) held property as tenants by the entirety. When they separated, the husband exercised his statutorily created paramount rights in the family home, denying the wife her equity in the property.

Issue: Does tenancy by the entirety, which is designed by statute to favor the husband, create a constitutionally impermissible classification?

Rule: Tenancy by the entirety, being but one option open to married persons seeking to take title in real estate, is constitutionally permissible.

Mann v. Bradley (1975)

Facts: Before their divorce, Aaron Mann (defendant) and his wife held property as joint tenants. The divorce agreement allowed the wife and children to live in the family house until the occurrence of certain events, whereupon it would be sold and the proceeds equally divided. None of the contingencies occurred during the wife's life. On the wife's death, the husband claimed to be sole owner by virtue of his right of survivorship. The administrator of the wife's estate sued to quiet title, arguing that the earlier agreement had converted the joint tenancy into a tenancy in common.

Issue: May a joint tenancy be terminated by a mutual agreement, explicit or implicit, of the parties?

Rule: A joint tenancy may be terminated by mutual agreement of the parties, which can be inferred from the manner in which the parties deal with the property.

Duncan v. Vassaur (1976)

Facts: A married couple, Edgar and Betty Vassaur, owned property as joint tenants. Betty murdered her husband and then argued that her right of survivorship left her sole owner of the property.

Issue: Does a surviving joint tenant lose her rights to survivorship when she murders her cotenant?

Rule: The murder of a cotenant by the other cotenant is inconsistent with the continued existence of the joint tenancy; thus, the joint tenancy is terminated at the time of the murder and right of survivorship will not be effective.

Centex Homes Corp. v. Boag (1974)

Facts: Centex Homes Corp. (plaintiff) contracted to sell a condominium to the Boags (defendants). When the Boags refused to honor the contract, Centex sued for specific performance.

Issue: Is the equitable remedy of specific performance available for the enforcement of a contract for the sale of a condominium?

Rule: Because damages sustained by a condominium vendor resulting from the breach of a sales contract are measurable, and the remedy at law is wholly adequate, specific performance is not an available remedy.

Dutcher v. Owens (1983)

Facts: A fire began in the commonly held area of a condominium complex. The Owenses sued in tort for property damage sustained while renting a condo from Dutcher. The trial court ruled that Dutcher's liability was pro rata to his ownership interest in the common areas. The appeals court partially reversed and held Dutcher jointly and severally liable.

Issue: Are condominium co-owners jointly and severally liable, or are they liable only for a pro rata portion of damages caused by a fire that originated in an area held as tenants in common?

Rule: The liability of a condominium co-owner is limited to his pro rata interest where such liability arises from those areas held by tenancy in common.

Holbrook v. Holbrook (1965)

Facts: By statute, Oregon abolished joint tenancy. Contemplating divorce, Mr. Holbrook and his wife (plaintiff), agreed to hold land "as joint tenants . . . with right of survivorship." Before his death, Mr. Holbrook conveyed "an undivided one-half interest" in the land to his nephew (defendant).

Issue: Where the common-law rule of severance has been abolished as well as the common-law joint tenancy, what will be the effect of an agreement purporting to create a joint tenancy?

Rule: Where the common-law rule of severance has been abolished by statute along with common-law joint tenancy, an agreement purporting to create a joint tenancy creates concurrent life estates with contingent remainders in the life tenants, remainder to vest in the survivor.

Porter v. Porter (1985)

Facts: Mary Jane Porter (plaintiff) was married to Denis Porter until 1976, when they divorced. Before the divorce, they acquired a house as joint tenants with a right of survivorship. The divorce decree temporarily granted Mary Jane exclusive possession of the house. After Denis Porter's death, the executrix of his estate sought partition, arguing that the divorce decree terminated the survivorship provisions of the original deed.

Issue: Does a divorce decree that temporarily divides possession of jointly held property destroy a joint tenancy with right of survivorship in real estate?

Rule: The mere temporary division of property held by joint tenants, without an intention to partition, will not destroy unity of possession and amount to a severance of the joint tenancy; consequently, a divorce decree that is silent with respect to property held jointly with a right of survivorship does not automatically destroy the existing survivorship provisions.

Brant v. Hargrove (1981)

Facts: The Brants (plaintiffs) were husband and wife, and were joint tenants with rights of survivorship. Before his wife's death, the husband, without his wife's consent or knowledge, encumbered his joint tenancy interest.

Issue: Does the granting of a deed of trust lien by a joint tenant on his joint tenancy interest sever the joint tenancy relationship?

Rule: The execution of a deed of trust by one joint tenant does not, in and of itself, operate to sever the joint tenancy.

Lerman v. Levine (1988)

Facts: The Levines (defendants) and Lerman (plaintiff) purchased a home as joint tenants. After relations deteriorated between the parties, Lerman left to reside elsewhere. Lerman sued to recover use and occupancy payments from the Levines.

Issue: Do one or more cotenants who use common property to the exclusion of another cotenant have a duty to account to the excluded cotenant for the benefit received in excess of their fair share?

Rule: When two or more persons hold property as joint tenants or tenants in common, if one of them occupies, receives or uses the property in greater proportion than the amount of his interest, any other party may bring an action for use and occupation against such person and recover such value as is in excess of his proportion. It is not required to show that an ouster occurred.

Massey v. Prothero (1983)

Facts: Massey (plaintiff) was the sister of Prothero (defendant). The two held real property inherited from their parents. Because one of their deceased brothers had failed to pay the taxes, the property was placed for sale at a tax sale. Prothero, without telling his sister, purchased the property at the sale.

Issue: May one cotenant extinguish the rights of others by buying the property at a tax sale?

Rule: A cotenant may not extinguish the rights of the other cotenants by buying the property at a tax sale.

Delfino v. Vealencis (1980)

Facts: The Delfinos (plaintiffs), tenants in common of 99/144 of an undivided interest in property, sought to partition the property with the defendant, who owned the rest of the property.

Issue: May a court order a sale to partition property jointly owned?

Rule: A partition by sale may be ordered only when: (1) the physical attributes of the land are such that a partition in kind is impracticable or inequitable; and (2) the interests of the owners would be better promoted by a partition by sale.

Central National Bank of Cleveland v. Fitzwilliam (1984)

Facts: The Fitzwilliams (defendants), husband and wife, were tenants by the entirety. When the husband failed to satisfy promissory notes owed to the plaintiff, Central National Bank, the plaintiff sought to conduct a foreclosure sale to satisfy the lien on the jointly held property.

Issue: When holding property as tenants by the entirety, may either spouse alienate that property absent the consent of the other spouse?

Rule: When property is held as a tenancy by the entirety, one spouse is unable, without the consent or acquiescence of the other, to convey, bind, encumber, sever, or otherwise alienate the property.

In Re Estate of Brown (1988)

Facts: The defendant Brown and his wife owned real property as tenants by the entirety. The defendant intentionally killed his wife.
Issue: Does a surviving tenant by the entirety retain title to real property after intentionally killing his spouse?
Rule: Because the survivor's interest is created by the deed creating the tenancy by the entirety, not the spouse's death, the survivor has a vested estate in fee simple regardless of the manner in which the spouse died.

Strong v. Wood (1981)

Facts: To have a deed canceled, Strong (plaintiff) sued the administrator of her husband's estate. She claimed she was defrauded when, just before their marriage, her husband conveyed title to his farm, keeping a life estate for himself only.
Issue: Is intent to defraud sufficient to find a fraudulent conveyance in contemplation of marriage?
Rule: Fraudulent intent is not sufficient to establish a spouse's right in property transferred before marriage. The claimant must also prove the fraudulent effect of the transferor's actions (i.e., reliance).

Kerwin v. Donaghy (1945)

Facts: The plaintiff, the widow of William Kerwin, sued her stepdaughter (defendant) to recover stocks, bonds, and deposits in banks, which had been transferred during William's lifetime to the defendant.
Issue: Does a spouse have an absolute right to dispose of personalty while living without the other spouse's knowledge or consent?
Rule: A spouse has an absolute right to dispose of any and all of his personal property while living, without the knowledge or consent of the other spouse.

Drapek v. Drapek (1987)

Facts: Pursuant to a divorce judgment, Celia Drapek was awarded a lump sum payment of $42,024.50 from her husband Mark Drapek, based on the judge's determination that Mark's medical degree was part of his estate.
Issue: How is a professional license or degree to be evaluated for purposes of distributing marital assets in divorce proceedings?

Rule: Although the earning capacity of the degree-holder may be considered in awarding alimony and dividing property a professional license or degree is not property subject to equitable distribution upon divorce or dissolution. Because assigning a present value to a professional degree would involve evaluating the earning potential created by that degree it is not a marital asset subject to division.

Sawada v. Endo (1977)

Facts: Endo (defendant) was liable for plaintiff's injuries. The defendant and his wife had owned a parcel of real estate as tenants by the entirety, but conveyed the land before trial. Unable to satisfy the judgment from the defendant's personal assets, the plaintiff sued to set aside the conveyance as a fraud on the defendant's judgment creditors.

Issue: Is one spouse's interest in real property held in tenancy by the entirety subject to levy and execution by his individual creditors?

Rule: The interest of a husband or a wife in an estate by the entirety is not subject to the claims of an individual's creditor during the joint lives of the spouses.

Pico v. Columbet (1859)

Facts: The plaintiff and the defendant were tenants in common. The defendant exclusively used the property, profited thereby, and retained the proceeds. The plaintiff sued to recover part of the profits.

Issue: Does a tenant in common have an action against a cotenant who exclusively profited from use of the commonly held property?

Rule: One tenant in common has no remedy against another tenant who profits from his exclusive use of the tenancy and receives the entire profits, unless the plaintiff was ousted from possession (when ejectment may be brought) or unless the defendant acted as bailee of plaintiff's interest by agreement (when the action of account will lie).

McKnight v. Basilides (1943)

Facts: Charles Basilides (defendant) owned property with his wife as tenants in common. Following his wife's death, Basilides exclusively used and profited from the land. Fifteen years later, the wife's legal heir, McKnight, brought suit demanding partition, Basilides claimed sole ownership by adverse possession and that the rents received were his alone.

Issue: May a cotenant of land held as a tenant in common acquire sole ownership of the land by adverse possession?

Rule: A tenant in common may obtain sole ownership of the tenancy by adverse possession only when the cotenants not in possession had actual knowledge that their rights were repudiated.

Riddle v. Harmon (1980)

Facts: Riddle (plaintiff) and his wife were joint tenants. The plaintiff's wife attempted to terminate the joint tenancy by conveying her interest from herself as a joint tenant to herself as a tenant in common. The plaintiff sued Harmon, the executrix of the wife's estate, to quiet title.
Issue: May a joint tenant unilaterally sever the joint tenancy without the use of an intermediary?
Rule: The common-law "strawman" device is no longer necessary. A joint tenant may unilaterally sever the joint tenancy without the use of an intermediary device.

Harms v. Sprague (1984)

Facts: Harms (plaintiff) and his brother took title to real estate as joint tenants. Before he died, the plaintiff's brother mortgaged his half interest. The plaintiff filed suit to quiet title and named as defendant Sprague, executor of the brother's estate.
Issue 1: Is a joint tenancy severed when less than all of the joint tenants mortgage their interest in the property?
Rule 1: A mortgage given by one joint tenant does not sever the joint tenancy.
Issue 2: Does such a mortgage survive the death of the mortgagor as a lien on the property?
Rule 2: The property right of a mortgaging joint tenant is extinguished at the moment of his death. Thus, the mortgage does not survive as a lien on the surviving tenant's property.

Wiggins v. Parson (1984)

Facts: Cooper named herself and her sister, Broadhead, joint tenants of a bank account. Later, she added the names of another sister, Parson, and a brother to the account. Cooper removed her own name from the account. Parson withdrew and kept all the money.
Issue: Does the complete withdrawal of funds from a joint tenancy account by one owner terminate the joint tenancy nature of the funds so as to destroy the right of survivorship in the funds?
Rule: The withdrawal of jointly owned funds by a joint owner and placement of the funds in other persons' names terminates the joint tenancy nature of the money and transforms it into a tenancy in common.

Johnson v. Hendrickson (1946)

Facts: Hendrickson was survived by her second husband and the children from both her marriages. All the survivors had an interest in certain land, which descended from her first husband.

Issue: When land is so situated that it cannot be partitioned among the various owners without prejudice to such owners, may a court order the sale of the land?

Rule: Where partition would cause the value of each cotenant's share to be materially less than the corresponding share of the money equivalent that could be obtained for the whole, then the court may order a sale of the property.

Spiller v. MacKereth (1976)

Facts: Spiller and MacKereth owned a building as tenants in common. When their lessee vacated the building, Spiller entered the space and began to use it as a warehouse.

Issue: Is a demand to vacate half of a building or pay half the rental value sufficient to establish an occupying co-tenant's liability for rent?

Rule: In the absence of an agreement to pay rent or of an ouster of a co-tenant, a co-tenant in possession is not liable to the other(s) for the value of his use and occupation of that property. Before an occupying co-tenant can be liable for rent, he must have denied his co-tenant the right to enter. A request that the occupying tenant vacate is not sufficient because he holds title to the whole and may rightfully occupy the whole unless the other co-tenant(s) assert their possessory rights.

Swartzbaugh v. Sampson (1936)

Facts: Swartzbaugh (plaintiff) and her husband owned land as joint tenants. The plaintiff's husband leased part of the land without her consent. The plaintiff sued to cancel the leases.

Issue: Can one joint tenant, who has not joined in a lease executed by her cotenant and another, maintain an action to cancel the lease where the lessee is in exclusive possession of the leased property?

Rule: When one cotenant of a joint tenancy executes a lease with a third party, the lease is a valid contract giving to the lessee the same right to possession of the leased property as the cotenant had.

United States v. 1500 Lincoln Avenue (1991)

Facts: The United States sought civil forfeiture of property containing a pharmacy, which was owned as a tenancy by the entirety by a husband, who was convicted for the illegal distribution of prescription drugs, and his wife, who did not know about or consent to the illegal activity.

Issue: In a tenancy by the entirety, is the government entitled to a forfeiture of an interest in property where one spouse is convicted for the illegal use of the property and the other spouse is completely innocent?

Rule: An innocent owner has a right to full and exclusive possession and use of the whole property during his lifetime, is protected against conveyance of and against a levy upon the property by any creditor of the spouse's former interest, and retains all survivorship rights.

In re Marriage of Graham (1978)

Facts: Mrs. Graham provided seventy percent of her husband's support while he earned an M.B.A. They filed for divorce six years after his graduation.

Issue: Is a graduate degree considered marital property subject to division upon the marriage's dissolution?

Rule: An educational degree is not encompassed by the concept of property and does not constitute marital property.

Elkus v. Elkus (1991)

Facts: Elkus was an opera singer, who during the course of her marriage saw a dramatic growth in her career which correlated to a significant increase in her income. During this time, her husband was highly involved in her career, sacrificing his own career to help her and to take care of their children.

Issue: In a divorce proceeding, does the career and/or celebrity status of a spouse constitute marital property subject to equitable distribution?

Rule: The extent to which the development of an individual's career can be attributed to a spouse's efforts and contributions is the factor that determines what constitutes marital property subject to equitable distribution.

Marvin v. Marvin (1976)

Facts: Plaintiff and defendant lived together for seven years without marrying. All the property that the couple acquired during this time was in the defendant's name. Plaintiff alleged that the two entered into an oral agreement that entitled her to half the property and to support payments.

Issue: What rights do the partners of nonmarital relationships have in the event that one dies or the couple separates?

Rule: Express contracts between nonmarital partners should normally be enforced. If there is no express contract, an inquiry should be made to determine whether the conduct of the parties demonstrates an implied contract, agreement of partnership or some other tacit understanding between the parties.

Hewitt v. Hewitt (1979)

Facts: The plaintiff and her boyfriend (defendant) lived together as an unmarried couple for 15 years.

Issue: Does a woman who alleges that she and her boyfriend lived as husband and wife have a claim to an equal share of the profits and property accumulated by the parties during the period of cohabitation?

Rule: Knowingly unmarried cohabitants do not acquire mutual property rights.

CHAPTER 6

Leaseholds: Landlord-Tenant Law

I. LEASEHOLDS

Leaseholds are created when the holder of a greater interest, the landlord, transfers possession to the tenant for a fixed or indeterminate period. The term must be for a lesser duration; at the expiration of the period, the right to possession reverts to the landlord. The common law did not regard leaseholds as one of the freehold estates in land discussed in Chapter 3. Thus a separate body of law developed around the leasehold.

II. PROPERTY OR CONTRACT?

A. One essential element of the law of landlord-tenant was that the promises in the lease were **independent covenants**: the landlord promised to deliver possession to the tenant and not to interfere with the tenant's use and enjoyment of the premises during the term; and the tenant promised to pay the rent. A breach of promise by one party did not excuse performance by the other. Thus if the tenant did not pay rent, the landlord had an action for the rent, but could not evict her. Likewise, if the landlord breached a promise not to interfere with the use of the premises, but entered, the tenant still had to pay the rent, and sue the landlord for damages.

B. A second was the doctrine of *caveat emptor*. Accordingly, it was the tenant who knew the purposes for which the premises were to serve, and she decided whether they were fir for the particular purposes. Landlord did not warrant fitness.

C. The tenant was assumed to be a jack (or jill) of all trades. The tenant was responsible to maintain the premises.

D. Landlord had no tort liability for injuries which occurred on the premises. Exceptions were to the common-law rules:
   1. Tort liability for latent defect known to landlord.
   2. Liability for common areas.
   3. The landlord was liable if he undertook to make repairs, and did so negligently causing loss.
E. Modern landlord tenant law has modified these principles extensively. The covenants are now thought to be **dependent**, so the tenant may withhold the rent should the landlord breach a covenant in the lease. Landlords of residential real estate and some types of commercial real estate warrant habitability or fitness. Maintenance is usually the landlord's obligation, particularly if the repair required is extensive.

III. CLASSIFICATION OF LEASEHOLDS

A. Term of Years
   1. Possession for a Determinate Period of Time
      This type of leasehold requires that both the beginning and ending date either be fixed or computable by formula, so that the term of the tenancy is certain.
   2. Duration
      a. This tenancy can be created for any length of time (e.g., 1,000 years or even one day).
      b. Some states limit duration by statute.
   3. Termination
      Because both parties know the ending date, this type of tenancy expires automatically, and no notice is required. However, it can be terminated earlier on the happening of some event or condition, and the lease may have a provision for renewal.
B. Periodic Tenancy
   1. Possession for an Indeterminate Period
      The tenancy will continue from period to period (i.e., renews itself automatically), unless and until one party terminates the arrangement with proper notice.
   2. Duration
      The period can be expressly agreed on or implied by the course of dealings between the parties: a week-to-week; a month-to-month. If there is no period specified in the lease, the court will examine the following factors:
      a. The Use of the Property
         Example: If the property in question is a farm with a yearly cycle, then the term will be one year.

      b. The Terms of the Rental Agreement
      Example: If rent is paid monthly, then the period will be one
      month. However, if annual rent is specified but payable in
      monthly installments, courts will have to determine whether
      the period should be one month or one year.

   3. Termination Requires Notice
      a. For a year-to-year tenancy, six months' notice was necessary
      for termination at common law. For tenancies with a period
      of less than a year, a full period's notice was required for
      effective termination (e.g., a month's notice for a month-
      to-month tenancy).
      Note: Most modern statutes require only 30 days' notice for
      the termination of any tenancy.
      b. Notice to terminate must stipulate the intention to termi-
      nate the tenancy on the final day of the period (i.e., if a
      month-to-month tenant provided notice of termination
      on March 24, the termination would not be effective until
      April 30).
      Note: Many states today have relaxed this requirement and,
      for example, allow a month-to-month tenancy to end after
      the 30-day notice period has expired.

C. Tenancy at Will
   1. Mutual Right of Termination
   This tenancy has no stated duration and may be terminated by
   either party at any time.
   2. Methods of Termination
      a. Expressly by either party
      Notice, however, was not required at common law. Modern
      statutes, however, give a tenant at will a right to prior notice.
      b. By Implication
      Death of one of the parties, conveyance of the property, or
      assignment of the lease terminates the tenancy.
   3. Creation of a tenancy at will may occur by express agreement.
   However, this type of tenancy usually arises by implication.
      a. Example: The tenant takes possession of the landlord's
      apartment without agreement as to the term or period
      when rent would come due.
      b. However, even if no period is specified, a court may still
      interpret the arrangement as a periodic tenancy, if some plau-
      sible period can be deduced (see above).

D. Tenancy at Sufferance
Strictly speaking, a tenancy at sufferance is not a tenancy at all, but
arises when a tenant remains in possession after a valid lease has
ended. This "holdover tenant" is liable for rent.

1. Right of Election

The landlord has the power to either bring an action to eject the tenant or bind the tenant to a new term.

2. Duration

Courts are in disagreement as to the nature and duration of the tenancy that is created when the landlord exercises his option to bind the tenant to another term. Some courts hold that the new tenancy is a term of years, while others hold that it is a periodic tenancy. Furthermore, some conclude that the duration should be measured by the rent computation period of the original tenancy, while others hold that the duration of the original lease (with a maximum of one year) should be the duration of the new tenancy.

3. A holdover may be excused for the following reasons:

a. Where the tenant remains in possession for a brief period. Example: The tenant was still packing the morning after the lease expired.

b. Where the holdover tenant remains due to no fault of his own.

c. Where landlord and tenant are renegotiating the lease, but a new lease is not signed before the expiration of the old.

IV. OBLIGATIONS OF A LANDLORD/TENANT'S RIGHTS

A. Covenant of Title

Landlord promises that he has a valid legal interest in the property to make the lease, and that he has not made a conflicting estate in another. If a third party held title to the leased premises that is superior to that of the landlord, the tenant may terminate the lease on discovery of this paramount title if he has not yet entered into possession of the premises. If the tenant has already taken possession, he may only terminate if the paramount title holder actually asserts his title.

B. Covenant of Possession

1. Traditional View

A landlord had no duty to deliver actual possession at the beginning of a tenant's lease term.

2. "American" Rule

Landlord is obligated to deliver legal but not actual possession.

3. "English" Rule (followed by most American courts) and the Uniform Residential Landlord and Tenant Act.

Landlord is obligated to provide both legal and actual possession. Under this rule, a tenant may sue a landlord for breach when a previous tenant "holds over."

4. An exception was made for the short-term lease of furnished premises — actual possession was covenanted.
C. Covenant of Quiet Enjoyment
   1. A covenant of quiet enjoyment is said to be implied in every lease. The tenant therefore has a right to terminate the lease if his right to quiet enjoyment is interfered with.
   2. Breach of the Covenant of Quiet Enjoyment
      a. Acts by Landlord
         The following acts, constituting a breach of the covenant of quiet enjoyment, must be done either by the landlord or by someone holding under the landlord to be actionable. Breaches by third parties such as other tenants are not actionable unless the third party is acting with the express or implied permission of the landlord.
         i. Total Actual Eviction
            The landlord physically ousts the tenant from the entire premises.
            Remedies: The tenant is relieved of all rent liability and has the right to sue for damages.
         ii. Partial Actual Eviction
            The landlord physically ousts the tenant from a portion of the rented premises.
            Remedies: The tenant is relieved of all rent liability and may continue to occupy the remainder of the premises rent-free.
            Note: This result is based on the notion that the landlord may not apportion his wrong.
         iii. Total Constructive Eviction
            The landlord's acts or omissions make it extremely difficult or impossible for the tenant to use any portion of the premises.
            Remedies: The tenant may terminate the lease and sue for damages, but he must abandon the premises within a reasonable time after the landlord's breach of the covenant.
         iv. Partial Constructive Eviction
            The landlord's acts or omissions make it extremely difficult or impossible for the tenant to use part of the premises.
            Remedies: The tenant's remedies are the same as for total constructive eviction.
   3. The continued evolution of the implied warranty of habitability has virtually eliminated the usefulness of the covenant of quiet enjoyment in residential leases. However, in commercial leases,

the covenant of quiet enjoyment remains a tenant's only avenue of relief.

D. Implied Warranty of Habitability

Landlords leasing urban *residential* property warrant that their premises will be maintained in a condition that satisfies applicable housing codes and that the premises are safe and habitable.

1. Applicable to residential but not to commercial leases (although a few jurisdictions do recognize an implied warranty of suitability in certain commercial contexts), and to both single and multiple dwellings.

2. The implied warranty may not be waived by the tenant.

3. Standards are greatly influenced by local housing codes, a substantial deviation from which will violate the warranty. However, in a jurisdiction without a code, the court will define habitability as premises that provide a healthy and safe living environment.

4. Multiple less serious violations may combine to constitute a material breach.

5. Conditions that interfere with safety or habitability may constitute a breach even if local housing codes have not been violated.

   a. Conditions existing prior to tenant's occupancy.

      i. Latent defects
         A tenant is protected by the implied warranty of habitability from those conditions that cannot be easily observed.

      ii. Patent defects
         Some courts and the Second Restatement hold that the tenant waives the warranty by entering the premises, unless the defect made the premises unsafe or unhealthy, or the landlord promised to repair the premises at a later date.

   b. Conditions that arise after the tenant enters.
      The landlord must make all repairs, unless the damages were caused by the tenant, a sudden natural force (tenant may terminate the lease but may not claim damages), or a third party (e.g., a burglar).

6. Some courts have held that the age of a building and the rent charged may be considered to determine whether the implied warranty of habitability has been breached.

E. Tenant's remedies for landlord's material breach of the implied warranty of habitability

1. Rescission: Tenant may terminate the lease, vacate the premises, and recover damages. (Some states require that the landlord be given notice and an opportunity to fix the defect, and that the tenant had been current on his rent prior to the defect.)

2. Recover Damages: Tenant remains, or may quit. If he remains he continues to pay the rent but offsets against the rent the difference between the fair market value of the premises if they were as warranted and the fair market value of the premises as is. If tenant quits, he can sue for the benefit of his bargain over the term.

3. Repair and Deduct: Tenant undertakes improvements that make the premises habitable and deducts the cost of repairs from the rent.

4. Rent Abatement: Tenant pays rent into an escrow account pending the outcome of the dispute. Court may set fair market value.

F. Various ways of measuring damages for a landlord's breach

1. Tenant accepts defective premises "as is." Damages equal actual rent or fair rental value of premises.

2. Percent reduction: Damages equal percentage of usage lost multiplied by the rent.

3. Actual expenses caused by breach.

4. Loss of bargain. Damages equal fair market value of premises as promised minus fair market value of premises "as is."

V. OBLIGATIONS OF A TENANT

A. Payment of rent.

B. Express promises to repair (no duty to reverse ordinary wear and tear).

C. Liability for waste.

D. Reasonable behavior in use of premises.

VI. LANDLORD'S REMEDIES

A. Deposit
A landlord may withhold a security deposit if the tenant abandons or misuses the property.

B. Eviction
A landlord may evict a tenant who has committed a material breach or is holding over.

1. Self-Help
Most states have abolished the common law right of a landlord to forcibly regain possession and to seize the chattels of a tenant who has not paid rent. Most states allow self-help without the use of force, although case law has limited this option so much that it is rarely of practical benefit to a landlord.

2. Summary Process

A legal procedure whereby a landlord can quickly (usually within 30 days) evict a tenant by proving that the lease had expired, or that the tenant had not paid rent.

C. Acceleration Clause

This is a contractual clause requiring a lump sum payment of all rents due on the remainder of the lease term in the event of a breach by the tenant. The tenant may remain on the premises after paying the accelerated damages.

D. Damages

A landlord may recover damages from a tenant who has abandoned the premises or has occupied a leasehold after the leasehold expired. The landlord is entitled to reasonable rent plus special damages caused by the holdover that the tenant could have foreseen.

1. When a tenant "holds over," the landlord may either bind the tenant to a periodic tenancy or evict the tenant.

2. When a tenant abandons the premises the landlord may accept the surrender of the premises, let the premises remain vacant, or re-let the premises on behalf of the tenant. If the landlord accepts a surrender, the tenant is released from his rent obligation. If the landlord elects to pursue either of the other options, he may sue for damages. Courts are split on the question of a landlord's duty to mitigate damages.

VII. TRANSFERS: ASSIGNMENT AND SUBLEASE

A. Absent a contractual agreement to the contrary, a landlord may transfer or sell his interest in a leasehold, and a tenant may assign or sublease his interest. Leases routinely prohibit the tenant from transferring the leasehold interest without the consent of the landlord. Most courts imply into the clause that landlord shall not unreasonably withhold consent.

B. Assignment and Sublease

1. A transfer of *all* of a tenant's interest is an assignment. A transfer of *less* than a tenant's complete interest is a sublease.

2. Assignment

a. Must be for the remaining term of the lease, under the same terms, accompanied by intent to substitute the assignee for the original tenant.

b. The assignor (i.e., original tenant) remains liable to the landlord for the rent. By virtue of the original lease, tenant remains in privity of contract with landlord.

      c. The assignee is in privity of estate with the landlord. Therefore, an assignee will be bound by all covenants that "run with the land," including landlord's warranties and the tenant's obligation to pay rent.

  3. Sublease

      a. A sublessee is liable to the sublessor (i.e., original tenant). The sublessor remains liable to the landlord.

      b. A sublease does not establish privity with the landlord, contract or estate. Therefore, the sublessee will not be bound by covenants that "run with the land." Arguably, he cannot enforce the landlord's expressed and implied covenants.

      c. Agreements not to assign a lease will generally be enforced, but a landlord may waive the assignment prohibition by his actions.

VIII. LIABILITY OF LANDLORD AND TENANT IN TORT

A. Liability of a Tenant

A tenant is liable to others for injuries sustained on his leased premises as if he were the owner of the property.

B. General Duties Owed by an Occupier of Land

  1. To invitee: Duty to inspect property and remedy all hazards.

  2. To licensee No duty to inspect and remedy hazards but must exercise reasonable care.

  3. To trespasser: No duty.

C. Liability of a Landlord

A landlord is generally not liable for injuries sustained by third parties on property he has leased except for injuries caused by:

  1. Latent defect known to landlord.

  2. Dangerous conditions in common areas.

  3. Repairs done negligently.

IX. NO-FAULT TERMINATION OF A LEASEHOLD

A. Condemnation

Condemnation will terminate a lease when the entire estate (not just part of the estate) is condemned by eminent domain.

B. Impossibility

The destruction of the premises, through no fault of the tenant, relieves the tenant of his duties under the lease.

C. Commercial Frustration

Where the landlord knows in advance of the tenant's proposed use for the premises and unforeseen circumstances arise after the lease has been executed which make the tenant's use of the premises no longer commercially viable, the tenant may terminate the lease.

D. Subsequent Illegality

If the purpose for which the property is leased becomes illegal after the lease is executed, the tenant may terminate the lease.

CASE CLIPS

I. Leaseholds /II. Property or Contract

Cook v. University Plaza (1981)

Facts: The plaintiffs and University Plaza entered into a "Residence Hall Contract Agreement" that stipulated that the parties did not intend a landlord-tenant relationship. The defendant reserved the right to require a resident to move from room to room.

Issue: Is a contractual agreement between students and a university dormitory a lease or a license?

Rule: The essence of a lease is transfer of possession, whereas a license is an agreement that merely entitles one party to use property subject to the management and control of the other party. Therefore, an agreement that allows a dormitory to move students from room to room at its discretion is a license because it fails to pass a possessory interest in specific property.

Sproul v. Gilbert (1961)

Facts: The plaintiffs held grazing privileges on lands owned by the federal government. The state of Oregon attempted to levy a tax on these privileges pursuant to a statute requiring taxation of property owned by the federal government and held by a person "under lease or other interest less than a fee." The plaintiffs brought an action for declaratory judgment arguing that their grazing privileges could not be classified as "a lease or other interest less than a fee" and therefore were not subject to the type of tax required under the statute.

Issue: Does the granting of grazing privileges on land owned by the federal government constitute a lease agreement or merely a license?

Rule: A lease is a transfer of an interest in land and is characterized by a grant of a right to exclusive possession. A license, by contrast, is a revocable privilege to use land in the possession of another. The exclusiveness of the possessory interest, the character of the land, and degree of control that the lessee exercises over the land are the determinative factors in characterizing an agreement as either a lease or a license. In this case, grazing privileges were found to be a sufficiently possessory interest in the land to constitute a lease.

Township of Sandyston v. Angerman (1975)

Facts: By agreement with the National Park Service, the defendants Mr. and Mrs. Angerman had exclusive, private use of a house on public land for a fixed period, though the Park Service reserved the right to terminate the agreement. In lieu of a rent payment the Angermans were obligated to restore the house. Arguing that the defendants were lessees, as opposed to licensees, the plaintiffs sued to collect taxes.

Issue: Does an agreement permitting exclusive use of a publicly owned house for a fixed period of time in exchange for a promise to restore the premises constitute a lease or a license?

Rule: A grant of exclusive possession of property for a fixed period of time constitutes a lease, whereas a license is merely a personal privilege to use the land of another for some particular purpose or in some specific way. A license is therefore a much more tenuous interest than a lease.

III. Classification of Leaseholds

Womack v. Hyche (1987)

Facts: Womack leased property to Hyche for a fixed minimum rent plus funds received from running a fishing camp on the property. Hyche had the option to renew the lease as long as the camp was run for a profit. When friction developed between the two parties, Womack instituted a declaratory judgment action to have the lease agreement voided.

Issue: May a lease for a term of years be valid when the renewal clause is so ambiguous as to create uncertainty regarding the duration of the lease?

Rule: Where a renewal clause fails to state with certainty a date on which the lease terminates, the lease is void as a tenancy of years and a tenancy at will results.

Arbenz v. Exley, Watkins & Co. (1905)

Facts: Arbenz and the defendant had a written lease for a period of more than five years. It lacked a seal and therefore was considered a year-to-year tenancy, ending at the close of the calendar year. After the property was destroyed by fire, the defendant, on Oct. 31, 1898, sent Arbenz a letter stating, "we have vacated the premises — and hereby surrender possession of same."

Issue: When is a notice of termination effective for a year-to-year tenancy?

Rule: To be an effective notice of termination of a year-to-year tenancy, notice must be given at least three months prior to the term's end and state a specific future date for termination.

Wright v. Braumann (1965)

Facts: The plaintiff and the defendant entered into an agreement to make a lease, contingent on the plaintiff's completion of a building. The defendant notified the plaintiff, before the premises being ready for occupancy, that he would not enter into a lease.

Issue: Does a lessor have a duty to mitigate damages when a lessee breaches a lease agreement?

Rule: A lessor has a duty to mitigate damages by making reasonable efforts to find another tenant.

Garner v. Gerrish (1984)

Facts: Garner's lease with Gerrish explicitly stated that Gerrish had the option to terminate the agreement at any time. Garner, assuming he had the power to do the same, brought suit to evict Gerrish.

Issue: Does a lease that grants the tenant the right to terminate the agreement at will create a determinable life tenancy or merely establish a tenancy at will?

Rule: A lease that expressly gives the right to terminate the agreement only to the tenant creates a determinable life tenancy.

Crechale & Polles, Inc. v. Smith (1974)

Facts: The plaintiff leased premises to Smith, the defendant, who, before the term's end, requested monthly extensions of the lease. Initially the plaintiff refused to extend the lease but later changed his mind and attempted to hold Smith to a full renewal.

Issue: May a landlord who initially elects to treat a holdover tenant as a trespasser later elect to treat the holdover as a lease renewal?

Rule: When a tenant continues in possession of the premises after the expiration of his lease term the landlord has the option of treating him as either a trespasser or as a tenant under the previous terms. However, having chosen one of the two options, the landlord may not change his mind and pursue the other.

IV. Obligations of a Landlord/Tenant's Rights

Hannan v. Deutsch (1930)

Facts: The defendant, a landlord, entered into a lease with the plaintiff, Hannan. When the lease term was to begin the defendant's prior tenant wrongfully held over. The plaintiff argued that the lease contained an implied covenant obligating the defendant to take legal action to oust the holdover tenant.

Issue: Is a landlord who leases property without any express covenant as to delivery of possession required to oust trespassers and wrongdoers to allow for entry by the tenant at the beginning of the term?

Rule: Under the "American Rule," absent an agreement to the contrary, the landlord has a duty to deliver only legal possession and not actual possession. The responsibility of ousting holdover tenants rests with the new tenant.

Note: Case law is divided between the above-stated "American Rule" and the "English Rule," which commands the opposite result.

Fetting Manufacturing Jewelry Co. v. Waltz (1930)

Facts: Fetting Manufacturing (defendant) was a tenant for a term of years. It remained on the premises for almost a month after the expiration of its tenancy. Waltz insisted that the defendant, by holding over, acquiesced to a lease for a full year.

Issue: Is a holdover tenant liable for the rent for an entire new term?

Rule: A tenant who holds over becomes, at the lessor's election, either a trespasser in the sense of being wrongfully in possession, or a tenant for another complete term subject to the terms of the original lease.

Mason v. Wierengo's Estate (1897)

Facts: Wierengo informed his landlord, Mason, of his intent to vacate the demised premises on the expiration of the lease. However, Wierengo died and the premises were not vacated on time. Mason sued Wierengo's estate for the rent of a full new term.

Issue: When a tenant holds over, is the presumption of a renting for another term rebutted by the holdover tenant's intent to vacate on time?

Rule: Absent some express or implied consent on lessor's part to a holding over on new terms, the tenant's intention to vacate on time does not affect the right of the lessor to elect to treat the holding over as a renewal of the lease for a new term.

Teitelbaum v. Direct Realty Co. (1939)

Facts: By the terms of his lease the lessee was to gain possession of certain premises on July 1, 1938, but the lessor's prior tenant wrongfully held over. The lessee brought suit for damages for failure to deliver possession of the premises.

Issue: Does a lessor have a duty, when the demised premises are wrongfully held by a third person, to take the necessary steps to put his lessee in possession?

Rule: If, at the time a lease begins, possession of the premises is held by a trespasser, there is no implied duty on the part of the lessor to oust the trespasser to enable the tenant to enter.

Adrian v. Rabinowitz (1930)

Facts: On April 30, 1934, Rabinowitz (defendant) and Adrian (plaintiff) entered into a lease whose term was to begin on June 15, 1934. Rabinowitz's prior tenant failed to vacate voluntarily. Rabinowitz began proceedings against the prior tenant, but Adrian did not take actual possession until July 9, 1934.

Issue: Does a lessor, in the absence of an express undertaking to that effect, have a duty to put the lessee in actual, as well as legal possession of the leased premises at the commencement of the term?

Rule: When the term of a lease is to begin in the future, there is an implied duty owed by the lessor that the premises shall be legally and actually open to the lessee's entry when the time for possession under the lease arrives.

Pines v. Perssion (1961)

Facts: Perssion agreed to lease a furnished house to Pines and three of his friends. When the lessees took possession of the house, they found it uninhabitable. They moved out and sued to recover their deposit.

Issue: Do leases contain an implied warranty of habitability?

Rule: The old rule of no implied warranty of habitability in leases is inconsistent with current conditions and legislative policy. This covenant and a lessee's covenant to pay rent are interdependent.

Berman v. Jefferson (1979)

Facts: Cynthia Jefferson leased an apartment for one year from Berman & Sons Inc. For several months, through no fault of the landlord, she experienced sporadic failures of heat and hot water and consequently withheld a portion of one month's rent.

Issue 1: At what point after a landlord's material breach of the warranty of habitability is a tenant entitled to a rent abatement?

Rule 1: A tenant's obligation to pay rent abates as soon as a landlord is given notice that a violation exists. A tenant is not required to allow a reasonable time for the landlord to make repairs.

Issue 2: How does lack of fault on the part of a landlord impact on a tenant's remedy of rent abatement?

Rule 2: A tenant is entitled to a rent abatement for a material violation of the warranty of habitability whether the landlord is at fault or not.

Reste Realty Corp. v. Cooper (1969)

Facts: After experiencing serious recurrent flooding and submitting numerous complaints to her landlord, Cooper vacated her leased premises

and refused to honor her lease. The plaintiff brought suit to recover the
remaining rent due under the lease.

Issue: Does a tenant have the right to vacate the premises when the landlord breaches the covenant of quiet enjoyment?

Rule: Where there is a covenant of quiet enjoyment, express or implied,
and it is breached substantially by the landlord, the doctrine of constructive eviction allows the tenant to vacate the premises. However, the tenant
must leave within a reasonable time after his right to vacate comes into
existence. What constitutes a reasonable time depends largely on the
particular circumstances of the case.

Franklin v. Brown (1889)

Facts: Franklin leased a furnished dwelling to Brown. The lease had no
express covenant of habitability. Due to noxious odors emanating from
adjoining premises, of which neither Franklin nor Brown were aware at the
time of the execution of the lease, Brown claimed that the premises were
uninhabitable. Brown argued that, because the dwelling was furnished,
Franklin impliedly covenanted they were fit for habitation. Franklin
brought suit to recover rent payments.

Issue: Does a lessor who leases a furnished dwelling impliedly covenant
against external defects detrimentally affecting habitability when the
defects were unknown to the lessor at the time of the execution of
the lease?

Rule: Absent fraud, an express warranty of habitability, or a covenant to
repair, there is no implied covenant that premises are fit for occupation or
are in safe condition.

Louisiana Leasing Co. v. Sokolow (1966)

Facts: The lessor, Louisiana Leasing Co., included a provision in the lease
stating that no ". . . tenant shall make or permit any disturbing noises in
the building by himself, his family (etc.)" and to so do "shall be deemed a
substantial violation" of the lease. The Sokolows, a young couple with two
children, resided in an apartment immediately above the Levins. The
Levins complained of the noise emanating from the apartment above
them and the Louisiana Leasing Co. brought suit to evict the Sokolows.

Issue: Pursuant to a covenant prohibiting noise, may a tenant be evicted
because another tenant complains of noise?

Rule: In urban apartment buildings with lease provisions regulating noise
a tenant who occupied the premises before another complaining tenant
cannot be evicted if the noise coming from his apartment is neither exces-
sive nor deliberate.

Milheim v. Baxter (1909)

Facts: Baxter leased premises from Milheim who, as owner of the adjoining premises, was aware that the premises were used for "immoral" purposes. On discovery of the happenings next door Baxter moved out, claiming wrongful eviction based on a breach of the lease's implied covenant of quiet enjoyment.

Issues: May a tenant be relieved of all responsibility under a lease and recover damages when the landlord breaches the implied covenant of quiet enjoyment?

Rule: Absent a provision to the contrary, all leases contain an implied covenant of quiet enjoyment and any wrongful act willfully done by the lessor justifying the tenant's abandonment of the premises is a breach of said covenant, thereby constituting a constructive eviction.

Marina Point, Ltd. v. Wolfson (1982)

Facts: The tenants, Stephen and Lois Wolfson, renewed their lease in January of 1974. In October of 1974 the landlord instituted a blanket ban on families with children. When the tenants failed to vacate the premises, the landlord commenced an unlawful detainer action.

Issue: May a landlord of an apartment complex refuse to rent an apartment to a family solely because the family includes a minor child?

Rule: Some states prohibit, by statute, all arbitrary discrimination by business establishments. Therefore, in those states, such a restriction aimed at children as a class is illegal.

Blackett v. Olanoff (1977)

Facts: The lessor leased premises to be used as a nightclub. The tenants of the lessor's nearby apartment building abandoned their apartments because of loud music and other disturbances emanating from the club. The tenants claimed that the lessor breached their implied warranty of quiet enjoyment. The terms of his lease with the club would have allowed the lessor to correct the disturbing conditions if he had undertaken to do so.

Issue: Does a lessor constructively evict his tenant when he permits a third party to substantially deprive his tenants of quiet enjoyment of the premises?

Rule: Where a lessor fails to eliminate a disruptive condition, which is within his power to eliminate, and which results in the deprivation of the tenant's right to quiet enjoyment, the lessor will be held to have constructively evicted the tenant.

Brown v. Southall Realty Co. (1968)

Facts: At the time a lease was executed Southall, the landlord, knew that several conditions existed on the premises that violated certain housing regulations. He brought suit to collect unpaid rent, and the tenant defended on the grounds that the lease was illegal and therefore unenforceable.

Issues: Is a lease illegal and therefore unenforceable where the condition of the premises violates housing regulations, and the landlord is aware of the violations at the time the lease is executed?

Rule: An illegal contract (i.e., lease), made in violation of the statutory prohibition designed for police or regulatory purposes, is void and confers no right on the wrongdoer.

Javins, Saunders and Gross v. First Nat'l Realty Corp. (1970)

Facts: The lessor, First National Realty Corp., sued for possession for nonpayment of rent. The tenants contended that they were equitably excused from paying rent because of nearly 1,500 violations of the Housing Regulations of the District of Columbia, arising after their leases were executed.

Issue: Is a tenant's obligation to pay rent independent of the landlord's obligation to comply with applicable housing regulations?

Rule: A warranty of habitability, measured by the standards outlined in the Housing Regulations for the District of Columbia, is implied by operation of law into leases of urban dwellings. Therefore, a tenant's rent liability is dependent on the landlord's compliance with his responsibilities under the implied warranty of habitability.

Habib v. Edwards (1965)

Facts: Habib sued Edwards for possession of premises that were leased to her on a month-to-month basis. He obtained a default judgment but Edwards moved to have it set aside due to excusable neglect of counsel. She also asserted the defense that Habib was merely retaliating because Edwards had previously reported housing code violations present on the property.

Issue: Does a tenant have a constitutional right to inform the authorities of housing code violations that can be asserted as a defense to a lessor's action to repossess?

Rule: A tenant has a constitutional right to inform the proper governmental authorities of violations of law, as well as the correlative right not to be injured or punished by the lessor or anyone else for having availed herself of her basic right to provide such information.

Note: The preceding was a trial court opinion. The case was remanded to the Landlord and Tenant Branch for a new trial. However, at trial the judge excluded evidence of retaliatory intent. The opinion that follows is the disposition of this case on appeal.

Edwards v. Habib (1967)

Facts: Habib sued Edwards for possession of premises that were leased to her on a month-to-month basis. He obtained a default judgment but Edwards moved to have it set aside due to excusable neglect of counsel. She also asserted the defense that Habib was merely retaliating because Edwards had previously reported housing code violations existing on the property.

Issue: Is evidence of a lessor's motive for evicting a tenant admissible?

Rule: In a month-to-month tenancy a notice by a landlord terminating the tenancy need give no reason whatsoever for the termination, and evidence as to the reason for the notice is inadmissible when, by the terms of the lease itself, the landlord may terminate for no reason at all.

Edwards v. Habib (1968)

Facts: Edwards, a month-to-month tenant, notified authorities of her landlord's multiple sanitary code violations. Habib, her landlord, promptly attempted to evict her.

Issue: May a landlord evict a month-to-month tenant for reporting housing code violations to the authorities?

Rule: Although a landlord may evict a month-to-month tenant for any legal reason or for no reason at all, he is not free to evict in retaliation for the tenant's report of housing violations to the authorities. However, the landlord is free to evict the tenant after the illegal purpose has dissipated.

Berg v. Wiley (1978)

Facts: The defendant, pursuant to a lease provision allowing him to retake possession of the premises on breach of any terms of the lease, locked out the plaintiff, Berg, and relet the premises. The plaintiff subsequently brought an action for wrongful eviction.

Issue: May a landlord resort to self-help to regain possession of leased premises?

Rule: If a tenant claims possession of the premises, and has neither abandoned nor voluntarily surrendered them, then the only course of action open to the landlord is to resort to judicial process.

Note: The above-stated approach is not yet the majority position.

Anderson Drive-in Theatre v. Kirkpatrick (1953)

Facts: Kirkpatrick leased farmland to the defendant knowing that the defendant planned to erect a drive-in theater. After the lease was executed, the defendant discovered that the land was unsuitable for this purpose. When Kirkpatrick sued to recover rent, the defendant contended that Kirkpatrick breached an implied warranty that the land was fit for the contemplated use.

Issue: Does a lease contain an implied warranty that leased premises are fit for the purposes for which they are let?

Rule: There is no implied warranty that leased premises are fit for the purposes for which they are let.

Davidow v. Inwood North Professional Group — Phase I (1988)

Facts: The plaintiff sued Dr. Davidow for unpaid rent on medical office space. The doctor argued that defects in the premises made the space unsuitable for use as a medical office.

Issue: Is there an implied warranty by a commercial landlord that the leased premises are suitable for their intended commercial purpose?

Rule: There is an implied warranty of suitability by the landlord in a commercial lease that the premises are suitable for their intended commercial purpose.

Swann v. Gastonia Housing Auth. (1982)

Facts: The Swans participated in the Gastonia Housing Authority's (GHA) public housing program. When the Swans' landlord refused to renew their lease they contended that the landlord must have good cause, and that they were entitled to a full hearing before the GHA on that issue. GHA, however, refused to deviate from its policy of allowing landlords to refuse to renew a tenant's lease with or without cause.

Issue: Does the Due Process clause of the Fourteenth Amendment guarantee to tenants, under 42 U.S.C. §1437, a right to a full and complete hearing by the GHA?

Rule: The Due Process clause will be invoked when a tenant is evicted pursuant to a state action. In such a case only a showing of good cause will permit a landlord to terminate a tenancy. However, a full-fledged hearing by the GHA is not mandated by the due process requirement of good cause.

Pennell v. City of San Jose (S. Ct. 1988)

Facts: A rent control ordinance enacted by the city of San Jose allowed a hearing officer to consider, among other factors, the "hardship to a tenant" when determining whether to approve a rent increase proposed by a landlord.

Issue: Does taking into consideration a tenant's hardship when reviewing a rent increase violate the Takings, Equal Protection, or Due Process clauses?
Rule: (Rehnquist, C.J.) The ordinance does not violate the Due Process clause because its purpose is to protect tenants from burdensome rent increases, which is a legitimate goal within the police power of the legislature. The Equal Protection clause is not violated because distinguishing between landlords is rationally related to the purpose of the ordinance. Because there is no record of a rent increase actually being denied because of the ordinance, it is premature to decide whether the ordinance violates the Takings clause.

Concurring in part, dissenting in part: (Scalia, J.) The ordinance effects a taking of property without just compensation because, while the other factors are rationally related to providing reasonable rents, the tenant hardship factor is aimed at a different social problem, one that the landlords did not cause. Thus, this problem should be borne by the public at large rather than by the landlords. In effect, the city is using rent regulation to establish a welfare program privately funded by those landlords who happen to have "hardship" tenants.

Cromwell Assocs. v. Mayor and Council of Newark (1985)

Facts: The City of Newark had a rent control ordinance which prohibited rent increases greater than 25% during any 12-month period. The plaintiff, an owner of a large apartment complex, claimed that the ordinance denied him a constitutionally mandated fair rate of return.
Issue: Is an ordinance that places a maximum limitation on annual increases, including increases granted pursuant to the hardship provision of the ordinance, constitutionally permissible?
Rule: When the maximum rent increase allowable by a rent control ordinance is insufficient to allow an efficient operator a fair rate of return, the ordinance is unconstitutional on its face.

Chicago Board of Realtors, Inc. v. City of Chicago (1987)

Facts: A group of property owners challenged the constitutionality of an ordinance enacted by the Chicago City Council, which codified the warranty of habitability. The new law established new responsibilities for landlords and gave more legal rights to tenants.
Issue: What are some relevant economic and policy concerns at issue when dealing with landlord/tenant ordinances?
Rule: (Posner, J.) A strong case can be made for the unreasonableness of the ordinance. The implication is that the initial consequence will be to reduce the resources landlords have to devote to improving the quality of housing, and increased costs to landlords will result in higher rents, largely hurting the people the ordinance was intended to help, the poor and the newer tenants.

Lindsey v. Normet (S. Ct. 1972)

Facts: Oregon's Forcible and Wrongful Detainer Statute precluded consideration of a tenant's defenses in a landlord's action to recover possession of the demised premises. Lindsey argued that the statute violated due process.

Issue: Is it a violation of constitutional due process to prohibit a tenant, in a summary proceeding, from asserting as an affirmative defense a lessor's violation of the implied warranty of habitability?

Rule: (White J.) Because a tenant can initiate a separate action against a lessor, states can constitutionally restrict the issues to be addressed in summary proceedings.

Barash v. Pennsylvania Terminal Real Estate Corp. (1970)

Facts: When the defendant lessor failed to adequately ventilate Barash's office during evening and weekend hours Barash refused to pay rent, but remained in possession of the leased premises.

Issue: Does a landlord's wrongful failure to supply a continuous flow of fresh air on evenings and weekends to offices leased by a tenant constitute an actual partial eviction relieving the tenant from the obligation to pay rent, or is it a constructive eviction requiring the tenant to abandon the premises before he may be relieved of the duty to pay rent?

Rule: An actual eviction occurs only when the lessor wrongfully ousts the tenant, either by physical expulsion or exclusion. A constructive eviction exists where, although there has been no physical expulsion or exclusion of the tenant, the landlord's wrongful acts substantially and materially deprive the tenant of the beneficial use and enjoyment of the premises. A tenant must abandon the premises to sustain a claim of constructive eviction.

Hilder v. St. Peter (1984)

Facts: The tenant leased an apartment from the defendant Stuart St. Peter that was in a terrible state of disrepair, and despite having ample notice of multiple health code violations the defendant failed to correct the problems. Instead of vacating the premises, the plaintiff paid all rents due and then sued for reimbursement of rent paid, together with compensatory and punitive damages.

Issue 1: Does a tenant have to vacate the premises in reliance on the covenant of quiet enjoyment before he can be released from having to pay rent?

Rule 1: The implied warranty of habitability has made reliance on the covenant of quiet enjoyment virtually obsolete in residential leases. It applies to all residential leases and does not require the tenant to move out to avoid paying rent.

Issue 2: What remedies are available to a tenant when the landlord has breached the implied warranty of habitability?

Rule 2: The tenant may withhold future rent, seek damages in the amount of rent previously paid, seek damages for discomfort and annoyance, seek punitive damages, or make repairs himself and deduct their cost from future rent.

Jack Spring, Inc. v. Little (1972)

Facts: The lessor sued in a summary proceeding to recover possession of demised premises for nonpayment of rent. The court prohibited the defendant, Little, from presenting evidence of violations of an implied warranty of habitability as an affirmative defense.

Issue: May a tenant assert a landlord's violations of an implied warranty of habitability as a defense in a summary proceeding?

Rule: The Forcible Entry and Detainer Act does not bar presentation of issues that are germane to the lessor's claims in a judicial proceeding, such as violations of an implied warranty of habitability.

Dickhut v. Norton (1970)

Facts: The lessor sued for possession of the demised premises. In defense, the tenant, who had an oral month-to-month lease, answered that the landlord brought suit only because the tenant had earlier notified the authorities of the unsanitary conditions of the premises. The lower court dismissed the tenant's defense as immaterial.

Issue: May a tenant, in an unlawful detainer action, assert as a defense an allegation that the landlord's attempt to terminate the tenancy and evict the tenant was motivated by retaliation for the tenant's complaint to the health authorities of a housing code sanitary violation?

Rule: A landlord cannot terminate a tenancy at will or a month-to-month tenancy as a means of retaliation, simply because a tenant has reported an actual housing code violation.

Orange County Taxpayers Council, Inc. v. City of Orange (1980)

Facts: The City of Orange enacted a rent-control ordinance requiring that the landlord's building be in "substantial compliance" with municipal housing regulations before a rent increase in rent controlled housing would be allowed.

Issue: Is a rent control ordinance that prohibits increases in rent without a certification that a dwelling is in "substantial compliance" with municipal housing regulations arbitrary and unreasonable?

Rule: A requirement that an apartment be in "substantial compliance" with local housing regulations before a lessor can charge higher rent is neither arbitrary nor unreasonable.

Seawall Associates v. City of New York (1989)

Facts: Seawall Associates challenged a city law prohibiting the demolition or conversion of single-room-occupancy properties and obligating the owners to lease them at controlled rents for an indefinite period. New York City housing officials defended the law on the basis that it was a valid effort to prevent homelessness.

Issue: Do uncompensated affirmative obligations and restrictions on use imposed by the state, which prevent an owner's development of his property, constitute an unconstitutional taking?

Rule: Uncompensated affirmative obligations and restrictions on property development constitute an unconstitutional taking when they drastically interfere with the property owner's right to possess and to exclude, or they deny an owner economically viable use of the property, or do not substantially advance legitimate state interests.

Flynn v. City of Cambridge (1981)

Facts: A city ordinance prohibited conversion of rent-controlled apartments to condominium units. Flynn challenged the ordinance as an unconstitutional taking of property.

Issue: Does an ordinance restricting an owner's use of his property automatically constitute a taking?

Rule: A government action does not constitute a taking when an owner's primary expectation concerning the use of his property is not frustrated and he is assured of a reasonable return on his investment.

V. Obligations of a Tenant

Sigsbee Holding Corp. v. Canavan (1963)

Facts: The landlord sought to evict Canavan for replacing old cabinets with new ones.

Issue: Under what circumstances will a tenant be held liable for waste?

Rule: A tenant will be held liable for waste if he materially and permanently changes the nature and character of the building, even if he increases the value of the property by doing so.

Commonwealth Building Corp. v. Hirschfeld (1940)

Facts: Hirschfeld, through no fault of his own, vacated a leasehold one day after the lease expired. The lease provided that the lessor could collect double rent if the tenant failed to vacate on time.

Issue: May a lessor treat a tenant as a holdover tenant for another complete term when the tenant involuntarily holds over?

Rule: A tenant who, through no fault of his own, involuntarily holds over cannot be bound to a new and complete term by the lessor.

Handler v. Horns (1949)

Facts: Horns leased premises in which he installed equipment used to carry on his trade.

Issue: May a tenant who has installed equipment used to carry on his trade remove the fixtures when his lease expires?

Rule: In the absence of an agreement to the contrary, a tenant may remove whatever he has erected or installed for the purpose of carrying on his trade, provided that it can be severed from the freehold without material injury thereto, and that such removal is effected before he yields possession of the premises.

United States National Bank of Oregon v. Homeland, Inc. (1981)

Facts: The plaintiff leased commercial space to Homeland, Inc., who subsequently abandoned the premises. The plaintiff succeeded in finding a new tenant for a longer term at a higher rate, but the second tenant also defaulted.

Issue: When a lessee of commercial space abandons the premises before the expiration of the lease, and the lessor relets the premises for a term extending beyond the expiration of the original lease and at a higher rent, does such reletting constitute a termination of the lease as a matter of law, thus freeing the first tenant from any claim for damages accruing subsequent to the reletting?

Rule: Reletting or attempting to relet by a commercial lessor at a higher rate and for a longer term than provided for in an original lease does not, as a matter of law, bar the lessor's claim for damages against a lessee who abandoned the premises.

Fifty States Management Corp. v. Pioneer Auto Parts Inc. (1979)

Facts: Fifty States Management Corp. and Pioneer Auto Parts Inc., parties of equal bargaining strength, freely negotiated for the inclusion of a clause in their lease whereby the rent for the remainder of the lease term would be accelerated upon breach of tenant's covenant to pay rent. The lease's term was 20 years. Pioneer missed two consecutive monthly rental payments and Fifty States brought suit to collect on the remainder of the payments due under the lease.

Issue: Will equity intervene to prevent enforcement of a provision in a 20-year lease between commercial parties providing for the acceleration of the rent due for the entire lease term on the tenant's default in the payment of a monthly rental installment?

Rule: Absent fraud or overreaching acceleration clauses in commercial leases are enforceable if the sum reserved for liquidated damages is no greater than the amount the tenant would have paid had he fully performed, and the tenant is entitled to possession on payment.

Jamaica Builders Supply Corp. v. Buttelman (1960)

Facts: A lease between Buttelman and Jamaica Builders Supply Corp. contained a provision which stipulated that certain acts by the tenant were prohibited and would automatically terminate the tenancy and result in forfeiture of rent already paid in advance. When Buttelman held over after the expiration of his lease term, the plaintiff corporation instituted summary proceedings to remove the tenant.

Issue: In determining whether a clause in a lease is a condition (requiring the landlord to take affirmative steps to terminate the tenancy) or a conditional limitation (an automatic termination of the lease on the happening of some event) should the court rely solely on the pertinent clause standing alone?

Rule: When determining whether a clause in a lease is a condition or a conditional limitation courts examine not only the language in the clause itself but also the language of the entire lease in an attempt to ascertain the parties' intent. Because the courts disfavor forfeitures, a clause will be held to be a conditional limitation only if there is a clear and unambiguous intention that when an event happens, the lease, by its terms, comes to an end.

VI. Landlord's Remedies

David Properties, Inc. v. Selk (1963)

Facts: Selk sold property to the defendant corporation, and the defendant allowed him to live on the land for over two months for a price of $1. When Selk failed to quit the premises after the agreed date, the defendant asked him to pay a monthly rent of $300.

Issue: What remedies may a landlord pursue when a tenant holds over after the term of the lease without responding to the landlord's demand that the tenant pay increased rent if the tenant continues in possession?
Rule: The landlord could choose either to claim damages for trespass in the amount of rental value or to bind the tenant to a new lease term.
Note: Courts are split on the duration of a tenancy so created.

The Liberty Plan Co. v. Adwan (1962)

Facts: The plaintiff lessor notified The Liberty Plan Co. that he would attempt to relet the premises that Liberty had vacated, but would continue to "hold you (Liberty) liable for loss of rent."
Issue: Is a tenant who vacates a leasehold released from liability when the landlord notifies the tenant of his intent to reenter and relet the premises?
Rule: When a tenant wrongfully abandons leased premises, a lessor may give notice to the tenant of his refusal to accept surrender and sublet the premises for the unexpired term.

Sommer v. Kridel (1977)

Facts: On May 19, 1972, the defendant James Kridel abandoned an apartment he had leased for a two-year period. Although the landlord had an opportunity to relet the apartment, he chose not to do so. Instead, he brought an action for payment of the entire rent that was due under the lease.
Issue: Is a landlord seeking damages from a defaulting tenant under a duty to make reasonable efforts to relet an apartment wrongfully vacated?
Rule: A landlord has a duty to make reasonable efforts to mitigate damages where he seeks to recover rents due from a defaulting residential tenant.

Lefrak v. Lambert (1976)

Facts: The Lamberts breached their lease by vacating the demised premises many months before its expiration. Lefrak, contending that a lessor has no duty to mitigate damages when a lessee breaches a lease, sought to recover 17 months' rent, covering the period during which the apartment remained vacant.
Issue: Does a lessor have a duty to mitigate damages when his tenant abandons the premises before the expiration of the lease?
Rule: A lessor must show that he attempted to mitigate damages by making a good faith effort to relet the premises within a reasonable time.
Note: The Appellate Division affirmed this judgment in 1978, but modified it to award the plaintiff damages for the entire seventeen months that

the apartment remained vacant. The Appellate Division found it unnecessary to rule on the question of a landlord's duty to mitigate damages because of its finding that Lefrak had in fact made good-faith efforts to relet the apartment.

Jordan v. Talbot (1961)

Facts: Jordan, Talbot's lessee, instituted a forcible entry and detainer action when, after falling behind in her rent, Talbot entered her apartment and refused to allow her back in. The lease gave Talbot a right of reentry upon the breach of any condition in the lease.

Issue: Is a landlord's contractual right to reentry a defense to a tenant's action for forcible entry and detainer?

Rule: Regardless of who has the right to possession, a landlord, absent a voluntary surrender of the premises by the tenant, can enforce his right of reentry only by judicial process. A landlord may not reenter the premises by self-help.

VII. Transfers: Assignment and Sublease

Jaber v. Miller (1951)

Facts: The lessee, Jaber (defendant), transferred his lease to Norber & Son "for the remainder of the term of said lease." Norber & Son transferred the lease to Miller (plaintiff), who contended Jaber's transfer constituted a subletting, not an assignment, under the common law.

Issue: Is the intent of the parties determinative when deciding if a transfer of a lease constitutes an assignment or a sublease?

Rule: The intention of the parties governs in determining whether an instrument is an assignment or a sublease.

Ernst v. Conditt (1964)

Facts: The plaintiff's original lease with Rogers was renegotiated between the parties to allow the defendant, Conditt, to take over the leased premises from Rogers. The modified lease provided that Rogers would "sublet" the premises to Conditt and be personally liable if Conditt failed to pay the rent.

Issue: Are the words "sublet" and "subletting" conclusive of the construction to be placed on a document when determining if it was a sublease or an assignment?

Rule: When determining if a document is a sublease or an assignment the words actually used by the parties are not dispositive. The parties' intent, gleaned from the whole instrument and the surrounding circumstances, is controlling.

A.D. Juilliard & Co. v. American Woolen Co. (1943)

Facts: A.D. Juilliard & Co., leased property subject to a covenant obligating the lessee to pay rent, but not restricting assignments. The lease was assigned several times without any covenant requiring the assignor, in the event of default by the assignee, to assume the obligation to pay rent for the unexpired term, American Woolen, one of the companies in the chain of assignments, itself assigned to another party who defaulted. A.D. Juilliard & Co. contended that American Woolen was responsible for payment.

Issue: Is the assignee of a lease of real property liable for the payment of stipulated rent for the entire unexpired term of the lease, notwithstanding that the assignee did not agree to assume such obligation and assigned the lease to another party before the expiration of the term?

Rule: In the absence of an assumption by the assignee of an obligation to pay off the remainder of the lease, the liability of an assignee to the original lessor rests in privity of estate, which is terminated by a new assignment of the lease made by the assignee.

Note: The original lessee always remains liable to the lessor, even if he assigns the lease.

Childs v. Warner Brothers Southern Theatres, Inc. (1931)

Facts: Childs leased premises imposing a covenant requiring its consent to an assignment by a lessee. The lessee, with Childs' consent, assigned the lease to Warner Brothers (defendant), Warner Brothers, in turn, attempted to assign the lease without Childs' consent.

Issue: If a lessor executes a lease to a given lessee, and the lease provides that the lessee shall not convey the lease nor sublet the premises without the written consent of the lessor, and thereafter, the lessor consents to an assignment of the lease, can such assignee subsequently make a valid reassignment of the lease without the consent of the lessor?

Rule: If a reasonable construction of a lease leads to the conclusion that a restriction against assignment and subletting operated upon the heirs and assigns of the lessee as well as on the lessee himself, the lessor, by consenting to one assignment, does not waive the restriction.

Dress Shirt Sales Inc. v. Hotel Martinique Associates (1963)

Facts: Dress Shirt Sales Inc. leased space from the defendant hotel. It vacated the leased premises before the term's end but continued to pay rent. The lease prohibited subleasing without the defendant's consent. The defendant refused to accept a sub-tenant found by Dress Shirt Sales. The two parties reached a settlement and agreed to terminate the lease, whereupon the defendant leased the premises, at a higher rent than he had with Dress Shirt Sales, to the party previously rejected.

Issue: Where no provision to the contrary is in the lease, may a lessor arbitrarily withhold consent to a subletting of the demised premises?

Rule: Unless the lease provides that the lessor's consent shall not be unreasonably withheld, a provision against subleasing without the lessor's consent permits the lessor to refuse arbitrarily for any reason or no reason.

Krasner v. Transcontinental Equities, Inc. (1979)

Facts: Kasner brought suit against several defendants for an unauthorized assignment of a lease in which he had a reversionary interest.

Issue: Is a tenant free to assign his leasehold interest in the absence of an express prohibition against assignment incorporated in the lease?

Rule: A lease agreement will be construed strictly against the drafter, usually the landlord, and a tenant will be free to assign the lease unless the lease itself prohibits it.

Kendall v. Ernest Pestana, Inc. (1985)

Facts: An express provision of a lease required the written consent of the defendant lessor before the plaintiff lessee could assign his interest. The defendant refused to consent to an assignment unless the assignee agreed to pay a higher rent.

Issue: May a commercial lessor unreasonably and arbitrarily withhold his consent to an assignment?

Rule: Where a commercial lease provides for assignment only with the prior consent of the lessor, such consent may be withheld only where the lessor has a commercially reasonable objection to the assignee or the proposed use.

Samuels v. Ottinger (1915)

Facts: Ottinger assigned his lease with the lessor's consent. The assignee, after paying one month's rent, defaulted on rent due for the next two years. The lessor sued Ottinger to recover the rent.

Issues: Is an original lessee absolved from liability to pay rent by an assignment when the assignee defaults on his obligation to pay the rent?

Rule: The obligation to pay rent remains with a lessee even after he assigns the lease to a third party.

Reid v. Wiessner & Sons Brewing Co. (1898)

Facts: Reid leased certain premises to Miller, who assigned the lease to Wiessner (defendant), who in turn assigned it to Jones. Jones failed to pay the rent due.

Issue: Does an assignee remain liable to a lessor when he is no longer in privity of estate with the lessor?

Rule: In the absence of an independent agreement, the liability of an assignee to the original lessor for rent is founded on privity of estate and such liability continues only so long as that privity exists.

Masury v. Southworth (1859)

Facts: The landlord leased real property to the lessee. The lease provided that the lessee would insure the building. The lessor's interest was assigned to the plaintiff and the lessee's interest was assigned to the defendant, who did not insure the leasehold.

Issue: Is a lessee's assignee bound by a covenant signed by the original lessor and lessee?

Rule: A covenant will bind an assignee if it benefits both parties to a lease, and the two original parties to the lease intended to have the covenant run with the land.

Davis v. Vidal (1912)

Facts: Dallas Brewery agreed to "sublet, assign, and transfer" property to Vidal, who defaulted on his rent payments. Dallas Brewery had reserved the right to "reenter and repossess said premises" in the event Vidal failed to pay rent. The original lessor was Antoinette Davis.

Issue: Does a lessor have an action against a transferee who, subject to a right of reentry in the original lessee, assumed the obligations of a lease?

Rule: A sub-lease is created when an original lessee retains a reversionary interest in the demised premises. Because there is neither privity of estate nor privity of contract between the original lessor and the sub-tenant, the original lessor cannot maintain an action for rent against the sub-lessee.

Gruman v. Investors Diversified Services, Inc. (1956)

Facts: Gruman's lease with the defendant corporation prohibited assignment or subleasing of the demised premises without Gruman's consent. Although the premises were abandoned by the defendant before the term's end, the defendant found a suitable sub-tenant. Gruman refused to consent to the proposed sublease.

Issue: Must a lessor, whose lease prohibits assigning or subleasing the premises without his consent, mitigate damages by accepting a suitable subtenant, or can the lessor arbitrarily refuse to accept the proffered subtenant?

Rule: Absent a contractual clause prohibiting a lessor from unreasonably withholding consent. The lessor may arbitrarily refuse to accept a suitable subtenant.

VIII. Liability of Landlord and Tenant in Tort

Sargent v. Ross (1973)

Facts: The tenant sued the landlord for negligently constructing a stairway from which the tenant's child fell to her death. The defendant asserted that she owed no duty to the child.

Issue: Does a landlord owe his tenants a duty of reasonable care with respect to the safety of the premises?

Rule: The doctrine of landlord tort immunity is abrogated. Henceforth, landlords are liable for injuries caused by their failure to exercise reasonable care.

O'Callaghan v. Walter & Beckwith Realty Co. (1958)

Facts: O'Callaghan sustained an injury on the lessor's premises. Her lease contained an exculpatory clause relieving the lessor of all liability for his negligent acts or omissions.

Issue: Is an exculpatory clause invalid in a residential lease?

Rule: An exculpatory clause in a residential lease is enforceable.

Sweney Gasoline & Oil Co. v. Toledo, Peoria & Western Railroad (1969)

Facts: Sweney Gasoline & Oil Co. leased property from the defendant railroad company. The property was damaged by the derailment of the lessor's train. The lease contained an exculpatory clause excluding lessor's liability for property damage caused by its negligence.

Issue: May lessors protect themselves by including exculpatory clauses in their leases?

Rule: Absent a contrary social policy or a social relationship militating against them, exculpatory clauses are enforceable.

Trentacost v. Brussel (1980)

Facts: The tenant, Florence Trentacost, was robbed and seriously injured in the hallway of her apartment building. Although the building was located in a high-crime area, its front door was not equipped with a lock.

Issue: Is a landlord who provides inadequate security for common areas of rental premises liable for failing to prevent a criminal assault upon a tenant?

Rule: A landlord has a legal duty to take reasonable security measures for tenant protection on his premises. Failure to provide adequate security gives rise to potential liability on grounds of both conventional negligence and the implied warranty of habitability.

Borders v. Roseberry (1975)

Facts: At the time of the letting of the premises the tenant knew that the landlord, Roseberry, had not reinstalled the gutters used for excess water removal from the premises. Borders, the tenant's social guest, slipped on the ice, which had accumulated as a result of the absence of gutters. He sued Roseberry in tort for his injuries.

Issue: May a tenant's social guest sue a landlord for negligence when both the landlord and the tenant knew of the defective condition?

Rule: When a landlord undertakes to make repairs to the premises he is only liable for tortious injury resulting therefrom when the tenant neither knows nor should know that the purported repairs have been negligently made or not made at all.

Kline v. 1500 Massachusetts Ave. Corp. (1970)

Facts: Sarah Kline was criminally assaulted and robbed by an intruder in the common hallway of an apartment house. She sued the defendant corporation in tort for damages.

Issue: Does a landlord have a duty to take steps to protect tenants from foreseeable criminal acts committed by third parties?

Rule: A landlord has the duty of taking protective measures to guard the entire premises and the areas under the landlord's control against the perpetration of criminal acts.

Johnson v. O'Brien (1960)

Facts: While visiting the defendant's tenant, the plaintiff fell from a stairway, sustaining injury.

Issue: Must a lessor, lacking actual knowledge of a latent defect but having information leading him to suspect a danger exists, inform the tenant of the danger?

Rule: When a landlord has information which would lead a reasonably prudent owner exercising due care to suspect that a danger exists on the leased premises at the time the tenant takes possession, and a tenant exercising due care would not discover the defect for himself, the landlord must disclose such information to the tenant.

Bowles v. Mahoney (1952)

Facts: Well after the lease was executed, Mahoney, a nephew of the lessee, was injured by the collapse of a retaining wall. The lessor of the premises, Mrs. Bowles, had built the wall.

Issue: Does a lessor have a duty to repair defects that develop after a lease is executed?

Rule: Absent any statutory or contractual duty, a lessor is not responsible for an injury resulting from a defect that developed during the term of a lease.

Faber v. Creswick (1959)

Facts: The Fabers leased premises from the defendant under a written lease providing that the defendant would "have the house ... in good order and repair at the beginning of this lease." Mr. Faber was the only signatory to the lease. A few days after moving into the house, Mrs. Faber was injured when she stepped on plasterboard so situated as to look like part of the floor, though it actually concealed a portion of a stairway.

Issue: When a lessor assumes a duty to repair the premises, is he liable in tort for injuries to third parties who have the tenant's consent to be on the premises?

Rule: If a landlord negligently performs the duty to repair that he had explicitly assumed, liability in tort arises for proximate consequential injuries suffered by both the tenant and third parties on the premises with the tenant's consent.

Feld v. Merriam (1984)

Facts: Plaintiffs Peggy and Samuel Feld were tenants in a large apartment complex. While returning home one evening they were abducted from the parking garage by armed felons. Subsequently, they brought suit against the owners of the complex alleging a breach of a duty of protection.

Issue: Under what circumstances does a landlord have a duty to protect tenants from the foreseeable criminal acts of third persons?

Rule: Absent an agreement, a landlord has no duty to provide protection for his tenants from acts of third parties. However, if a landlord undertakes to provide security services, whether by agreement or voluntarily, he must perform the task in a reasonable manner. The duty is not that of an insurer but of reasonable care under the circumstances.

Becker v. IRM Corp. (1985)

Facts: The plaintiff, a tenant in an apartment complex owned by the IRM Corp., sustained serious injuries when he fell against a shower door that was made of untempered glass. He sued the defendant in negligence and strict liability.

Issue 1: What is the nature of a residential landlord's liability for injuries sustained by a tenant as a result of a latent defect on the premises?

Rule 1: A landlord engaged in the business of leasing dwellings is strictly liable in tort for injuries resulting from a latent defect in the premises when the defect existed at the time the premises were let to the tenant.

Issue 2: Does a residential landlord owe his tenants a duty of inspection of the premises before they are leased?

Rule 2: A landlord, in the exercise of due care, has a duty to conduct a reasonable inspection of the premises at the time of letting, whether he has knowledge of a defective condition or not.

IX. No-Fault Termination of a Leasehold

Stroup v. Conant (1974)

Facts: As a prospective tenant, the defendant assured the plaintiff that he planned to use the premises for the operation of a variety store. Some time after the lease was executed, the landlord discovered that the defendant had opened an adult bookstore. She filed suit to have the lease rescinded.

Issue: May a lease be rescinded when a prospective tenant misrepresents his proposed use of the premises?

Rule: When a landlord relied on a misrepresentation of the planned purpose for which the premises were leased, the landlord may rescind the lease.

Warshawsky v. American Automotive Products Co. (1956)

Facts: The defendant's landlord sued for rent due when the defendant failed to pay rent. The defendant asserted as a defense the fact that his use of the premises as set forth in the lease was thwarted because it was contrary to a zoning ordinance.

Issue: May a tenant defend against an action for rent on the grounds that the use to which he had contemplated putting the premises is prohibited by a zoning ordinance?

Rule: Where a lease is restricted to a legal use, a zoning ordinance prohibiting that use is not a defense to an action for rent.

College Block v. Atlantic Richfield Co. (1988)

Facts: College Block leased land to the Atlantic Richfield Company (ARCO) on the condition that ARCO operate a gas station on that property and pay as rent a minimum monthly amount plus an amount determined by the quantity of gas delivered. When ARCO stopped operating the gas station, it paid College Block all of the minimum monthly payments remaining on the lease. College Block brought suit alleging that ARCO was also responsible for the additional sum it would have received had the gas station remained in business.

Issue: Where rent is based on a minimum payment plus a percentage of the lessee's revenues, does the lease contain an implied in law covenant of continued operation?

Rule: A covenant of continued operation will be implied in commercial leases containing a specified minimum payment plus a percentage of the lessee's revenues only when the guaranteed minimum is not substantial, i.e., when the specified minimum fails to provide the lessor with what was reasonably expected.

Kulawitz v. Pacific Woodenware & Paper Co. (1945)

Facts: The plaintiff leased space from the defendant in which he operated a furniture store. The lease contained a covenant not to compete, prohibiting the defendant from leasing other space to anyone planning to conduct the same type of business as the plaintiff. The defendant leased space to another who sold several of the same products as the plaintiff, and the plaintiff brought suit for violation of the restrictive covenant.

Issue: Is a tenant whose lease contains a noncompetition clause released from his obligations under the lease when his landlord breaches the agreement?

Rule: When a lessor breaches a noncompetition covenant, the tenant is entitled to rescind the lease and is relieved of further rent liability.

Teodori v. Werner (1980)

Facts: The tenant, Werner, asserted that Teodori's breach of their lease's noncompetition clause was a valid defense to actions for ejectment and rent payments due.

Issue: Will a landlord's breach of a lease's noncompetition clause provide a tenant with a defense to the landlord's actions for ejectment and sums due?

Rule: Absent an agreement to the contrary, a tenant's rent obligation and a landlord's promise under a noncompetition clause are interdependent. Therefore, a tenant is relieved from his rent obligation if the landlord materially breaches one of his obligations under the lease.

Marini v. Ireland (1970)

Facts: Because the lease between Marini and Ireland lacked a covenant imposing a duty on the landlord to repair the premises, Marini contended that Ireland could not offset the cost of certain repairs that she had made against her rent.

Issue: May a tenant offset the cost of necessary repairs against rent owed?

Rule: Pursuant to an implied warranty of habitability, if a landlord fails, within a reasonable period of time, to make repairs and replacements of vital facilities necessary to maintain the premises in a livable condition, the tenant may cause the same to be done and deduct the cost thereof from future rents.

Lloyd v. Murphy (1944)

Facts: In August 1941, Lloyd leased to Murphy premises to be used solely for selling new cars and gasoline. Due to the start of the Second World War, the government severely restricted sales of new automobiles. Despite Lloyd's willingness to waive the lease restriction, Murphy repudiated the lease.

Issue: What facts must be proved by a tenant seeking to avoid his rent obligation based on the doctrine of commercial frustration?

Rule: To successfully use the doctrine of commercial frustration, a tenant must prove that the risk of the frustrating event was not reasonably foreseeable and that the value of counterperformance by the landlord is totally or nearly totally destroyed.

Albert M. Greenfield & Co., Inc. v. Kolea (1976)

Facts: The plaintiff leased a building to the defendant for the purpose of operating a used car lot and repair shop. The building was subsequently destroyed by fire, and the plaintiff brought an action for rent payments remaining on the lease term.

Issue: Does the common law rule that the lessee must, absent an express provision to the contrary, continue to pay rent even if the leased premises are destroyed retain its viability in today's property law?

Rule: If there is no express allocation of risk within the lease and it is evident to the court that the true subject of the lease was a structure, and not the land on which it stood, the court should relieve the parties of their respective obligations when the building no longer exists.

Leonard v. Autocar Sales & Service Co. (1945)

Facts: Leonard leased premises to the defendant corporation for a 20-year term. The state temporarily condemned the premises. The defendant corporation vacated and refused to pay rent.

Issue: Is a tenant liable for rent during the time that the exclusive possession and temporary use of the leased premises has been taken by the government?

Rule: For a tenant to be excused from the payment of rent because of the condemnation of the demised premises, it is essential that the estate of the landlord be extinguished by the condemnation proceedings.

CHAPTER 7

Nuisance

I. NATURE OF A NUISANCE

A nuisance is a nontrespassory invasion by an actor that interferes with another person's use and enjoyment of land (private nuisance), or one that adversely impacts a right common to the general public (public nuisance).

Examples: Nuisances results from inherently noxious acts: a factory emitting smoke or odors; a business which creates loud noise; a farmer whose pesticide leaches onto the land of another; a landlord who allows his apartment to be shelter drug users.

The more modern approach to nuisance is to recognize that it is not the character of the use that creates a nuisance, after all smoke-emitting factories in industrial parks, noisy neighbors, farms in an agricultural area, and even drug-infested apartments do not usually negatively impact neighbors who use their property in a similar manner. Nuisances arise, therefore, when there are land use conflicts, where nonconforming uses operate in close proximity.

Example: A pig in the parlor, rather than in the barnyard.

A. Interest Protected

Nuisance law protects a person's use and enjoyment of his property. Contrast this concept with trespass, which applies to cases in which a person physically invades the property of another.

B. Intent Requirement

Nuisance liability can arise either from intentional acts that interfere with another's use and enjoyment of land or from acts in which the person knows that the unwanted interference will result from her conduct.

C. Entitlements

Nuisance law in the past focused on whether the landowner had some legal entitlement, a right to be free from the harm visited. Rules developed regarding the right in a landowner to access to the free flow of air or light to her land, lateral and adjacent support, water rights, and the like.

D. Reasonableness

Modern nuisance law balances the costs and benefits of the actor's conduct: Does the economic benefit outweigh the costs? If so, perhaps the actor's conduct should be permitted, but the neighbors whose property has become less valuable should receive damages. If not, perhaps an injunction should issue to prevent the overall negative consequence of the actor's conduct.

II. PUBLIC NUISANCE

A public nuisance is an interference with a right that is common to the general public or community.

Examples: Blocking a public highway, polluting a municipal beach, violating a local statute, engaging in illegal activities.

A. Elements
   1. Injury is to the public at large.
   2. Harm must be substantial.

   Unlike trespass, where nominal damages are awarded even if no harm is done, a nuisance action requires proof of actual damages.

B. If an individual plaintiff wants to recover damages that he suffered from a public nuisance, he must show that he suffered a different kind of harm than the public (not just more of the same harm).

   Example: The defendant blocks a road, delaying all commuters, and the plaintiff suffers a heart attack because of his irritation.

III. PRIVATE NUISANCE

The Restatement of Torts (Second, 1977) sec. 821D defines nuisance as a "nontrespassory invasion of another's interest in the private use and enjoyment of land. Even those with non-possessory interests like leaseholds and servitudes can recover."

A. Liability Under the Restatement
   1. One is liable if his conduct is the "legal cause of an invasion," and the invasion is intentional and unreasonable, or "unintentional but actionable under the rules controlling liability for negligent or reckless conduct" (sec. 824).
   2. The conduct may be an act or omission where there is a duty to act.
   3. An act is intentional if it is undertaken purposefully or knowingly (sec. 825).
   4. The act is unreasonable if the "gravity of the harm" of the conduct outweighs its social utility **or** the harm is "serious" and the

actor can compensate the injured party and still continue his enterprise (sec. 826).

   a. In assessing reasonableness a court will **either** balance the harm to the plaintiff against the benefits of the defendant's conduct.

   Example: The defendant's oil refinery may cause pollution, but oil is a necessary commodity.

   b. **Or** allow the interference to continue if the actor compensates the person whose interests have been negatively impacted

5. To determine whether the gravity of the harm outweighs the social utility, the court will consider the following factors with respect to the harm (sec. 827):

   a. The extent of the harm.

   b. The character of the harm.

   c. The social value of the use that is damaged by the actor.

   d. The suitability of the use given the character of locality

   e. The ability of the occupier to avoid the harm.

6. To determine whether the gravity of the harm outweighs the social utility, the court will consider the following factors with respect to the harm of the conduct (sec. 828):

   a. The social value attached to the actor's conduct.

   b. Its suitability for the area.

   c. The impracticality of avoiding the harm of locality

7. Whether the harm is severe, whether it is practical to avoid, and whether it is unsuitable to the area, are considerations (secs. 829A, 830, and 831, respectively).

8. Likewise, "first in time," and therefore whether a party came to the nuisance is relevant though not controlling (sec. 840D).

B. Liability at Common Law

   1. Nuisance "Per Se"

   Actionable no matter where it is done.

   Example: A factory spills toxic chemicals.

   2. Nuisance "per accidens"

   Actionable only because of surroundings.

   Example: An oil refinery in the middle of a residential neighborhood.

IV. REMEDIES

A plaintiff has three possible remedies against a nuisance:

A. Abatement by Self-Help

In some cases a plaintiff is allowed to use minimal force to cure the nuisance himself if the defendant refuses to do so.

B. Injunction

An injunction will only be granted if the plaintiff succeeds in proving that the gravity of the harm to him outweighs the social utility of the actor's conduct.

C. Damages

Damages will be granted if the harm is serious and the actor can continue operations and pay the party claiming a nuisance the lost value of the land injured.

1. Temporary

Compensation for past harm. The plaintiff must bring successive actions if the interference continues.

2. Permanent

Compensation for past and future harm. The plaintiff needs to bring only one action. Generally permanent damages are awarded in cases where the nuisance will be permanent but an injunction is not issued.

V. DEFENSES

A. "Coming to the Nuisance"

This is really a variation on the "assumption of risk" doctrine.

1. Old Rule

The presence of the defendant's enterprise in an area before the plaintiff's arrival constituted a complete defense to a nuisance action, even if the defendant's activity substantially interfered with the plaintiff's use and enjoyment of his land.

2. Restatement

"Coming to the nuisance" is only one factor to look at in the balancing test.

B. Conduct of Others

When several parties combine to produce a nuisance, each party is liable only for the damages it actually caused.

C. Contributory Negligence

Applies only if the plaintiff claims that the defendant negligently created the nuisance.

D. Legislative Authority

Compliance with local zoning laws and regulations is persuasive, although not conclusive, evidence that an activity was not a nuisance.

CASE CLIPS

I. Nature of a Nuisance

Rose v. Chaikin (1982)

Facts: The Roses sought to enjoin the defendants from operating a noisy windmill in a residential area.
Issue: Can noise alone constitute a private nuisance?
Rule: Noises that injuriously affect the health and comfort of ordinary people to an unreasonable extent can, considering all the circumstances, constitute a private nuisance.

Morgan v. High Penn Oil Co. (1953)

Facts: The plaintiffs brought suit against the High Penn Oil Company, alleging that its oil refinery was a nuisance because it emitted noxious gasses in close proximity to the plaintiffs' property.
Issue: For a claim of nuisance to be actionable, must the alleged tortfeasor, if conducting a legal enterprise, have behaved negligently?
Rule: A nuisance exists when a person's conduct substantially interferes with another's interest in the use and enjoyment of his land, whether such interference is the result of negligent conduct or not.

Armstrong v. Francis Corp. (1956)

Facts: By artificially draining water from its land, the Francis Corp. caused damage to downstream owners.
Issue: Does a landowner have an absolute right to drain surface water from his land?
Rule: A landowner is legally privileged to make a reasonable use of his land even though the flow of surface waters is altered thereby and causes some harm to others, but he incurs liability when his harmful interference with the flow of waters is unreasonable.

Evans v. Merriweather (1842)

Facts: Evans purchased land directly upstream from Merriweather. He diverted water to such an extent that Merriweather did not receive any.
Issue: To what extent may riverbank proprietors use the water flowing on their land?
Rule: A riparian owner may use all the water necessary to meet his domestic needs, but, where he uses water for a commercial use or irrigation, his consumption is limited to a reasonable use.

Ferguson v. City of Keene (1968)

Facts: Although flight paths did not cross over her land, Ferguson claimed that the noise from the defendant's airport damaged her land and made her life unbearable, thereby constituting a taking for which she should have been compensated.

Issue: Does an action for inverse condemnation lie where noise from a city-owned airport damages nearby land, even if no flight paths cross over the land?

Rule: Where a flight path does not cross directly over property no taking of the property results, even when the enjoyment of the property is diminished by noise emanating from a nearby airport.

II. Public Nuisance

Spur Indus., Inc. v. Del E. Webb Development Co. (1972)

Facts: Del E. Webb Development Co. developed a huge tract of land for residential purposes and subsequently sued Spur Industries in a nuisance action to enjoin further operation of its large cattle feedlot located nearby. The plaintiff alleged that the odors emanating from the feedlot constituted both a public nuisance and a private nuisance. This clip addresses the former.

Issue: Does the use by Del Webb constitute a public nuisance?

Rule: Arizona law regards as a public nuisance any conditions that constitute a breeding place for disease carrying animals as a public nuisance.

III. Private Nuisance

Fountainebleu Hotel v. Forty-Five Twenty-Five Corp. (1959)

Facts: Defendant proposes to construct a building that will shadow plaintiff's pool.

Issue: Does a property owner, absent a contract or a statute, have a right to the free-flow of light and air over its property?

Rule: The English doctrine of "ancient lights" is not generally accepted law in the United States. Therefore use of land such as a building is not a nuisance *per se* even though it impedes the flow of sunlight to a neighbor's land.

Prah v. Maretti (1982)

Facts: Defendant proposes to build a house on his lot that will "shadow" the solar reflectors on his neighbor's roof.

Issue 1: Will the proposed house, if constructed where the defendant plans to locate it constitute a nuisance at common law?

Rule 1: Although the court remands for a factual determination, it regards blocking a solar reflector's access to the sun as a nuisance if the trial court, in considering the facts, finds that the "gravity of the harm" to the plaintiff outweighs the "social utility" of the actor's conduct.

Issue 2: If the court does find an actionable nuisance, what is the appropriate remedy.

Rule 2: Under the Restatement sec. 826 (a), an injunction preventing the actor's conduct is an appropriate remedy.

Estancias Dallas Corp. v. Schultz (1973)

Facts: The air conditioning unit of the defendant's apartment complex produced such high levels of noise that the Schultzes, owners of adjoining property, brought suit for injunctive relief.

Issue 1: When facts constituting a private nuisance are found by the judge or jury, must there be a further balancing of the equities involved?

Rule 1: Before injunctive relief can be granted the court must balance the injury to the defendant or the general public if an injunction is issued against the injury to the complainant if an injunction is denied.

Issue 2: Under what circumstances will a court, after balancing the equities, refuse to enjoin a private nuisance?

Rule 2: An injunction prohibiting a nuisance will be denied only when it is found that the continued operation of the nuisance is *strictly necessary* for the benefit of others.

Crest Chevrolet v. Willemsen (1986)

Facts: Defendant regrades his land so that the flow of water is reversed. Instead of water flowing from the plaintiff's land to his, water from defendant's land flows to plaintiff's land and damages his parking lot.

Issue 1: May defendant regrade his land in such a way as to divert the water, a "common enemy," to his neighbor's land?

Rule 1: The "common enemy" doctrine is replaced by the Restatement rule.

Issue 2: Is the nature of the harm serious, and will the defendant be able to continue his operation even though he is required to compensate plaintiff for its losses?

Rule 2: Where the actor could have avoided damage to his neighbor's land by including that land in the regrading project, he should have done so. The harm caused by the regrading is serious and the actor could compensate his neighbor for damages by merely passing along the cost to his own customers.

Von Henneberg v. Generazio (1988)

Facts: Generazio built a berm on his land which prevented water from draining from Von Henneberg's land and caused that land to flood.
Issue: Does the reasonable use doctrine apply to Generazio's actions?
Rule: The reasonable use doctrine holds that a landowner incurs liability when his harmful interference with the flow of surface waters is unreasonable.

Hendricks v. Stalnaker (1989)

Facts: Local ordinance requires that wells and septic tanks be separated by at least 100 feet. Hendricks applied for a permit to build a septic tank; Stalnaker, a well. Stalnaker builds his well first, and Hendricks is thereafter unable to locate the septic tank on his property, given its configuration, more than 100 feet from Stalnaker's well.
Issue: Is the well a nuisance?
Rule: Although the uses are inconsistent, both are of equal utility. Hendricks cannot therefore demonstrate that the gravity of the harm to him outweighs the social utility of the well.

Boomer v. Atlantic Cement Co. (1970)

Facts: Individual property owners brought suit against the Atlantic Cement Company requesting damages and an injunction. They alleged that in the course of its operation the cement plant was emitting dirt, smoke, and vibrations, which were causing injury to their property.
Issue: Must a court grant an injunction whenever substantial damage results from the operation of a nuisance?
Rule: If the court, after balancing the equities, determines that an injunction would impose a grossly disproportionate economic loss on the enterprise that is creating the nuisance, it may allow the enterprise to pay permanent damages to the aggrieved property owners in lieu of an injunction.

IV. Defenses

Bove v. Donner-Hanna Coke Corp. (1932)

Facts: Bove bought land near an industrial area and built a residence there. Subsequently the defendant built a coke oven across the street, which Bove sought to enjoin as a private nuisance.
Issue: Although a particular enterprise, claimed to be a nuisance, began operations after a residence was built, must the enterprise be enjoined when the residence was built in an area suited for and already used for industrial purposes?

Rule: Equity will not issue an injunction when the complainant claims that her peace and comfort have been disturbed by a situation which existed, at least to some extent, at the very time complainant bought her property and where it was foreseeable that the condition would worsen.

Spur Indus., Inc. v. Del E. Webb Development Co. (1972)

Facts: Del E. Webb Development Co. developed a huge tract of land for residential purposes and subsequently sued Spur Industries in a nuisance action to enjoin further operation of its large cattle feedlot located nearby. The plaintiff alleged that the odors emanating from the feedlot constituted both a public and a private nuisance to the people living in their newly constructed homes. Del E. Webb further alleged that the odors were substantially hurting sales.

Issue 1: When the operation of a business is lawful in the first instance, but becomes a nuisance by reason of the encroachment of a nearby residential area, may the business be enjoined from further operation?

Rule 1: A change in the composition of the area surrounding a business may cause the business to become a nuisance subject to being enjoined from further operation.

Issue 2: Is a developer of a new residential area in a previously agricultural one required to indemnify the operator of a business that has been enjoined from further operation due to the actions of the developer?

Rule 2: A developer who, with foreseeability, converts a previously agricultural or industrial area into a residential one, thereby necessitating an injunction against a lawful business, must indemnify the owner of the business for a reasonable amount of the cost of moving or shutting down.

CHAPTER 8

Private Land-Use Arrangements

I. EASEMENTS

A. Definition

An easement is a nonpossessory interest in another's land. Easements benefit one parcel of land, the *dominant* tenement, and burden another, the *servient* tenement. There are various types.

1. Affirmative Easement

Entitles the easement holder to enter the servient tenement for a specified purpose.

2. Negative Easement

Entitles the holder to compel the possessor of the servient tenement to refrain from using his property in a specified manner.

3. Easement Appurtenant

Benefits the holder in his use and enjoyment of a particular parcel of land.

4. Easement in Gross

The benefit to the holder is personal and independent of his use and enjoyment of a particular parcel of land.

5. Profit

A right to enter another's land to remove its product, such as minerals or crops.

B. Creation

An easement may be created in any of the following ways:

1. Easement by Grant

   a. A written conveyance may expressly grant or reserve an easement, but it must be reasonably clear regarding the scope of the easement. Express easements must comply with the statute of frauds.

      b. Expressly granted easements will be valid if the parties unambiguously include the following elements:
        i. Location
        ii. Dimensions
        iii. Special uses allowed or disallowed

2. Easement by implication

For an easement by implication to arise, the dominant and servient estates must have been owned by the same person at some earlier time.

Requirements:

    a. The use, claimed to be an easement by implication, must have existed before the time when the two estates were severed from each other.

    b. It must also have been apparent and continuous prior to the severance.

    c. Lastly, it must be reasonably necessary for the use and enjoyment of the dominant tenement.

Note: The requirements are more carefully scrutinized when the original owner has transferred the servient tenement and retains the dominant tenement, claiming that he impliedly reserved an easement at the time of severance.

3. Easement by necessity

Will arise only if the two parcels of land were, at one time, owned by the same person. No prior use is required, but a showing of strict necessity is mandatory.

Example: A parcel of land is so situated that it is impossible for the owner to have access to a road without a right of way across someone else's property.

4. Easement by prescription

    a. An easement by prescription will arise when the claimant's use is open, notorious (not concealed), continuous (regularly used), exclusive (of other claimant, though titleholder can also use), and adverse (non-permissive) for the period of time required by the statute of limitations. The statute of limitations will begin to run when the servient tenement's owner gains a cause of action against the adverse user, that is, the time at which the use commences.

    b. Easements by prescription are "close relatives" of adverse possession, and similar rules regarding the disability and tacking doctrines will apply.

C. Scope of easements

1. Prior location, dimension, and special uses determine the scope of implied and prescriptive easements.

   2. The scope of an easement by necessity is strictly confined to the
      necessity.
   3. Easements may be enlarged by prescription.
   4. Reasonably foreseeable normal changes in use will be permitted if
      the resultant increased burden on the servient tenement is not
      unreasonable.
   5. The servient tenement's owner may grant an identical easement to
      a third party if the granted easement is not inconsistent with the
      original easement holder's interest.
D. Transfer of easements
   1. An easement appurtenant automatically passes to the new owner
      on conveyance of the dominant, unless the parties agree
      otherwise. An appurtenant easement is not terminated by transfer
      of the servient tenement.
   2. If the servient tenement is subdivided or conveyed in whole or in
      part, the burden of an easement appurtenant remains with those
      portions of the property, subdivided or conveyed, that are subject
      to the easement, unless and until the subdivision burdens the
      easement to a greater extent than contemplated by the parties
      to a grant or the use that gave rise to an easement by prescription,
      implication, or necessity.
   3. Except for commercial easements, an easement in gross is gener-
      ally not transferable, but they may be divisible so long as the
      additional holder uses the interest together (in one stock).
E. Termination of easements may occur in the following ways:
   1. Written release.
   2. Prescription.
      The holder of the servient interest blocks the prescriptive ease-
      ment for the prescriptive period.
   3. Abandonment.
      The holder must manifest an intent by conduct (not words alone)
      to permanently discontinue using the easement.
   4. Merger (i.e., common ownership of the servient and dominant
      tenement).
   5. When the purpose for the original creation of the easement no
      longer exists.
   6. When creating document prescribes conditions governing the
      easement's duration.
   7. Forfeit (i.e., the servient tenement's burden dramatically increases
      and cannot be alleviated).
   8. When the easement is by necessity and the necessity no longer
      exists.
   9. Estoppel (i.e., the owner of the servient tenement changes his position
      in reliance on the words or conduct of the easement holder).

II. LICENSE

A. Generally

A license is a privilege (and sometimes even regarded as an interest in property — Restatement (sec. 512) to enter or use the property of the licensor. A license allows its holder to an act on the land of another which, without the license, would be a trespass.

Elements:

1. A license need not be created in a writing, and is frequently created orally.
2. A license is usually personal and therefore non-transferable.
3. A licensor may revoke a license at will by an express or implied manifestation of an intent to so do.
4. A licensee may surrender a license at will.

B. Revocation by Operation of Law

A license will be revoked by operation of law if:

1. The licensor dies.
2. The licensor conveys the subject property.
3. The licensee attempts to transfer the license.

C. Irrevocable Licenses

1. When in justifiable reliance on the continuation of a license, the licensee makes substantial expenditures in reliance on its continuation on the land of the licensor, or in most jurisdiction (see Restatement secs. 514, 519(4)); even on his own land, the licensor will be estopped from revoking a license for a period of time necessary for the licensee to recoup expenditures made in reliance.

   Example: Smith gives Jones a license to reach his land by using a road on Smith's land. Jones repairs the road, and builds the house. Smith is estopped from revoking until Jones' has used the road for a substantial period of time, until he has "amortized" the cost of the access way to his own land.

2. A license coupled with an interest is irrevocable to the extent necessary to protect that interest (Restatement secs. 514 and 519(3)).

   Example: A licensee has a chattel on the licensor's land. The licensor cannot revoke the license in an attempt to prevent the licensee from entering his land to reclaim the chattel.

D. Public Events

Paying an entry fee (e.g., to play golf) or buying a ticket to an event (e.g., to the movies) creates a revocable license. If a license is improperly revoked by a licensor, the licensee may sue for breach of contract but he will not have any remedies under the laws of property.

III. REAL COVENANTS

A. Generally

A covenant running with the land (i.e., a real covenant) is a contract between two landowners, binding the successor in interest of each, that restricts one owner's use of his land (the burdened estate) in a manner benefiting the other's land (the benefited estate). Covenants may be either affirmative or negative. **Traditionally, they are enforceable in law for damages.** Successor of promissee can therefore recoup the lost value to her land if the successor of the promise fails to perform.

B. Requirements for a Covenant to Run with the Land

1. Running of the **Burden**

   a. The promise must be in writing (the statute of frauds must be satisfied).

   b. The promise between the original parties must be one that would be enforceable in contract between them.

   c. The original parties must have intended that the promise bind their respective successors in interest. Usually the agreement will so specify or indicate that the promissory "covenants for herself, her heirs, or assigns."

   d. The covenant must "touch and concern" the land.

      i. A covenant "touches and concerns" a particular parcel of land if the burden or benefit imposed by the covenant is connected to the land and therefore confers some value on the land.

      ii. The covenant must "touch and concern" both the burdened and benefited estates for the burden to run with the land. However, some courts will allow a burden to run with the land even if the benefit is in gross. Restatement Third sec. 3.2 (2000) has abolished the requirement.

   e. A buyer of the burdened estate must have notice of the covenant prior to acquiring his interest. Notice is proved by requiring that there must be horizontal privity at the time the burden is created and successors to the burden must be in vertical privity with the promissor.

      i. Horizontal privity exists when the covenant is incident to a conveyance of an interest in the burdened property. Horizontal privity is absent if two property owners simply agree to restrict the use of their respective property by an ancillary, unregistered written agreement.

      ii. Vertical privity exists when the present owners of the burdened and benefited property have acquired the land through a recognized legal transfer: usually a deed, will

or through intestate succession. For a burden to run with
the land, an assignee must acquire the entire interest in
the estate.

Example: An assignee acquiring a life estate from his predecessor in title, who held a fee simple absolute, does not
comply with the vertical privity requirement.

2. Running of the **Benefit**

   a. The covenant must be in writing; the statute of frauds must
be satisfied.

   b. The promise between the original parties must be enforceable in contract.

   c. The original parties must have intended that the promise
bind their respective successors in interest. Usually the agreement will so specify or indicate that the promissory "covenants for herself, her heirs, or assigns."

   d. The covenant must "touch and concern" the land. It is sufficient that the covenant "touch and concern" only the benefited
land, that it confers some economic benefit on the land. Restatement Third sec. 3.2 (2000) has abolished the requirement.

   e. There need only be vertical privity of estate.

     i. There must be privity of estate between the assignee
and the original promisee. However, the assignee need
not succeed to the identical estate of his predecessor in
interest.

     ii. Horizontal privity is not required.

C. Termination

Real covenants may be terminated in any of the following ways:

1. Release.

2. Prescription.

3. Merger (i.e., the burdened and benefited parcels become commonly owned).

4. Abandonment.

The beneficiary must, by conduct, manifest an intent to permanently discontinue using the servitude.

5. Government action (e.g., condemnation) though holder may
share in award.   *emurent domain*

6. Conditions change to such an extent that the purpose of the
covenant is no longer furthered by its continued existence.   *necessity —*

IV. EQUITABLE SERVITUDES

A. Generally

An equitable servitude is an interest recognized in equity (**and therefore enforceable by an injunction**) of one property owner (the

benefited estate) in the land of another (the burdened estate). Formal requirements are unnecessary to create an equitable servitude.

B. Elements

For an equitable servitude to <u>bind a subsequent purchaser,</u> the following requirements must be met:

1. <u>An agreement</u> that is a promise with respect to land use. The agreement may be implied in cases of restricted residential subdivisions, carried out pursuant to a general scheme. When a developer subdivides a tract of land, putting restrictive covenants on some, but not all, of the parcels, implied reciprocal servitudes arise. The grantees of each of the plots of land so subdivided may enforce the restrictive covenant against each other, whether the covenant was expressly in their deed or not, provided that the following conditions are met:

   a. The subdivision was carried out pursuant to a <u>general scheme.</u>

   b. The grantees seeking enforcement purchased their lots in reliance on their <u>right to enforce</u> the restrictive covenant.

   c. The grantee against whom enforcement is sought had actual or constructive <u>notice</u> that the land may be subject to a restrictive covenant.

2. The <u>original parties</u> must have <u>intended</u> that the promise <u>bind</u> their respective <u>successors</u> in interest. Usually the agreement will so specify or indicate that the promissory "covenants for herself, her heirs, or assigns."

3. The promissor's successor in interest must have <u>notice</u>, actual or constructive.

4. The <u>burden</u> must <u>"touch and concern"</u> the burdened estate. It is sufficient that the covenant "touch and concern" only the benefited land, that it confers some economic benefit on the land. Restatement Third sec. 3.2 (2000) has abolished the requirement.

C. The following <u>may prevent enforcement</u> of an equitable servitude:

1. Laches (delay in bringing suit).

2. Estoppel.

3. Plaintiff has unclean hands (plaintiff has himself committed a violation of a similar servitude).

4. The servitude's purpose is against public policy.

5. Plaintiff has tolerated similar violations of the servitude.

6. Changed conditions render the enforcement of the servitude

D. Termination

Equitable servitudes may be terminated in any of the following ways:

1. Release.

2. Prescription.

3. Merger (i.e., the burdened and benefited parcels become commonly owned).

4. Abandonment.
   The beneficiary must, by conduct, manifest an intent to permanently discontinue using the servitude.
5. Government action (e.g., condemnation).
6. Conditions change to such an extent that the purpose of the
   servitude is no longer furthered by its continued existence.

CASE CLIPS

I. Easements

Mitchell v. Castellaw (1952)

Facts: A grantor conveyed two of her three lots and, without using terms of art, reserved an express easement on one of the lots conveyed. Castellaw, the grantor's devisee, sued to establish the easement's validity.

Issue: Are words of inheritance or other words of art essential to a valid reservation of an appurtenant easement?

Rule: Neither words of inheritance nor other words of art are essential to the valid reservation of an appurtenant easement, even one of unlimited duration.

Willard v. First Church of Christ Scientist (1972)

Facts: Petersen bought land that was subject to an easement reserved for the benefit of the defendant, a third party to the transaction. He then sold the land to Willard with no mention of the easement in the deed. Willard subsequently brought suit to quiet title.

Issue: May a grantor reserve an easement for the benefit of a third party?

Rule: A grantor's intent is dispositive in the interpretation of his conveyance. Therefore, if there is enough evidence to indicate that the grantor intended to reserve an easement for the benefit of a third party the easement will be upheld.

Note: Jurisdictions are split on this issue with some courts adhering to the old common law rule that a grantor may not reserve an easement for the benefit of a third party.

Midland Valley Railroad Co. v. Arrow Indus. Mfg. Co. (1956)

Facts: Midland Valley Railroad Co. and Arrow Industrial Mfg. Co. both acquired their land from a common grantor. The grant to the plaintiff Midland Valley Railroad Co. conveyed by deed "a strip of land for a right of way" located across land now owned by the defendant corporation. The defendant corporation asserted that the grant created an easement rather than an estate in fee. Pursuant to Oklahoma statute every estate conveyed by deed was in fee simple, unless limited by express language.

Issue: Is an estate in land conveyed by deed without language of express limitation an estate in fee simple or merely an easement?

Rule: The intent of the parties to a conveyance, gleaned from the four corners of the granting instrument, is the controlling factor in deciding whether the conveyance is an estate in fee simple or an easement. Where it appears that the intent of the parties was to convey a described strip of land, rather than a right of way over a strip of land, the conveyance is considered a fee estate rather than an easement.

Stoner v. Zucker (1906)

Facts: The defendant had a license from the plaintiff to build, use, and maintain an irrigation ditch on the plaintiff's land. After the defendant spent $7,000 building the ditch, the plaintiff revoked the license.

Issue: Is an executed parol license revocable at the will of the licensor, when it has already involved the expenditure of money, and when the very nature of the license is one of continuous use?

Rule: Where a licensee enters under a parol license and expends money, or its equivalent in labor, in the execution of the license, the license is irrevocable and will continue for so long time as its nature requires.

Granite Properties Limited Partnership v. Manns (1987)

Facts: The plaintiff sold a lot to the Mannses, while retaining two lots on either side of the Mannses' property. The plaintiff had used driveways situated between its land and that of the Mannses, which had been there before the land was sold to the Mannses. The plaintiff therefore argued that an implied easement over the driveways had arisen due to the plaintiff's prior use.

Issue: For an easement to be implied from a prior existing use, must the use be one that was absolutely necessary to the grantor's beneficial enjoyment of his land?

Rule: For an easement to be implied from a prior existing use, the use need only be reasonably necessary.

Holbrook v. Taylor (1976)

Facts: The Taylors owned land adjacent to the Holbrooks. From 1944 to 1970 the Holbrooks had allowed a road, running through their property, to be built and improved by successive owners of the adjoining property, including the Taylors. The Taylors filed suit to establish their right to use the road as an irrevocable license.

Issue: When a licensee makes substantial expenditures to a roadway over another's land on the faith of the license, and the licensor consents to or tacitly approves of such use, is the licensor estopped from revoking the license?

Rule: The right of revocation of a license is subject to the qualification that where the licensee has exercised the privilege given him and erected improvements on the faith or strength of the license, it becomes

·irrevocable and continues for so long as the nature of the license calls. In effect the license becomes a grant through estoppel.

Shepard v. Purvine (1952)

Facts: Plaintiffs were close friends and neighbors of the defendants. The parties entered into an agreement, but plaintiffs did not insist on a deed, accepting defendants' word as they would a written instrument.
Issue: When an individual enters into an agreement with a close friend, is it negligent not to insist on a formal transfer of rights?
Rule: When one makes an oral agreement with a close friend or neighbor, the license promptly acted on is just as valid and binding, and irrevocable as a deeded right of way.

Henry v. Dalton (1959)

Facts: Henry filed suit when the respondent revoked his license.
Issue: Is a license revocable where the intention is to confer a continuing right, and money has been expended by the licensee on the faith of the license?
Rule: A parol license to perform an act on the property of a licensor is revocable at his option.

Finn v. Williams (1941)

Facts: Finn's land was entirely surrounded by Williams' land, from which it was originally severed, and by land owned by third parties. From the date of severance, Finn had a permissive right of ingress and egress over the land of a third party. He brought suit to establish his right of way over Williams' land by virtue of an easement by necessity, created at the time of severance.
Issue: Where an owner of land conveys a parcel thereof, which has no outlet except over the grantor's retained land or land owned by third parties, does an easement by necessity arise, and if so, may it lie dormant through several transfers of title?
Rule: Where an owner conveys a parcel of his land which has no outlet except over the grantor's retained land or that of third parties, an easement by necessity arises over the grantor's remaining land. Although this easement may lie dormant through several transfers of title, it still passes with each transfer as appurtenant to the dominant estate and may be exercised at any time by the titleholder of the dominant estate.

Van Sandt v. Royster (1938)

Facts: Under the plaintiff's house was a sewer drain that flooded his cellar. The document that originally conveyed his land did not expressly reserve an easement for the passage of sewer pipes under his property. Therefore, on discovery of the leakage, he brought an action to enjoin the defendants from using the underground sewer drain.

Issue: To establish an easement by implied reservation in favor of the grantor must the easement be one of strict necessity?

Rule: If land may be used without an easement, but cannot be used without disproportionate effort and expense, <u>strict necessity is not a requirement for finding an implied easement by reservation.</u>

Romanchuck v. Plotkin (1943)

Facts: Romanchuck bought lot 1310 from Plotkin, who also owned lot 1312. At the time of the sale, the sewage from lot 1310 passed through lot 1312 to a public sewer on Humboldt Avenue. After the sale, sewage from lot 1310 caused sewage to collect in the basement of lot 1312. Plotkin sued to enjoin Romanchuck's use.

Issue: Was an easement by implication created on severance when Plotkin sold to Romanchuck? *Particioning land, created an implied easement*

Held: Where there is the partition of property, and at the time of partition, one part of the property is used for the benefit of another, an easement by implication is created if the use was apparent and was reasonably necessary. *@time of partition: apparent reasonably necessary benefit another ⟩ implied easement.*

Othen v. Rosier (1950)

Facts: The plaintiff Albert Othen could enter and exit his property only by traveling across a roadway on the defendant's land, which the defendant also used. The common grantor of both parcels first conveyed the defendant's parcel and then, more than two years later, conveyed the plaintiffs. The plaintiff claimed that the common grantor impliedly reserved an easement for himself, and consequently he, as the successor in interest, also held an easement.

Issue 1: What are the requirements that must be met before an easement can be said to have been created by implied reservation?

Rule 1: Before an easement can be held to have been created by implied reservation it must be shown that (1) there was a unity of ownership of the alleged dominant and servient estates; (2) the easement is a necessity, not a mere convenience; and (3) the necessity existed at the time of severance of the two estates.

Issue 2: Can a prescriptive easement arise when both the owner and the claimant use a roadway?

Rule 2: For a prescriptive easement to be created the claimant must be using the roadway under a claim of right. Use of a roadway by both the owner and the adverse claimant is sufficient evidence that the claimant's use of the roadway is merely permissive, and not under a claim of right.

Krzewinski v. Eaton Homes, Inc. (1958)

Facts: The Krzewinskis bought a lot from Eaton Homes, Inc. pursuant to a plat that showed their lot abutting a through street. Eaton Homes refused to complete the street and the Krzewinskis sought specific performance.

Issue: Where a vendee buys a lot with reference to a plat that shows that the property abuts a planned street, does an implied easement for the use of the road arise?

Rule: Where a deed describes the lot conveyed by reference to a plat, the grantee acquires an implied easement to use the road that extends to the whole street shown so far as it was owned by the grantor when the deed was executed.

Campbell v. Great Miami Aerie No. 2309 (1984)

Facts: Campbell's and defendant's adjoining properties were once owned by a common grantor. The sewage system serving both pieces of property was located on Campbell's property. When each party purchased its respective property the placement of the sewage system was not known to either of them. Alleging trespass, Campbell sued for damages and a permanent injunction to prevent the defendant from using his sewage facilities. The defendant claimed that he had an implied easement.

Issue: Where a sewage system serving adjoining properties previously owned by a common grantor is located on one parcel, does the other parcel retain an implied easement upon severance of the two parcels?

Rule: For an implied easement to arise there must have been a severance of the unity of ownership of an estate. The easement shall have been long continued and obvious before the separation. The easement must be reasonably necessary to the beneficial enjoyment of the land, and the servitude shall be continuous. Absent actual or constructive notice of the easement by the party sought to be charged with knowledge of it, no implied easement arises.

Roy v. Euro Holland (1981)

Facts: The predecessors of Roy purchased a tract of land that was landlocked: The new owner could not reach a public road without traveling across land retained by the grantor. No easement was expressly created in the grant.

Issue: Was an easement created by necessity?

Rule: Easements by necessity are created on severance if the transferred property is rendered landlocked. The owner has a right of ingress and egress over land remaining in the hands of the grantor.

Lunt v. Kitchens (1953)

Facts: Under license from Lunt's predecessor in title, the Kitchenses used a driveway for a period of time satisfying the statutory period for adverse claims. However, the Kitchenses never communicated to Lunt's grantor their intent to repudiate the license and claim the driveway under color of right.

Issue: Where a landowner consents to the use of his land by another, will a prescriptive easement arise after passage of the statutory period?

Rule: If a landowner consents to the use of his land by another, the right created is a license and the presumption of adversity will not arise through mere conforming use by the licensee. A prescriptive easement can only arise from a license when the licensee openly renounces the license and uses the property under a claim of right.

Dartnell v. Bidwell (1916)

Facts: Bidwell claimed a prescriptive easement over Dartnell's land. Before the expiration of the statutory period, Dartnell notified Bidwell in writing that she did not acknowledge Bidwell's right of way across her property. She subsequently brought an action for trespass. Bidwell argued, in defense, that the writing was not sufficient to interrupt the running of the statutory period.

Issue: Is an owner's acquiescence essential to the creation of a prescriptive easement and if so, may the owner interrupt the running of the statutory period by actions that fall short of actual entry and ousting of the adverse claimant?

Rule: An owner's acquiescence is one of the essential elements in the creation of a prescriptive easement. In this context acquiescence is understood to mean passive assent, submission, or consent by silence. Therefore, an owner may interrupt the running of the statutory period by demonstrating his nonacquiescence. A notice in writing served or delivered to the adverse claimant is sufficient for this purpose. No physical intrusion by the owner is required.

Hester v. Sawyers (1937)

Facts: The defendant built, used and maintained a road that traversed the plaintiff's land. His tenants, visitors, and those doing business with him had used the road daily and openly without interruption or objection from anybody, and without obtaining anybody's permission. He claimed that he had established a prescriptive easement over the plaintiff's land.

Issue: May an easement be acquired by prescription?

Rule: An easement by prescription arises where the user makes open, uninterrupted, peaceable, notorious, and adverse use of another's land under a claim of right, which use continues for a period of years set by the statute of limitations and is with the knowledge or imputed knowledge of the owner.

Shanks v. Floom (1955)

Facts: The predecessors in title to Shanks and Floom orally agreed to build a common driveway on the medial line of their adjacent properties. The Shanks brought suit to enjoin the defendants from using the common driveway.

Issue: Is it necessary to show that there was a heated controversy or ill will to establish the required hostility for a prescriptive easement?

Rule: All that is required to fulfill the hostility requirement of a prescriptive easement is that the use be inconsistent with the rights of the title owner and not subordinate or subservient thereto.

Fischer v. Grinsbergs (1977)

Facts: The parties, neighboring landowners, shared a driveway that was largely on the property of the defendant, and had been constructed by previous owners. Each party used the drive as an access way for automobiles from the street to their garage in the rear of their lot. Defendant built a fence on the property line allowing him the use of the drive, but essentially precluding plaintiff uses. Plaintiff brings an action to enjoin the defendant's interference with her "easement by prescription"?

Issue: Was the plaintiff's use, and the use by the plaintiff's predecessor in interest, adverse?

Rule: The burden to show permissive rather than adverse use is on the landowner where there has been open, continuous, and exclusive use of an easement used by both sets of homeowners.

Parker & Edgerton v. Foote (1838)

Facts: After the defendant built an edifice on his own land that blocked the plaintiff's light, the plaintiff, whose windows were unobstructed for 24 years, claimed an easement by prescription to light.

Issue: May an easement of light be acquired by prescription?

Rule: In the case of light, because there is neither an adverse user nor any use whatsoever of another's property, no foundation is laid to support a presumption of adverse use against a rightful owner. Therefore, a prescriptive easement to light cannot arise.

Romans v. Nadler (1944)

Facts: By occasionally trespassing on Nadler's land to clean his gutters and paint his house, the plaintiff claimed a prescriptive easement on Nadler's land.
Issue: Will sporadic and occasional use satisfy the element of continuity needed to establish a prescriptive easement?
Rule: Because the requirement of continuity essential to establishing a prescriptive easement depends on the nature and character of the right claimed, sporadic and occasional use will not constitute continuous use.

Amarillo v. Carlotta (1950)

Facts: The defendant built a wall on her property that partially blocked light and air from entering the plaintiff's home.
Issue: Will an implied easement of light and air arise absent an absolute necessity?
Rule: Absent an absolute necessity, an implied easement of light and air cannot be created.

Skinks v. Wean (1933)

Facts: Wean, owner of the servient estate, proposed to erect a building with an 8-foot-high clearance over Skinks's right of way, and to lay out a new way for Skinks's use. Skinks sued to enjoin the construction of the building.
Issue: Where a general easement with a definite location is conveyed, may a court defer to the requirements of reasonableness to alter the terms of the easement?
Rule: In defining the scope of an easement, the rule of reason is applied to provide a detailed definition to rights created by general words, and it may not be used to compel the easement holder to abandon a right of way, even if continued use of it is unreasonable.

Miller v. Lutheran Conference & Camp Sass's (1938)

Facts: The plaintiff Frank C. Miller acquired an easement in gross that granted him an exclusive right to use a lake for recreational purposes. He subsequently assigned a 1/4 interest in the easement to his brother. Before the brother's death, he and the plaintiff were business partners who jointly operated and proportionately shared the receipts from recreational activities on the lake. The assignee's executors licensed the defendant to use the lake and collect receipts from such use. The plaintiff thereupon sought an injunction against the defendant's use of the lake.

Issue 1: Can an easement in gross be established by prescription?

Rule 1: As long as all of the requirements for a prescriptive easement are met, an easement in gross can be established by prescription.

Issue 2: Are easements in gross assignable and/or divisible?

Rule 2: An easement in gross is assignable when the parties to its creation manifest a clear intent that it be so. Furthermore, an easement in gross is divisible as long as the beneficiaries make common use of the easement.

Bang v. Forman (1928)

Facts: The defendants held an express easement appurtenant granting them beach access. They subdivided their three lots to which the easement was appurtenant into 26, granting all beach access.

Issue: May a grantee of a dominant estate increase the burden on the servient estate beyond that contemplated at the time the easement was created?

Rule: Where land is granted to which an easement is appurtenant, the right is appurtenant to every part of the dominant estate subsequently conveyed, provided the servient estate is not burdened to a greater extent than was contemplated at the time the easement was created.

Carlson v. Libby (1950)

Facts: The plaintiff's predecessor in title conveyed an easement to the defendant's predecessor in title but reserved a right for itself and its successors to use the railroad siding constructed on it.

Issue: Is a covenant that materially affects the value of the land in question a real or personal covenant?

Rule: If a covenant touches the land involved to the extent that it materially affects the value of that land, it is a real covenant running with the land, if it is in accord with the intent of the parties.

Henley v. Continental Cablevision (1985)

Facts: The plaintiffs' predecessors in title were granted the right to construct and maintain electric, telephone, and telegraphic service for five lots and to grant easements for those purposes. They, in turn, conveyed easements to electric and telephone companies to provide those services. Subsequently, Continental Cablevision acquired licenses from both those utilities to use the easements for the purpose of transmitting television programs.

Issue: Are easements in gross apportion able?

Rule: Where a grant of an easement in gross excludes the grantor's participation in the rights granted, divided use of the rights granted is presumptively allowable.

Stanton v. T.L. Herbert & Sons (1919)

Facts: In his grant of land to Stanton the grantor reserved a right to remove sand from Stanton's property. The grantor assigned his right to two other parties. Stanton brought suit to enjoin the defendants from removing the sand.

Issue: Is an incorporeal hereditament (a profit a prendre) assignable and divisible?

Rule: A profit a prendre, although assignable, is not divisible and an attempted division destroys the reservation.

Loch Sheldrake Associates v. Evans (1954)

Facts: The plaintiff's grantor reserved a right to draw water from a lake that he conveyed to the plaintiff. He then conveyed this right, along with other property, to the Evanses. The Evanses drew water from the lake in large quantities, and for purposes not encompassed by the grantor's original reservation. The plaintiffs brought suit requesting damages and an injunction.

Issue: May water rights not appurtenant to any particular parcel of land be used by their owner in any manner or at any location?

Rule: Water rights duly granted by deed, not appurtenant to any particular parcel of land, may be used by the owner at any place or in any manner, so long as he does not interfere with or impair the rights of others.

Martin v. Music (1953)

Facts: Music granted Martin an easement to construct and maintain a sewer line under his land. In return, Martin granted Music an easement that allowed him to hook up to the sewer line. Subsequently, Music sold his property to several grantees, each of whom wanted to hook up to the sewer line. Martin brought an action for a declaration that the right to use the sewer line was personal to Music, and that Music's grantees did not acquire this right from him.

Issue: May a dominant estate be divided, thereby increasing the burden on the servient tenement?

Rule: A dominant estate may be divided or partitioned, and the owner of each part may claim the right to enjoy the easement as long as no additional burden is placed upon the servient estate.

Farmer v. Kentucky Utilities (1982)

Facts: Utility holds an easement by prescription in gross to run wires over plaintiff's land. The company enters onto servient land to clear underbrush.

Issue: Is their entry a trespass?

Held: The utility company has also obtained a secondary easement (to enter and clear) to service the primary easement (the wires).

Bang v. Forman (1928)

Facts: The defendants held an express easement appurtenant granting them beach access. They subdivided their three lots to which the easement was appurtenant into 26, granting all beach access.

Issue: May a grantee of a dominant estate increase the burden on the servient estate beyond that contemplated at the time the easement was created?

Rule: Where land is granted to which an easement is appurtenant, the right is appurtenant to every part of the dominant estate subsequently conveyed, provided the servient estate is not burdened to a greater extent than was contemplated at the time the easement was created.

Pasadena v. California-Michigan Land & Water Co. (1941)

Facts: A municipal water-vending service had easements from various property owners to lay water pipes. A private competitor, the defendant, received permission from the owners of the servient estates to lay its pipe in the same areas where the municipal company held its easements. The plaintiff sued to enjoin the defendant water company's installation of its equipment.

Issue: Is the owner of a servient estate prohibited by law from granting an easement over the exact parcel of land that is already subject to an easement granted to a third party?

Rule: Where the easement is founded on a grant, only those interests expressed in the grant and those necessarily incident thereto pass from the owner of the fee. The owner of the servient estate may make any use of the land, including a transfer of his rights to a third party, that does not unreasonably interfere with the easement.

Lindsey v. Clark (1952)

Facts: By deed, the Clarks had an easement for a right of way on the south side of the Lindseys' lot. The Clarks mistakenly used a strip of land on the north side of the Lindseys' lot to gain access to their land. The Lindseys instituted a suit to enjoin the Clarks from using the north side strip.

Issue: May an express easement be abandoned by mere non-use of the easement?

Rule: To constitute abandonment of an easement, there must be acts or circumstances clearly manifesting an intention to abandon (in addition to non-use).

Kanefsky v. Dratch Construction Co. (1954)

Facts: Kanefsky bought a lot from the defendant. The deed included a portion of a common driveway, but the grantor reserved an easement in the driveway and retained title to a narrow strip of land parallel to it. The defendant sold his interest and the successor in title used the driveway to transport a developer's equipment.

Issue: May the owner of a dominant tenement extend an easement to benefit other land owned by him?

Rule: An easement cannot be extended by the owner of the dominant tenement to benefit land to which it was not originally appurtenant.

Cameron v. Barton (1954)

Facts: When he conveyed his land, the original grantor created an easement over the lot subsequently acquired by the plaintiff. Over time, the defendant's use of the dominant tenement changed and, consequently, so did the nature of the easement.

Issue: Does normal change in the use of a general easement of a right of way constitute an unacceptable deviation from the terms of the original grant?

Rule: In ascertaining, in the case of an easement appurtenant created by conveyance, whether additional or different uses of the servient tenement required by changes in the character of the use of the dominant tenement are permitted, it is assumed that the parties to the conveyance contemplated a normal development of the use of the dominant tenement.

Glenn v. Poole (1981)

Facts: The Pooles had a prescriptive easement across the plaintiff's land. Originally, it was used for hauling operations conducted by horse drawn wagons and by light trucks. When the Pooles' business changed, they increased their use of the road.

Issue: Does the use made during the prescriptive period permanently fix the scope of an easement obtained by prescription?

Rule: The use made of a prescriptive easement may change over time to accommodate normal developments in accord with common experience, provided the variations in use are not substantial and are consistent with the general pattern formed by the adverse use.

Matthews v. Bay Head Improvement Ass'n (1984)

Facts: One of Bay Head's neighboring communities instituted this suit because its residents were prohibited form gaining access to the ocean and the beachfront in Bay Head, which was controlled and supervised by the Association.

Issue: What are the rights of the public to use non-municipality-owned beaches?

Rule: The public must be given access to and use of privately owned beaches as is reasonably necessary. The public's rights on private beaches are not co-extensive with the rights enjoyed in municipal beaches, but private landowners may not in all instances prevent the public from exercising its rights under the public trust doctrine. Where a beachfront property is controlled by a quasi-public body, membership must be open to the public at large.

II. License

Baseball Publishing Co. v. Bruton (1938)

Facts: Baseball Publishing Co. and Bruton executed a writing granting the plaintiff company the "exclusive right and privilege to maintain" a sign on the wall of Bruton's building. Bruton later refused to honor the agreement and the plaintiff corporation brought suit for specific performance.

Issue: May a contract to give a license be enforced by a court of equity through the granting of specific performance?

Rule: In the absence of fraud or estoppel, there cannot be specific performance of a contract to give a license because a license is revocable at will and conveys no interest in land. However, when a writing gives one the "exclusive right" to maintain a sign on another's property for a term of years, an easement in gross arises and specific performance may be granted.

Marrone v. Washington Jockey Club (S. Ct. 1912)

Facts: After buying an admission ticket, Marrone was forcibly prevented from entering a racetrack. He brought a suit for trespass.

Issue: Is an admission ticket a conveyance of an interest in property?

Rule: (Holmes, J.) An admission ticket does not by itself convey an interest in property, but rather is a revocable license. Therefore, the plaintiff does not have an absolute right, enforceable at equity, to enter on the property, and his only remedy is to sue for breach of contract.

Note: Most courts no longer require acquiescence as an element in establishing a prescriptive easement. Consequently, a protest alone will not block a prescriptive easement.

Ricenbaw v. Kraus (1953)

Facts: Ricenbaw's predecessor in title was orally granted permission to construct a drain on the land of the predecessor in title of the defendant. The defendant attempted to revoke the license.

Issue: Is a license revocable at will?

Rule: A mere license, whether created by deed or parol, is revocable at will, except where the license is executed and where, by reason of expenditures by the licensee on the strength of the license, it would otherwise be inequitable to permit the licensor to effect a revocation. In such a case a court of equity may rule that the license became an easement by virtue of the financial outlays of the licensee undertaken in reliance on the apparent validity of an otherwise invalid parol easement.

Crimmins v. Gould (1957)

Facts: The defendant held an express appurtenant easement to use a road owned by Crimmins. To service a nearby nondominant parcel that he owned, the defendant extended Crimmins' road so that it joined a road that the defendant built through the nondominant parcel that connected with a public road.

Issue: May an express easement appurtenant be extinguished?

Rule: Where the burden of the servient estate is increased through changes in the dominant estate that increase the use and subject it to use of property to which it is not appurtenant, an easement will be extinguished if the unauthorized use cannot be severed and prohibited.

III. Real Covenants

Caullett v. Stanley Stilwell & Sons, Inc. (1961)

Facts: A developer conveyed one acre to the plaintiff, inserting a clause in the deed that "The grantors reserve the right to build or construct the original dwelling or building on said premises." The plaintiff brought suit to quiet title, arguing that such a covenant cannot run with the land.

Issue 1: Where a burden is placed on land and the corresponding benefit is personal to one of the parties, does the burden run with the land?

Rule 1: Where a benefit is clearly personal to the grantor, and not enhancing or otherwise affecting the use or value of any retained land, the covenant does not run with the land.

Issue 2: Can a covenant be enforced as an equitable servitude where the benefit is in gross and neither affects retained land of the grantor nor is part of a neighborhood scheme of similar restrictions?

Rule 2: Because the existence of a dominant estate is essential to the validity of the servitude granted, a benefit purely personal to the grantor does not burden the conveyed premises, but obligates the grantee only personally.

Gallagher v. Bell (1986)

Facts: The Gallaghers and the Bells acquired their respective property from a common grantor. Subsequently the two parties covenanted that the Gallaghers, in return for an easement across the Bells' property, would contribute to the cost of certain improvements that were required. The Gallaghers then sold their property to Deborah Camalier, agreeing to indemnify her for any financial outlays that the Bells would demand of her in relation to the covenant. The Bells later brought suit against the Gallaghers when the Gallaghers refused to honor the covenant. The Gallaghers defended on the ground that their covenant with the Bells ran with the land and, having sold the property, they were no longer bound by the covenant.

Issue 1: What conditions must be satisfied for the burden of a covenant to run with the land?

Rule 1: For the burden of a covenant to run with the land, three conditions must be met. The covenant must "touch and concern" the burdened land, the original parties to the covenant must have intended that the covenant run with the land, and there must be privity between the parties, such that the person claiming the benefit or being subjected to the burden is a successor to the estate of the original person so benefited or burdened.

Issue 2: Can an original covenantor escape the burden of a covenant that runs with the land by conveying his burdened estate to a third party?

Rule 2: The continuing liability of an original covenantor on a covenant of the type involved here will end on his conveyance of the burdened property if the parties so intended.

Wheeler v. Schad (1872)

Facts: Wheeler's predecessor in title conveyed land and water rights to the defendant's predecessor. Six days later, they agreed to jointly build and maintain a dam. When the dam was damaged, the defendant refused to contribute to its repair.

Issue: When covenanting parties not in privity of estate enter into a covenant concerning land, does the covenant run with the land?

Rule: For a covenant to run with the land, it is necessary that it touch and concern the land. A covenant imposing a burden on the land can only be created where there is privity of estate between the covenantor and covenantee, and a promise made after a conveyance does not satisfy the privity requirement.

Malley v. Hannah (1985)

Facts: Each of the parties acquired their property through a chain of title derived from a single original owner. The restrictive covenant in defendants' chain of title limited residential construction to single-family homes.

Issue: What must be shown to enforce a restrictive covenant?

Rule: A restrictive covenant is enforceable if the owner of the dominant estate derived the property from the original grantor who received the benefit, and the owner of the servient estate derived that property from the original grantee who took it subject to the covenant. Furthermore, the original grantor must have intended that the covenant run with the land.

Neponsit Property Owners' Ass'n, Inc. v. Emigrant Indus. Savings Bank (1938)

Facts: The Neponsit Property Owners' Association sought to enforce a covenant requiring owners of lots on a certain tract of land to pay an annual fee for the general upkeep of the area. The defendant argued that such a covenant cannot run with the land and therefore was not binding on successors to the original purchasers.

Issue 1: Does an affirmative covenant to pay money for use in connection with, but not on, the land that is purportedly subject to the burden of the covenant run with the land?

Rule 1: One of the requirements for a covenant to run with land is that it must "touch" or "concern" the land. This requirement is satisfied if the covenant, in its effect, substantially alters legal rights that otherwise would flow from the ownership of land and which are connected with the land. Whether a particular covenant is sufficiently connected with the use of land to run with the land is generally a question of degree.

Issue 2: Does a property owners' association, which technically owns no interest in property, have standing to enforce a covenant that runs with the land?

Rule 2: To give deference to function over form, the court may recognize a corporate entity, created solely for the purpose of advancing the common interests of the property owners, as having standing to bring suit to enforce a covenant that runs with land.

Eagle Enterprises, Inc. v. Gross (1976)

Facts: The plaintiff's predecessor in title included a covenant in all the deeds of a subdivision requiring lot owners to purchase water from it. The deed stipulated that the covenant run with the land. Gross, a subsequent purchaser of one of the lots, refused to comply.

Issue 1: Will an affirmative covenant run with the land if it does not touch and concern the land?

Rule 1: To run with the land, an affirmative covenant must touch and concern the land, i.e., it must relate in a significant degree to the ownership rights of the parties.

Issue 2: Will an affirmative covenant without a time limitation run with the land?

Rule 2: An affirmative covenant that lacks an outside time limitation and purports to bind all future owners, regardless of the use to which the land is put, creates a burden in perpetuity that is an undue restriction on alienation. It is therefore unenforceable.

Rodgers v. Reimann (1961)

Facts: The plaintiff's grantor sold a lot to the defendant, whose deed contained a restrictive covenant. The plaintiff sought to enforce the covenant.

Issue: Is a prior grantee entitled to enforce a covenant inserted in a deed from his grantor to a subsequent grantee?

Rule: To be entitled to enforce a covenant between his grantor and a subsequent grantee, a prior grantee must show that the covenant in the subsequent grantee's deed was intended to benefit the prior grantee's land and that the subsequent grantee entered into the covenant with notice of both the restriction imposed on the land he is purchasing and the extent to which others may enforce it.

Whitinsville Plaza, Inc. v. Kotseas (1970)

Facts: When selling a portion of his property, the defendant covenanted not to use his remaining land in competition with the grantee. Whitinsville Plaza, Inc. succeeded to the grantee's interest and sought an injunction when the defendant breached the covenant.

Issue: Does the benefit of a covenant not to compete run with the land?

Rule: Reasonable covenants against competition may run with the land when they serve a purpose of facilitating orderly and harmonious development for commercial use.

Shell Oil Co. v. Henry Ouellette & Sons Co. (1967)

Facts: When conveying a portion of its land, the defendant corporation covenanted not to use his remaining land in a manner competitive with his grantee's use of the conveyed parcel. A subsequent grantee leased land to Shell Oil, which erected a gas station. The defendant granted Mobil Oil

Co., who planned to open a gas station, an option to buy part of its remaining land.

Issue: Does the benefit of a covenant not to compete inure to a lessee of a subsequent grantee of the covenantor?

Rule: A covenant not to compete is personal and does not inure to the benefit of remote or successive grantees.

Note: This case represents a minority view. Since this decision, Massachusetts has modified its position.

Dick v. Sears-Roebuck & Co. (1932)

Facts: The plaintiff conveyed a lot opposite his business with a covenant not to compete. A subsequent grantee, whose deed contained a similar covenant, leased the premises to the defendant. The defendant's lease did not refer to the covenant and the defendant's business entered into competition with the plaintiff's.

Issue: Does the burden of a covenant not to compete run with the covenantor's land?

Rule: Because a covenant not to compete restrains the use to which land may be put in the future as well as in the present, and may likely affect its value, it touches and concerns the land and therefore runs with the covenantor's land if reasonable and consistent with the parties' intent.

Suttle v. Bailey (1961)

Facts: The original grantor placed restrictive covenants in all of the grantees' deeds to lots in a subdivision. However, he retained the right to alter or annul the covenants. The plaintiffs, owners of two of the lots in the subdivision, sought to enforce one of the restrictions against the defendants, owners of two adjoining lots.

Issue: Does a general reservation by the grantor of the power to dispense with restrictive covenants make the covenants personal?

Rule: A reservation by the grantor of a right to amend or annul restrictive covenants makes the covenants personal between the grantor and his individual grantees. Therefore, the covenants do not run with the land, and one grantee may not enforce a covenant against another.

Joslin v. Pine River Development Corp. (1976)

Facts: A subdivision's restrictive covenants limited the type and number of buildings that could occupy a lot owned by the defendant corporation.

Issue: Are restrictive covenants to be strictly construed, so that no restrictions may be implied from those expressly stated to permit the free use of land?

Rule: The policy of strictly construing restrictive covenants is no longer operative. Rather, in giving the covenant effect, courts must consider the surrounding circumstances as well as the conduct and intent of the parties.

Rhue v. Cheyenne Homes, Inc. (1969)

Facts: Pursuant to a restrictive covenant, a subdivision required that all buildings be approved by an architectural control committee. There were, however, no specific standards to guide the committee's determinations. Cheyenne Homes, Inc. sought an injunction prohibiting Leonard Rhue from moving an architecturally nonconforming house into the subdivision.
Issue: Are restrictive covenants that mandate the approval of an architectural control committee of all buildings erected or placed on a lot in a subdivision enforceable, if no specific standards are contained in the covenant to guide the committee?
Rule: So long as the intention of a covenant is clear, a covenant mandating the prior approval of an architectural control committee as to the appropriateness of erecting or placing a building on a lot is enforceable, even absent specific guidelines for the committee, when a refusal to grant approval is reasonable, made in good faith, and is neither arbitrary nor capricious.

Waldrop v. Town of Brevard (1950)

Facts: Grantor conveyed a portion of his land to the defendant. The deed expressly waived any right to sue the defendant over the use made of the land and granted the defendant the right to use the land as a garbage dump. Thirty-five to forty homes were later built on the grantor's remaining land. Waldrop, one of these homeowners, sued the defendant alleging that the garbage dump was a nuisance.
Issue: Will changed conditions justify the non-enforcement of a covenant?
Rule: Changed conditions may, under certain circumstances, justify the nonenforcement of restrictive covenants. However, the type of covenant between the grantor and the Town of Brevard may be viewed as granting the Town an easement over the remaining property of the grantor. In the case of a duly recorded easement, changed conditions will not prevent its enforcement.

Burton v. Chesapeake Box & Lumber Corp. (1950)

Facts: Burton's lease contained a covenant requiring the lessee to insure against fire loss, but it contained no covenant obligating Burton to use the insurance proceeds to rebuild. Burton's lessee conveyed his interest in the lease to the defendant.

Issue: Does a covenant in a lease requiring the lessee to insure against fire loss, when not coupled with a covenant requiring the lessor to rebuild, run with the land?

Rule: A bare covenant to insure without a reciprocal obligation from the lessor to rebuild does not run with the land.

Keppel v. Bailey (1834)

Facts: The Kendalls, lessees of an ironworks, joined a joint stock company with the plaintiffs and others. They agreed to bind themselves and their successors to using a certain railroad. Bailey, with notice of this agreement, acquired the Kendalls' interest and attempted to use another railroad.

Issue: May one bind his successors to a covenant entered into with third parties with whom he has no privity of estate?

Rule: Absent privity of estate between a covenantor and covenanted, neither can bind their successors to their covenant.

Petersen v. Beekmere, Inc. (1971)

Facts: The defendant, a community association, sought to compel the plaintiff, a subsequent purchaser with notice, to comply with a covenant requiring owners and their grantees to contribute to the maintenance of a lake in a subdivision.

Issue: May an affirmative covenant be enforced in equity?

Rule: An affirmative covenant is enforceable in equity as an equitable servitude against a subsequent grantee who takes with notice.

Oliver v. Hewitt (1950)

Facts: Oliver included an anti-competition covenant in a recorded deed between himself and the defendant's predecessor in interest. Subsequently, the defendant, having actual and constructive notice of the existence of the agreement, leased the premises to Boyd, who also had constructive notice. Neither the deed to the remote grantee nor Boyd's lease referred to the covenant. Boyd entered into competition with Oliver.

Issue: Is a personal covenant enforceable in equity against a subsequent purchaser with notice?

Rule: A personal covenant will be held valid and binding in equity on a purchaser taking the estate with notice.

Lauderbaugh v. Williams (1962)

Facts: Contrary to an agreement entered into by the plaintiff and other landowners requiring future purchasers to be members of the Lake Watawga Association, the plaintiff deeded her land to a non-member.

Issue: Is an agreement among landowners that restrains alienation based on lack of membership unreasonable?
Rule: A restrictive covenant that lacks standards of admissibility to the association is an unreasonable restraint on alienation.

Kell v. Bella Vista Village Property Owners Ass'n (1975)

Facts: The plaintiffs, landowners in a planned community, contended that an assessment covenant was invalid for vagueness and indefiniteness.
Issue: Is an assessment covenant containing a formula to calculate the assessment invalid as a restraint on alienation?
Rule: Assessment covenants that contain a formula for calculating the amount of, and purposes for, an assessment are valid and binding if applied alike to all units of a subdivision and are not restraints on alienation.

Osborne v. Hewitt (1960)

Facts: Due to changes in the surroundings, the Osbornes sought the nullification of a subdivision's restrictive covenants.
Issue: When substantial change occurs in an area surrounding a subdivision with restrictive covenants, will the covenants be nullified when the benefits they were intended to secure are still realizable?
Rule: Restrictive covenants on a subdivision will be enforced, notwithstanding change in the surrounding area, if the change in the character of the neighborhood is not such as to make it impossible to secure, in a substantial degree, the benefits sought to be realized through the adherence to the restrictive covenants.

Rick v. West (1962)

Facts: Restrictive covenants required a tract of land to be used for residential purposes only. By the terms of these covenants, the plaintiff reserved the right to modify the covenants in case of "special unforeseen conditions," provided the "spirit and intent" of the covenants is maintained. The defendant, owner of a half-acre tract, refused to release the plaintiff from the covenant when he desired to sell 15 acres to a hospital.
Issue: May restrictive covenants mandating a general plan of development be abandoned by a grantor who reserves the right to modify the covenants?
Rule: A limited reserved right by the grantor to modify restrictive covenants does not alone justify abandonment of a general plan of development when the restriction is not outmoded and still affords real benefit to the grantees.

IV. Equitable Servitudes

Tulk v. Moxhay (1848)

Facts: Tulk, the plaintiff, sold land with a covenant requiring the vendee, his heirs, and assigns to keep the land in an "open state, uncovered with any buildings." The defendant eventually acquired the property through a deed that was silent about the covenant, but he had actual notice of the covenant's existence.

Issue: Will a party who had notice of a restrictive covenant be permitted to use land in a manner inconsistent with the terms of the covenant?

Rule: If a restrictive covenant is attached to property by the owner, no one purchasing with notice of that covenant can stand in a different situation from the party from whom he purchased.

London County Council v. Allen (1914)

Facts: Allen covenanted with the plaintiff that he would not improve his lots, on which the plaintiff planned to build roads. Subsequently, Allen's assignee breached the covenant.

Issue: Where a benefit is in gross, will equity enforce the running of a burden as an equitable servitude?

Rule: A covenantee must have land for the benefit of which the covenant is created, both at the time of the creation of the covenant and afterward, for the burden of the covenant to run with the land at equity.

Sprague v. Kimball (1913)

Facts: Kimball conveyed several contiguous lots, and included in all but one deed restrictive covenants for the mutual advantage and protection of all the lot owners. Sprague, an owner of a restricted lot, sought to enforce the covenant as to the unrestricted lot.

Issue: Must an equitable servitude be evidenced by a writing to be enforceable?

Rule: As a property interest, an equitable servitude must be evidenced by some sufficient instrument in writing. Otherwise it is unenforceable.

Sanborn v. McLean (1925)

Facts: The lot owned by the McLeans (defendants) originally belonged to an individual who, at one time, owned all the other lots comprising the immediate neighborhood, 53 of the 91 lots which he eventually sold were burdened with restrictive covenants expressly providing that all structures be built for residential purposes only. The deed held by the defendants, however, had no such express restriction.

Issue 1: May a grantor, who burdens certain lots with reciprocal negative easements, convey other lots of the same original tract without the restrictions?

Rule 1: If the owner of two or more lots, so situated as to bear the relation, sells one with restrictions of benefit to the land retained, the servitude becomes mutual, and, during the period of restraint, the owner of the lots retained can do nothing that is forbidden to the owners of the lots sold.

Issue 2: Is the existence of a visible uniform plan of use sufficient to give a purchaser of a lot in a subdivision constructive notice of land use restrictions?

Rule 2: When a purchaser's visual examination of the premises clearly indicates that lots are occupied in strict accordance with a general plan, he has constructive notice that a reciprocal negative easement may exist and is under a duty to make certain inquiries.

Snow v. Van Dam (1935)

Facts: In 1907 the grantor conveyed part of his land to be subdivided with restrictions limiting construction to residential units. In 1919 he conveyed the remainder of his land with similar restrictions. The defendant Van Dam acquired a lot in the common grantor's last conveyed subdivision and built a commercial establishment, which the prior purchasers in the first subdivision sought to enjoin, claiming a violation of the restrictions.

Issue: When a grantor divides property into two subdivisions with common restrictions on use, can purchasers in one subdivision enjoin later purchasers in the separate subdivision from using their land in a manner which violates the common restrictions?

Rule: If there is a scheme of restrictions existing when the sale of lots begins that includes both the prior purchasers' land and the grantor's remaining unsold land, the prior purchasers acquire a right to enforce the restrictions against subsequent purchasers. However, the individuals seeking to enforce the restrictions must bear the burden of proving the existence of a scheme of restricted usage.

Nahrstedt v. Lakeside Village Condominium Ass'n, Inc. (1992)

Facts: Nahrstedt, a Lakeside resident, and owner of three cats, sued the Association over its restriction against the ownership of pets.

Issue: Under what circumstances is an equitable servitude enforceable?

Rule: The enforceability of equitable servitudes is a mixed issue of law and fact and can only be resolved in the context of the specific facts of a case.

Restrictions are enforceable when they prohibit conduct that interferes with or has a reasonable likelihood of interfering with the rights of other owners to the peaceful and quiet enjoyment of their property.

Merrionette Manor Homes Improvement Ass'n v. Heda (1956)

Facts: As assignee of the benefit of certain covenants, a homeowner's association with no legal title to realty in a subdivision sued to enforce a burden imposed on Heda's (a purchaser with notice) dwelling unit.

Issue: Does an association of homeowners organized as a nonprofit corporation, whose membership consists of the owners of real property within an area subjected to planned and uniform restrictive covenants, have sufficient interest to bring suit to enjoin alleged violations of these covenants?

Rule: Regardless of privity of contract or estate, a homeowner's association may equitably enforce covenants in a deed against purchasers with notice.

Shelley v. Kraemer (S. Ct. 1948)

Facts: Shelley's property was impressed with a restrictive covenant prohibiting occupancy or ownership of his house by blacks.

Issue: Does the Equal Protection Clause of the Fourteenth Amendment prohibit judicial enforcement by state courts of restrictive covenants based on race or color?

Rule: (Vinson, C.J.) The granting of equitable judicial enforcement of restrictive covenants that deny property rights available to other members of the community is prohibited by the Equal Protection Clause of the Fourteenth Amendment.

Barrows v. Jackson (1953)

Facts: Contrary to a restrictive covenant prohibiting the sale to or occupancy of her house by blacks, Jackson sold to a black.

Issue: Can a restrictive covenant that prohibits a homeowner from selling his home to blacks be enforced at law by a suit for damages against a co-covenantor who allegedly broke the covenant?

Rule: The awarding of damages by a state court for the breach of a restrictive covenant that prohibits the sale of property to blacks constitutes state action under the Fourteenth Amendment. Hence, it is an unconstitutional denial of equal protection of law.

McMillan v. Iserman (1983)

Facts: The defendant owned a lot in a subdivision subject to restrictive covenants, which also allowed three-fourths of the subdivision's property owners to amend the restrictions at any time. After letting his land for the purpose of a group home for the mentally impaired, the deed restrictions were amended to exclude this type of use.

Issue 1: Are amended deed restrictions enforceable when they impose a harsher restriction than any imposed in the original deed restrictions, and when they become effective after a lot owner has detrimentally relied on the absence of such restrictions?

Rule 1: Although amended deed restrictions may be more restrictive than those contained in the original deed restrictions, they are inapplicable to a lot owner who has, prior to the amendment, committed himself to a certain land use which the amendment seeks to prohibit, provided the lot owner both justifiably relied on the existing restrictions (i.e., had no notice of the proposed amendment), and will be prejudiced if the amendment is enforced as to his lot.

Issue 2: Are restrictive covenants discriminating against the mentally impaired unenforceable as against public policy?

Rule 2: Deed restrictions prohibiting residential facilities for the mentally handicapped are manifestly against the public interest and unenforceable as against public policy.

CHAPTER 9

Eminent Domain and Inverse Condemnation

I. EMINENT DOMAIN

The power of government to acquire land in private hands is recognized in the Fifth Amendment to the U.S. Constitution and made applicable to the states by the Fourteenth Amendment: ". . . nor shall private property be taken for public use without just compensation."

A. The "Public Use" Requirement

1. Government may only acquire private land if the proposed use is for the public benefit.
2. The land acquired may be for direct government use.
   Examples: A military base; a state office building; city hall.
3. Although more controversial, land may also be acquired for ultimate occupation by private entities, so long as the project confers an underlying benefit, generally economic to the public. Acquiring property without the developers having to negotiate a sale with each landowner allows projects to proceed less expensively and more expeditiously.
   Example: Urban renewal projects with mixed ownership housing or shopping centers.
4. The legislature makes the ultimate determination as whether a proposed project is for a public use, and therefore land comprising it can be acquired by eminent domain.
5. Courts review the legislative judgment using rational basis scrutiny. Could a rational legislature have determined that the proposed project is for public benefit and not private gain?
   Some states have through their own constitutions limited the use of eminent domain to projects in which government will own the land public. Likewise some state statutes have been adopted to

limit the extent to which private economic development projects have access to the "Takings Power."

B. "Just compensation"

Just compensation is defined as what a willing buyer would pay a willing seller for property acquired.

1. Landowner receives fair market value of land and fixtures.

2. Landowner does not receive compensation for business "good will," lost profits, or relocation expenses.

3. Undivided fee rule: if land acquired is leased, the compensation is divided between the two interests, landlord and tenant. The leasee receives fair market value of the lease (the benefit of his bargain — the difference between fair rental value of the premises and rent reserved in the lease over the remaining period of the leasehold) and the landlord is paid the residue.

4. Under certain circumstances, where the tenant has a going concern on the condemned premises, the so-called "capitalization of income" calculation is made, allowing tenant to value the lease by factoring in the return on the tenant's investment in the property.

II. INVERSE CONDEMNATION

Condemnation is said to be inverse where a landowner claims that a government action has devalued a private property interest so that compensation should be owed. In eminent domain the government acts to acquire privately held land; in cases of inverse condemnation, the landowner brings an action against the government charging that government action is tantamount to a taking, and therefore the landowner should receive compensation.

A. Takings by Trespass

1. Where a government constitutional provision, law, administrative regulation, or its interpretation compels a permanent physical occupation of her land, a taking occurs, and the property owner must be paid just compensation.

2. If the landowner can regulate the time, place, and manner of the required occupation, a taking has not occurred.

3. Just compensation is calculated as the loss in value of the premises occasioned by the required physical occupation (fair market value prior to the invasion less fair market value after the invasion).

4. Exactions: Under the "police power," government may prohibit development of land if a proposed project is harmful to the public interest. Where government requires a landowner to convey a property interest to it in return for permission to develop, a landowner may claim that a taking occurs except if there is a nexus

between the damage to the public interest occasioned by the development, and the property interest exacted by government in return for the development permit.

  a. The nexus between damage to the public interest need not be exact. But it must be "roughly proportional."

  b. The burden is on the government to show that the development will harm the public interest (that denying the permit is a valid exercise of the police power) and that the exaction is tailored to address the harm to the public interest created.

III. REGULATORY TAKINGS

A. Government regulation will frequently limit a property owner's use of her land.

  1. Holmes conundrum: "Government could hardly go on ... if it had to compensate landowners every time its actions occasioned a loss in value of a parcel of land; but we are in danger of forgetting ..." that government should not legislate to obtain benefits for the public at the expense of private property owners.

  2. When the regulation too greatly diminishes the value of private property it will occasion a taking.

  3. However, where the use of the property is considered a nuisance, barring the objectionable conduct is not a nuisance.

  4. Thus the issue is "how much is too much" and "how objectionable must the conduct be." The issue is when in "fairness and justice," the public should pay to limit a landowner's exploitation of her property.

  5. This very amorphous standard has led to a case-by-case approach based on the "particular circumstances" of the cases.

B. Current jurisprudence holds that a government regulation will not be a taking if either the landowner's primary expectations for the property have not been thwarted and/or there is some reciprocity of advantage to the owner through the regulation.

  1. Primary expectations address whether the purpose for which the property was bought is still permitted and provides the owner with an adequate return on her investment.

  2. Reciprocity of advantage means that the regulation, though it may diminish the value of the property owners land also confers some benefit to her.

    a. Where the effect of a government regulation prohibits the landowner from using property in any way, a taking has occurred unless the proposed use of land would violate some background principle of common law nuisance.

b. Where an individual purchases property for development, and at the time of purchase her proposed use is not barred by law, a subsequent statute whose effect is to preclude any productive use of the land constitutes a taking.

c. Moratoria on development for the purposes of determining the environmental impact of development do not require compensation if the time set aside for study is not unreasonably long.

d. A landowner cannot, for the purposes of claiming that a regulation renders land completely valueless, subdivide a parcel rendering some section valueless if some part can still be developed.

e. A slow consideration process emanating from a government development permit granting board may constitute a taking, particularly if the process sends vague or contradictory messages.

CASE CLIPS

I. Eminent Domain

Berman v. Parker (S. Ct. 1954)

Facts: As part of the District of Columbia's redevelopment of blighted land, the Land Development Agency sought to acquire Berman's lot, which was used as a department store. Part of the project was for low-income hosing. Berman claimed that Congress did not have the authority to exercise the takings power through the agency, and in circumstances in which private individuals rather than the government itself might occupy the land acquired.

Issue: Was the purpose of the exercise of eminent domain within the "public use" requirement of the Fifth Amendment?

Rule: The legislature in pursuance of the police power has the latitude to determine how best to deal with urban blight. The mere fact that the land was not destined for direct government occupation does not bar it from exercising the power of eminent domain.

Hawaii Housing Authority v. Midkiff (S. Ct. 1984)

Facts: The Hawaii legislature authorized a government agency to purchase the underlying freehold estate of private landowners, and transfer the estate under a specified procedure to owners of the private owners of leasehold estate. The purpose of the program was to lower what the legislature regarded as Hawaii's excessively high land prices.

Issue: Was the purpose of the exercise of eminent domain within the "public use" requirement of the Fifth Amendment?

Rule: The court held, following *Berman*, that redressing an adverse economic climate was of benefit to the public; and therefore a "rational" legislature could conclude the program conferred a benefit on the public in general, regardless of the private-to-private nature of the land transfer.

Kelo v. New London (S. Ct. 2005)

Facts: The city of New London sought to acquire through eminent domain houses occupied by the plaintiff for an economic development zone in the city that would largely be occupied by private entities.

Issue: Was the purpose of the exercise of eminent domain within the "public use" requirement of the Fifth Amendment?

Rule: A divided court reconfirmed both *Berman* and *Midkiff*— the property taken need not be itself blighted and the property condemned can pass through the government's taking from private to private hands.

II. Inverse Condemnation

Pruneyard Shopping Center v. Robbins (S. Ct. 1980)

Facts: Shopping center owner sought to exclude from his property individuals who were soliciting signatures for a petition. The activists cited free expression rights protected under the California Constitution.

Issue: Have owners the right to exclude others from property owned been taken so as to require "just compensation"?

Rule: A commercial property owner has not lost the right to exclude where he retains the ability to regulate the time, place and manner of the political activity that he required to permit on his land.

Loretto v. Teleprompter Manhattan (S. Ct. 1982)

Facts: A city ordinance required landlords of buildings with a given number of tenants to allow Teleprompter to affix cables and other equipment on the landlord's property.

Issue: Have owners the right to exclude others from property owned been taken so as to require "just compensation"?

Rule: Permanent physical trespasses, regardless of how minimal, always occasion a taking and therefore require the property owner to be paid "just compensation."

Nollan v. California Coastal Commission (S. Ct. 1987)

Facts: In return for a permit to rebuild and expand an existing house on land adjacent to the coastline, the California Coastal Commission required the property owner to deed an easement to allow the public to cross the dry sand adjacent to his seawall.

Issue: Is this exaction, which limits the landowner's right to exclude, a taking requiring just compensation?

Rule: Where government in exercise of its police power may limit development, it may condition a building permit on an exaction, but only where there is a nexus between the lost suffered by the public due to the development and the nature of the exaction. The exaction must in some way lessen the loss suffered by the public due to the development.

Dolan v. City of Tigard (S. Ct. 1994)

Facts: In a follow-up case to *Nollan*, Dolan was required to dedicate land to a flood plain, provide access to the land to the public, and deed land for a bikeway to expand the size of her premises.

Issue: Is this exaction, which limits the landowner's right to exclude, a taking requiring just compensation?

Rule: The exaction required to allow development must be roughly proportional to the harm to the public interest jeopardized by development. The increased parking space that the development authorized would create more water runoff justifying the demand for land dedicated to the flood plain, However, "rough proportionality" did not justify that the land be open to the public. Likewise, there was no showing that the store would result in increased bike traffic justifying the dedication of a bikeway.

Sparks v. Douglas County (1995)

Facts: In return for a development permit, a landowner was required to dedicate strips of land for road improvement.
Issue: Is the exaction, which limits the right to exclude, a taking requiring just compensation?
Rule: There is a sufficient connection between the development and an increase in traffic shown by a detailed report commissioned by the county to justify the exaction, even if the full impact of the development may occur sometime in the future.

III. Regulatory Takings

Penn Coal v. Mahon (S. Ct. 1922)

Facts: Penn Coal transferred the surface rights to Mahon, but retained the "third estate," the right to mine coal under the surface. The legislature passed the Kohler Act, which prevented mining in such a way so as to cause subsidence. In effect, Penn Coal could not mine under Mahon's land without providing lateral support.
Issue: Is the Kohler Act, as applied to Penn Coal, taking of its property estate without "just compensation?"
Rule: While property use may be regulated, if such regulation too greatly diminishes property value, the regulation will be a taking requiring "just compensation." Because the parties had contracted to allow Penn Coal the right to mine even if it did cause subsidence, the Kohler Act also rewrites the agreement between parties. The Kohler Act transfers the coal company's property to Mahon.

In a powerful dissent (Justice Holmes wrote the majority), Justice Brandeis looks at the Kohler Act as a nuisance case. The Kohler Act merely forbids Penn Coal to use its property in such a way so as to endanger the lives and property rights of others.

Keystone Coal v. DeBenedictis (S. Ct. 1987)

Facts: The Subsidence Act prevents the mining of coal in such a way so as to cause subsidence to pre-existing public buildings.

Issue: Is this repackaging of the Kohler Act a taking?
Rule: Given the proportion of coal that must remain in the ground, about 2% of the Coal company's estate must, given modern technology, remain in the ground.

Penn Central v. City of New York (S. Ct. 1978)

Facts: The Landmarks Preservation Commission designates Grand Central Station a landmark. This requires its owner to seek approval for alterations to the building. Penn Central submits seriatim two designs for a tower over the station, and both are rejected. Penn Central claims a taking.
Issue: Is the Landmarks Preservation law a taking as applied to Penn Central's property?
Held: A governmental regulation is not a taking unless it thwarts a property owner's primary expectations for the property. Penn Central can still use the property for the purposes for which it purchased it: a railway station. In addition, the Landmarks Preservation Commission awarded transferred development rights to Penn Central allowing them to build additional floors on other buildings that they own, floors in excess of standard height restrictions.

Lucas v. South Carolina Coastal Council (S. Ct. 1992)

Facts: Lucas purchased two beachfront lots in 1986. Two years later the Beachfront Management Act prevented construction on the lots. Lucas challenged the act as a taking.
Issue: As applied to Lucas's lots, is the Beachfront Management Act a taking?
Rule: Where a government regulation renders an owner's land valueless, it is taking requiring just compensation, unless the regulation identifies a background principle of nuisance law. In short, the regulation is a taking unless it prohibits a use of land that would have been prohibited anyway because it constituted a common law nuisance.

Monterrey v. Del Monte Dunes (S. Ct. 1999)

Facts: Over a number of years, a development company made successive applications to build. Each was rejected, citing concerns that the company addressed in the next application. Developer eventually sued.
Issue: As applied to Dunes's property, was the administrative process a taking?
Rule: A lengthy administrative process that seems conducted for the purposes of delay can render land valueless under the Lucas standard.

Palazzolo v. Rhode Island (S. Ct. 2001)

Facts: Developer purchases land consisting largely of salt marshes. The state thereafter prohibited the filling in of such land. Developer applies for a permit to build but is denied. Developer charges that his land is rendered valueless.

Issue: As applied to Palazzolo, does the regulation render his land valueless?

Rule: Because parts of the upland area could be developed, the land in question was not rendered valueless. One may not regard land as divided into discrete segments to claim that a part has been rendered valueless by a regulation.

Tahoe Sierra v. Preservation Council v. Tahoe Regional Planning Agency (S. Ct. 2002)

Facts: To assess the affect of development on the ecology of Lake Tahoe, the agency adopted a 32-month moratorium on building. Owners seek compensation for the lost value of their land during the period.

Issue: Is the moratorium a taking, rendering the property valueless for the period in question?

Rule: A moratorium along the order of the one enforced here cannot be said to render the property valueless even for the period of the study, and therefore cannot be the basis of a Lucas-style claim for compensation.

CHAPTER 10

Public Land Use Planning/Zoning

I. THE LOGIC OF ZONING

The purpose of zoning is twofold: to promote reasoned growth and to regulate the way in which certain land is exploited. The former is often called comprehensive zoning; the latter, amenity zoning. Amenity zoning has already been addressed in the section on inverse condemnation: the landmark's law in New York, and the beachfront management law in South Carolina both limited land use, leading their owners to demand "just compensation." In the former, the political subdivision drafts a master plan and a board to administer it. Both will be addressed.

II. GENERAL THEMES

A. The power to zone is derived from the police power, the obligation of government to protect the public form harm.
B. State legislatures authorize localities in the jurisdictions to zone according to the mandates set out in the legislation.

III. CUMULATIVE ZONING

A. Purposes
  1. To promote reasoned growth, zoning plans limit the amount of land that can be devoted to certain uses.
     Example: By limiting the amount of land for residential uses, a zoning plan can regulate population growth. Likewise, limiting the amount of land dedicated to industrial or commercial uses may slow industrialization and commercialization of areas
  2. To assist the municipality in efficiently providing services, disparate uses are congregated.

Example: By creating residential zones, schools can be clustered there to limit the need for transportation. Intensive fire fighting equipment can be located in industrial zones. Parking lots can be built in commercial zones.

3. To separate non-conforming uses. As we learned, nuisances can be the wrong thing in a particular place (e.g., the pig in the parlor).

Example: Zoning can make certain that residential areas are isolated from industrial, commercial or agricultural areas.

B. Constitutionality

In the 1920s, the Supreme Court held that comprehensive zoning was valid, even though it might limit land use values. If the value of land is too greatly diminished by the zoning, the owner may claim compensation.

IV. OTHER PERMISSIBLE PURPOSES OF ZONING

A. Regulation of adult entertainment sites. Cities may regulate the operation and venue of erotic dancing, video and bookshops because of the connection between these operations and crime. Although protected free expression, erotic "speech" can be limited by anti-skid row laws that limit the number of outlets in a particular area or require them to be a certain distance from houses of worship and schools. Such regulation is regarded as by the Supreme Court as content neutral, and therefore the city must only show through surveys that there is a connection between adult entertainment sites and crime.

B. Limiting signs on houses and businesses. Advertisements constitute commercial speech, and the Supreme Court has been reluctant to allow cities to ban signs in windows and land in general. Signs evincing support for a political candidate or cause cannot be banned, but the Court has struck down prohibitions against "for sale" signs and other commercial messages.

C. Limiting single family residential housing to a legislatively defined family. The Supreme Court has allowed a zoning law to define the family narrowly for the purposes of single-family housing districts to exclude unrelated individuals, so long as the definition adopted does not exclude blood relations from being constituted as a family. Members of a religious order that stresses communal living can be excluded. Some state supreme courts have found stronger "freedom of association" rights in their state constitutions.

D. Limitations on multi-family housing. Some state courts have found a right to affordable housing within communities and have required zoning plans to allocate sufficient land allocated for multifamily housing.

E. Historic landmarks and districts can be designated by zoning boards or by specially designated committees which can mandate that owners maintain structures, limit alterations to existing buildings, and determine whether new constructions should be permitted.

F. A wide variety of environmental laws regulate the uses of coastland, wetlands, habitat of endangered species, and the deposit of hazardous waste on lands.

G. Zoning laws may not be used to exclude racial minorities from communities.

V. THE OPERATION OF ZONING LAW

A. Zoning law regulates:
  1. The size and shape of lots,
  2. The buildings that can be placed on them,
  3. The types of activities that can be maintained on them.

B. Zoning law allows special exceptions to be granted by the zoning board to allow conforming buildings in use areas.
  Example: Schools in residential areas.

C. Developers may seek to rezone particular parcels. The zoning board may agree, but require certain limitations on building or dedications of land to the city. This so-called "contract zoning" infuses flexibility into the zoning plan, but may appear to allow boards to make random and arbitrary adjustments to the overall design.

D. Floating zones are unmapped zoning conditional use districts that "settle" in a particular area upon the petition of a developer. These floating zones may also appear but may appear to allow boards to make random and arbitrary adjustments to the overall design.

E. Variances from the zoning are permitted when the zoning law would impose a particular hardship on a parcel and the proposed use would not impair the purpose of the zoning plan.

F. Spot zoning is the selective re-zoning of individual parcels. It ought not to be permitted, if the re-zoning is contrary to the over all plan.

VI. RETROACTIVITY OF ZONING

A. Where zoning plans are adopted but affect existing developed land, zoning boards allow non-conforming uses to remain in place so long as the use was lawful when commenced. Sometimes the non-conforming use can remain perpetually, and be "grandfathered"; other times it may remain for a period until the investment costs have been amortized.

B. An owner who builds in reliance on existing zoning laws is protected from later changes in zoning law so long as his reliance is in good faith. This so-called vested right does not apply where there are grounds to believe that a change in the zoning regulation is imminent.

CASE CLIPS

I. Cumulative Zoning

Village of Euclid v. Ambler Realty (S. Ct. 1926)

Facts: Ambler owned land in Euclid. The village thereafter by ordinance adopted a comprehensive zoning plan which classified some land of its land for residential rather than commercial/industrial uses. Ambler claims that it was holding the land for industrial uses and seeks to enjoin enforcement of the comprehensive zoning plan.

Issue: Is a comprehensive zoning plan a valid exercise of the police power, and therefore in principle within the powers of state and local government to adopt?

Rule: State and local government has the power to adopt comprehensive zoning plans pursuant to the police power. Particular application of the comprehensive zoning plan to parcels of land held by private parties, however, might be the proper subject of an injunction.

Nectow v. City of Cambridge (1928)

Facts: As a follow-up case to Euclid, plaintiff had land which was zoned residential but was located in an industrial area. Plaintiff sought to enjoin its enforcement.

Issue: As applied to the particular lot in question, was the zoning plan a valid exercise of the police power?

Rule: The ambit of the police power is not unlimited, and the individual circumstances of a lot may render the application of the zoning law too economically burdensome so as to render an injunction against its enforcement a suitable remedy.

II. Other Permissible Purposes

Young v. American Mini-Theatres (S. Ct. 1976)

Facts: Detroit, in common with other major cities, adopted an anti-slid row zoning law that forbade the operation of adult bookstores within 100 feet of other specified regulated uses, such as, for example, liquor stores. They were, however, not entirely banned from the city.

Issue: Does the ordinance unduly impinge on free expression?

Rule: So long as not banned from the community, cities may regulate the time, place and manner of adult bookstores.

Alameda City of Los Angeles v. Alameda Books (S. Ct. 2022)

Facts: A zoning law prohibited the establishment of more than one adult entertainment business in a individual building. Alameda Books operated both an adult video arcade and an adult bookstore in the same building.
Issue: Does the ordinance unduly impinge upon free expression?
Rule: Applying intermediate scrutiny, the court held that Los Angles had demonstrated a link between crime and adult outlets through a survey. Thus the law's purpose was not to regulate expression, but its secondary effects. It was therefore a valid regulation of time, place and manner of adult entertainment.

City of Lidue v. Galleo (S. Ct. 1994)

Facts: The city prohibited signs in residential areas that were not address designations, for sale signs, and signs warning of hazardous material. Plaintiff posted a small sign in his window expressing political views. The town argued that other means of expression were available to the plaintiff, and this was a time, place, and manner restriction.
Issue: Is the prohibition of signs a violation of free speech when small signs conveying a political message are included within the ban.
Rule: A blanket prohibition by government which constrains the ability of individuals to make political statements through the use of signs on their property violates freedom of expression.

Haskell v. Washington Township (1988)

Facts: The town zoned all abortion clinics in one zone and buildings offering the delivery of medical services in another zone, thereby rendering abortion clinics financially unviable. No other abortion clinic was able to function within the town. Haskell sued to enjoin enforcement of the ban on his clinic offering other medical delivery in his abortion clinic.
Issue: Was the zoning regulation a valid exercise of the police power?
Rule: The zoning regulation was held invalid, because it was adopted in bad faith and to further a particular personal belief.

Charter Township of Delta v. Dinolfo (1984)

Facts: To prevent overcrowding, the township adopted districts in which no other buildings could be located other than single-family dwellings, and defined the family as a group related by blood or marriage. Only one unrelated person could live in the single family house (other than servants). Plaintiffs, to live out their commitment to their religion, live communally, and were therefore excluded from the district.

Issue: Is the ordinance a valid exercise of the police power?

Rule: In *Belle Terre*, the Supreme Court permitted narrow definitions of the family for the purposes of creating single-family residential districts, so long as they were not unduly restrictive in preventing family members from co-residence. Based on its own state constitution, the court found no rational basis for the classification, that is, that the zoning ordinance was irrational in that it advanced none of its articulated goals.

Anderson v. City of Issaquah (S. Ct. 1993)

Facts: Plaintiffs sought approval for a building in the historical district. Their application was denied, largely because the commissioners felt that the proposed building was not keeping with the character of the community. Plaintiffs attacked the vague nature of the requirements.

Issue: Was the zoning criteria too vague to be enforceable?

Rule: The ordinance, which did not use recognized architectural terms of art, but rather subjective standards, did not give meaningful guidance to property owners as to appropriate form that buildings could assume.

III. The Operation of Zoning Law

Village of Arlington Heights v. Metropolitan Housing Development Corporation (S. Ct. 1977)

Facts: Petitioners sought the rezoning of land from single- to multiple-family use. After hearings, the petition was denied. The petitioners claimed that the purpose of denying the alteration violated the equal protection clause.

Issue: Did petitioners prove that the underlying purpose of the denial was based on a desire to exclude minorities from the community?

Rule: Where the board followed existing practice in determining whether to allow the rezoning variances, the petitioners could not demonstrate that there was a discriminatory purpose which underlay the decision.

CHAPTER 11

The Sale of Land

I. THE STATUTE OF FRAUDS

Contracts for the transfer of interests in real property must be in writing to be enforceable. When one says a contract "falls within" the statute, it will be enforced only if it is in writing. A contract that "falls outside the statute" will be enforced even if it is not in writing.

A. Contracts for an interest in land that require a writing:
  1. Contracts for the sale of timber, minerals, and oil must be written if the buyer will remove the same after title to the land passes to him.
  2. Promises to give a mortgage as security for a loan must be in writing. Assigning rights to a mortgage may be oral.
  3. Leases of land for more than one year.
  4. Easements.

B. A contract which by its terms is incapable of being performed within one year is unenforceable if not in writing.
  1. The one-year period begins to run from the signing of the contract, not from the beginning of performance.
  2. The fact that performance within a year is very unlikely will not place a contract within the statute as long as the agreement may theoretically be performed within a year.

C. The contents of the writing: a contract or memorandum will satisfy the statute of frauds if the writing contains the following elements:
  1. The parties.
  2. The price or other consideration for the purchase.
  3. A description of the property.
  4. Expression of an intent to transfer.
  5. Signature of the party to be charged.
  Note: Under UCC §2-201 the requirements of a writing are satisfied if a memorandum is "sufficient to indicate that a contract for sale has been made between the parties, and it is signed by the party against whom enforcement is sought."

D. Exceptions: Oral promises to convey will be enforced:
1. Where there has been substantial steps by the buyer to complete the transaction; or
2. Where buyer relies on seller's oral promise to convey and economic loss would be suffered if seller was not ordered to convey (promissory estoppel); or
3. Where the seller would be unjustly enriched if he were not ordered to convey.

II. MARKETABLE TITLE

Unless otherwise specified, a contract for the sale of real property implies that the seller will deliver marketable title at the closing. Marketable title is "ownership that is free from encumbrances and any reasonable doubt" as to its validity so that a prudent and experienced businessman would be willing to accept performance of the contract for sale.

There are a number of common defects that may make a title unmarketable:
A. Defects in the chain of title:
1. Wrong names listed in recorded documents.
2. Improper description of the property in recorded documents.
3. Defective or invalid recording of documents of title.
4. Forged documents of title.
5. Inability on the part of the vendor to establish a record.
6. Adverse possession has been perfected.
B. Outstanding encumbrances:
1. Mortgage.
2. Lien.
3. Covenant.
4. Easement.
5. Encroachments by neighboring property owners.
6. Unexpired lease.
7. Structures in violation of zoning law.

III. TIME

Time is not usually "of the essence" in contracts for the sale of real property. A party may enforce a contract even though he is not unreasonably late (usually a few weeks will be considered not unreasonably late) in tendering performance. Although time is not of the essence, a party that is late in tendering performance may be liable for damages.
A. Suits for damages (action in law) will assume that time was "of the essence."

B. Suits for specific performance (action in equity) will *not* assume that time was "of the essence."
C. Time may become "of the essence" if the parties expressly agree to that effect, or one party gives notice that time will be important, or circumstances show that time was important.

IV. RISK OF LOSS ON EXECUTION OF A CONTRACT FOR SALE: EQUITABLE CONVERSION

A. Majority rule: The buyer bears the risk of loss between the time the contract was signed and the closing.
   1. Note: This rule relies on the doctrine of equitable conversion that establishes equitable ownership in land at the time a contract is signed. Legal title remains with the seller who has a lien for the sale price. The reasoning of this rule is that a buyer has a right to specific enforcement of the contract after the signing. "Equity regards as done, that which ought to be done."
   2. Exceptions
   In the following two situations, risk of loss will not pass to the buyer even though the majority rule is followed:
      a. Title was not marketable at the time the contract was signed; or
      b. The loss was caused by the seller's negligence.
B. Minority rule: Risk of loss remains with the seller until legal title is conveyed regardless of who retains possession between signing and closing.
C. Uniform Vendor and Purchaser Risk Act (another minority view): Seller bears the risk of loss until the possession or title shifts to the buyer.

V. INSTALLMENT CONTRACTS

Most sales of real property involve a small down payment by the purchaser who borrows the balance of the purchase price from the lender; lender may retain the property if the purchaser defaults. Under an installment contract, the lender is the seller, and the purchaser does not receive a deed to the property until he makes the final payment.
A. Default by Buyer
   Judicial proceedings are not necessary; the seller retains the deed and all payments previously made by the buyer.
B. Some states have enacted statutes to mitigate the harsh legal effects of a default by the buyer.

Examples:
1. Foreclosure Safeguard
   When a buyer has paid a substantial portion of the loan he has the rights of a mortgagor (see below).
2. Redemption
   Buyer may pay off the loan balance and keep the land despite his default.
3. Reinstatement
   Buyer pays the amount of his default and continues the contract as if the breach never occurred.
4. Restitution
   Buyer recovers payments in excess of damages incurred by the lender as a result of the default.

VI. MORTGAGES

A. Definitions
   1. Mortgagor
      Borrower who gives the mortgage.
   2. Mortgagee
      Lender who receives the mortgage.
   3. Mortgage
      A document giving a lender a security interest in real property, which allows the mortgagee to arrange for a sale of the property if a borrower defaults on a loan.
B. The mortgage: rights in property subject to mortgage.
   1. Lien theory states that when a buyer finances a purchase of property by using a mortgage he receives a deed to the property. (Contrast with an installment sale.) The lender has a lien on the property in exchange for the loan. The lender has the right to foreclose on the property in case the borrower defaults. After all payments have been made, the lien is exonerated.
   2. Title theory states that under this conceptualization of the mortgage, the lender holds title. The borrower holds the equity of redemption, because on repayment of the loan, the borrower has the right to demand that the lender convey title.

VII. DEEDS

A. Definition of a Deed
   A deed is a written document that effectuates a transfer of real property.
B. A deed will be effective if:
   1. It is delivered by the grantor.

      2. It is accepted by the grantee.

      3. It is valid.

  C. Delivery of a Deed

      1. A deed need not be physically delivered to satisfy this requirement. Conduct or words of a grantor that indicate his present intent to make the deed operative will satisfy the requirement of delivery. Intent is the key.

      2. Manual Delivery

        a. If the deed was physically transferred to the grantee, a presumption in favor of delivery will be created.

        b. If the grantor retains physical possession, a presumption against delivery will exist.

      3. A grantor's attempts to revoke a delivery previously effectuated will be futile because title passes at the moment a deed is delivered.

      4. Delivery of the deed to the county recorder's office will be a valid delivery.

      5. Delivery will be effective even if the deed contained a condition. Example: A deed specifies that the grantee must live until age 21. Delivery will be effective if the grantee is 18 years old, and he will have a contingent estate.

      6. Fine-Line Distinction: Revocation of Deed vs. Revocation of Estate

      If a grantor delivers a deed that by its terms reserves a right of revocation in the grantor, the grantor retains a right to revoke the estate, and he may do so, but he may not revoke the delivery after it was accomplished.

      7. Escrow

      A delivery in escrow is a delivery to an impartial third party who holds the deed until certain conditions are met. The delivery will be effective if the grantor relinquishes all control. Title will pass when the conditions of escrow are fulfilled, not when the deed physically passes from the third party to the grantee.

  D. Acceptance by the Grantee

  The grantee must accept the deed. Such acceptance is presumed.

  E. Validity of a Deed

  The following information is required on the face of the deed:

      1. Words of conveyance.

      2. Description of the property. The following are methods of description:

        a. By metes and bounds: "calls and distances" in relation to a "monument" (a landmark).

        b. By government survey.

        c. By a particular map.

3. Names of grantee and grantor
4. Signature of the grantor (seals have not been required for a long time).
   a. Some states require attestation (a disinterested witness) or acknowledgment (notarizing).
   b. Consideration is not required.

VIII. COVENANTS OF TITLE

There are two types of deeds.

A. Quitclaim Deed

Grantor conveys whatever title he owns without warranty as to his title.

B. Warranty Deed

Grantor makes representations concerning titles. There are six general classes of covenants.
   1. Grantor warrants that his conveyance is free of encumbrances: liens, mortgages, easements, etc.
   2. Grantor warrants that he will make any conveyance within his power to perfect grantee's title. This covenant is rarely used today.
   3. Grantor warrants her right to convey, a personal covenant that she has the legal right to convey.
   4. Grantor covenants that grantee's use or enjoyment of the property will not be disturbed by a third party.
      a. This covenant is a "real" covenant and will run with the property.
      b. This is the broadest covenant.
      c. Damages for breach are limited to the value of the property.

IX. APPLICABILITY OF COVENANTS TO FUTURE GRANTEES

Covenants that "run with the land" may be enforced by a future grantee against a transferor. Whether a covenant will run with the land depends on whether it is a "present" or "future" covenant.

A. Present Covenants

Covenants that are breached at the moment the conveyance is made. They generally do not run with the land.
   1. Covenant of seisin.
   2. Covenant of right to convey.
   3. Covenant against encumbrances.

B. Future Covenants
   Covenants that are only breached when a party is later evicted.
   Future covenants always run with the land.
   1. Covenant of quiet enjoyment.
   2. Covenant of warranty.
   3. Covenant of further assurance.

CASE CLIPS

I. The Statute of Frauds
Shaughnessy v. Eidsmo (1946)

Facts: The Shaugnessys (plaintiffs) leased land by oral agreement from Eidsmo (defendant). Eidsmo also gave the plaintiffs an option to buy the demised premises. Before expiration of the lease, the Shaugnessys performed their part of the option, and exercised the option, but no contract was ever written. Eidsmo refused to complete the sale.

Issue: Does possession and part performance of an oral option to purchase leased premises constitute a defense to the Statute of Frauds?

Rule: The taking of possession, coupled with the making of part payment, in reliance on and with unequivocal reference to the vendor-vendee relationship constitutes a defense to the Statute of Frauds.

Burns v. McCormick (1922)

Facts: J.A. Halsey (decedent) orally promised the plaintiffs that in return for their services he would give them his house. After his death, neither deed nor will existed to evidence the agreement.

Issue: Must a vendee's conduct be unequivocally referable to a contract for sale of land when the vendee seeks specific performance of an oral agreement to sell the same?

Rule: For equity to decree specific performance, acts of part performance must be solely and unequivocally referable to a contract for sale of land.

Hickey v. Green (1982)

Facts: Green (defendant) orally agreed to sell a lot to the Hickeys (plaintiffs). Green accepted a deposit from the Hickeys who, in reliance on the contract, contracted to sell their home. Green, although aware of the plaintiffs' sale of their home, repudiated the contract.

Issue: Does a vendee's reasonable reliance upon an oral contract to sell land constitute a defense to the Statute of Frauds?

Rule: A contract for the transfer of an interest in land may be specifically enforced notwithstanding failure to comply with the Statute of Frauds if it is established that the party seeking enforcement, in reasonable reliance on the contract and on the continuing assent of the party against whom enforcement is sought, has so changed his position that injustice can be avoided only by specific enforcement.

Pearson v. Gardner (1918)

Facts: Pearson (plaintiff) orally agreed to sell land to the Gardners (defendants). The Gardners refused to complete the contract after taking possession, making partial payment and so altering the premise's character as to diminish its value.

Issue: May a vendor seeking specific performance rely on the vendee's part performance as grounds to avoid the Statute of Frauds?

Rule: A vendor may seek specific performance of a contract that has been part performed on the grounds of mutuality.

Ward v. Mattuschek (1958)

Facts: The Mattuschek brothers (defendants) executed a contract with a real estate broker granting the broker an exclusive right to sell land. The contract, signed by the defendants, contained the essential terms of the defendants' offer to sell. The broker found Ward, a buyer, who unconditionally accepted. The Mattuscheks subsequently refused to convey the property. Ward sued for specific performance.

Issue: Is a contract between a seller and real estate broker granting the broker the right to sell the land and stating therein the essential terms of seller's offer invalid under the Statute of Frauds?

Rule: A contract between a vendor and broker that states the essential elements of the seller's offer is sufficient to take a contract of sale between vendor and vendee out of the Statute of Frauds.

Niernberg v. Feld (1955)

Facts: The Felds (plaintiff) and the Niernbergs entered a sales agreement to transfer land. Before the agreement was performed, the parties orally rescinded the contract.

Issue: Must a rescission of a written executory sales contract of real estate be in writing?

Rule: An executory contract involving title to, or an interest in, lands may be rescinded by a mutual parol agreement.

King v. Wenger (1976)

Facts: King (plaintiff) and Wenger (defendant) executed an informal memorandum in which they agreed to a transfer of real estate. The parties, however, contemplated negotiating, drafting, and executing a formal contract in the future.

Issue: Are parties bound to an informal agreement when they were negotiating with an understanding that the terms of the contract were not fully agreed on and a written formal agreement was contemplated?

Rule: Parties to an informal agreement are not bound thereby when the intent of the parties was that the terms of the contract were not fully agreed on and a written formal agreement was contemplated.

Gerruth Realty Co. v. Pire (1962)

Facts: A land sale contract contained a "subject to financing" clause. Pire (defendant) could not get financing and refused to complete the contract.

Issue: May a land sale contract be held void for indefiniteness when there are insufficient facts surrounding the transaction for a court to construe with reasonable certainty a "subject to financing" clause?

Rule: When a land sale contract contains a "subject to financing" clause, and a court cannot infer the terms of the clause either from the evidence or by means of current practices in the community, the contract is void for indefiniteness.

II. Marketable Title

Wallach v. Riverside Bank (1912)

Facts: Wallach desired to purchase certain property from Riverside Bank. To carry out the transaction Wallach (plaintiff) agreed to accept from Riverside Bank a quitclaim deed to certain property, then refused to complete the transaction because the defendant's title was clouded.

Issue: Must a vendor provide marketable title to a vendee who signed a land sales contract to accept a quitclaim deed?

Rule: A vendor always covenants by implication to give a good title, unless such a covenant is expressly excluded by the terms of the contract.

Bartos v. Czerwinski (1948)

Facts: Bartos (plaintiff) agreed to purchase realty if the defendant would provide marketable title. Bartos then refused to accept the conveyance unless the defendant took certain actions to clear the title. When the defendant refused, Bartos sued for specific performance.

Issue 1: If a possible outstanding interest in a property in one other than the vendor exists, is the vendor's title marketable?

Rule 1: A title is unmarketable if a reasonably careful and prudent person, familiar with the facts, would refuse to accept the title in the ordinary course of business because of a doubt or uncertainty that could reasonably form the basis of litigation.

Issue 2: Where a vendor who contracts to convey land by quitclaim deed fails to convey marketable title, is the vendee entitled to specific performance?

Rule 2: The equitable remedy of specific performance is not one of right, but rests in the discretion of the court. Where a vendor who contracts to convey land by quitclaim deed fails to convey marketable title, and clearing title would require substantial action, the court may deny specific performance.

Luette v. Bank of Italy Nat. Trust & Savings Ass'n (1930)

Facts: The plaintiff agreed to buy land from the defendant provided the defendant would supply marketable title. The installment contract provided that the land would be conveyed only when paid in full. The plaintiff sought rescission prior to closing, claiming that the defendant was not then in possession of a marketable title.

Issue: May a vendee, before the date when the vendor will be required to convey title under an installment contract, seek to rescind on account of an uncertainty as to the state of the vendor's title?

Rule: There can be no rescission by a vendee of an executory contract of sale merely because of lack of title in the vendor prior to the date when performance was due.

Cohen v. Kranz (1963)

Facts: Cohen (plaintiff) contracted to purchase Kranz's house. Before the closing date, Cohen (vendee) notified Kranz (vendor) that the title was unmarketable and demanded return of his down payment. Neither party tendered, nor demanded performance. Cohen sued to recover the deposit.

Issue: May a vendee, who does not tender his performance recover his deposit when the vendor's title is curably defective?

Rule: A vendee is barred from recovering his deposit from a vendor whose title defects were curable in a reasonable time and whose performance was never demanded.

Kramer v. Mobley (1949)

Facts: Mobley (plaintiff) contracted to purchase land from Kramer. Mobley notified Kramer of a cloud on Kramer's title. Kramer offered to institute a quiet title action and reimburse Mobley in the amount of the disputed lien on the property if Mobley would complete the transaction. Before he would complete the contract, Mobley insisted Kramer pay the purported lienholder and obtain a release. When Kramer refused, Mobley sued for the benefit of his bargain.

Issue: When a vendor's title is defective, may a vendee recover the difference between the contract price and the market value of the property, either at the time of breach or at the time fixed for delivery, when the vendor acted in good faith and was guilty of no positive or active fraud?
Rule: A vendee of real estate is not entitled to damages for the loss of his bargain on the inability of the vendor to obtain a good title if the vendor acted in good faith and was guilty of no active nor positive fraud in the transaction.

Smith v. Warr (1977)

Facts: Warr (defendant) contracted to sell land to Smith. The defendant was unable to convey the land because a third party successfully asserted an adverse possession claim. The plaintiff sued for benefit-of-the-bargain damages.
Issue: Is the correct measure of damages for a breach of contract for the sale of real property out-of-pocket loss, or benefit-of-the-bargain damages?
Rule: The measure of damages where the vendor has breached a land sale contract is the benefit-of-the-bargain damages, i.e., market value of the property at the time of the breach, less the contract price to the vendee.

Clay v. Landreth (1948)

Facts: Landreth (defendant) contracted to purchase land from Clay, Rezoned between the time of making the contract and the time for delivery of the deed, the land became unusable for its intended purpose. Clay sued for specific performance.
Issue: Will a contract for the sale of land be specifically enforced when the agreed purpose for which it was bought and sold was defeated?
Rule: Equity will not compel specific performance if hardship and injustice would be forced on one of the parties through a change in circumstances not contemplated by the parties when the contract was made.

Johnson v. Davis (1985)

Facts: The Davises contracted to buy a house from Johnson. When Davis asked about damage to a window and the ceiling, Johnson stated that the problem was corrected and that the roof and ceiling had never been a problem. Davis then gave Johnson an additional deposit. Davis later observed water entering the house from various parts of the ceiling and elsewhere.
Issue: Does the seller of a home have a duty to disclose latent material defects to a buyer?

Rule: When the seller of a home knows of facts materially affecting the value of the property that are not readily observable and are not known to the buyer, the seller is under a duty to disclose the defects to the buyer.

Lempke v. Dagenais (1988)

Facts: The Lempkes purchased a garage from the original owners. Shortly afterward, they noticed structural problems that were undiscoverable at the time of purchase.

Issue: May a subsequent purchaser of real property sue the builder or contractor on the theory of implied warranty of workmanlike quality for latent defects?

Rule: A subsequent purchaser may sue a builder or contractor under an implied warranty of workmanlike conduct for latent defects which manifest themselves within a reasonable time after purchase and which cause economic harm.

Frimberger v. Anzellotti (1991)

Facts: A wetlands area was filled without a permit and in violation of state statute. Unaware of the violations, Frimberger conveyed the property to Anzellotti by warranty deed, free of all encumbrances, but subject to all building and zoning restrictions as well as easements and restrictions of record.

Issue: Does a latent violation of a restrictive land use statute or ordinance, existing at the time a fee is conveyed, constitute a breach of the warranty deed covenant against encumbrances?

Rule: Encumbrances cannot be expanded to include latent conditions on property that are in violation of statutes or government regulations.

Lohmeyer v. Bower (1951)

Facts: The buyer (Lohmeyer) sued to rescind a contract for the sale of land on the grounds that the land contained violations of both private and public restrictions. The contract provided that the defendant would convey merchantable title.

Issue: Is a title to real property marketable when the property is in such a condition that it does not comply with public and/or private restrictions?

Rule: Title to real property is unmarketable when the violation of a land-use restriction imposed by covenant is of substantial character and may expose the party holding title to the risk of litigation.

III. Time

Kasten Construction Co. v. Maple Ridge Construction Co. (1967)

Facts: Maple Ridge Constr. Co. (plaintiff) contracted to purchase land from Kasten Constr. Co. The contract specified that settlement was to be made in 60 days but did not stipulate that time was of the essence. Maple Ridge performed most of its contractual duties before the closing date. Five days after the contract's expiration, Maple Ridge notified the defendant of its intention to complete the contract, but that an additional three weeks would be required to complete a title examination. The defendant, in response, repudiated the contract. Maple Ridge sued for specific performance.

Issue: When a contract for the sale and purchase of realty fails to expressly state that time is of the essence and circumstances surrounding the transaction do not imply such an intent, what will be the effect of a deadline?

Rule: In a case involving specific performance, time is not of the essence of the contract of sale and purchase of land unless a contrary purpose is disclosed by its terms or is indicated by the circumstances and object of its execution and the conduct of the parties.

Doctorman v. Schroeder (1921)

Facts: A land sale contract executed by Schroeder (defendant) and Doctorman (plaintiff) provided that time was of the essence, and further, if the plaintiff failed to complete payment by a certain hour, Doctorman would forfeit the down payment and terminate the contract. The plaintiff was unable to raise the amount required, and sued to recover the down payment.

Issue: May equity relieve a defaulting party of the consequences flowing from a land sale contract when the agreement distinctly provides that time is of the essence, and that the purchaser's rights shall cease unless payment is made at the time stipulated?

Rule: When parties to a land sale contract expressly provide that time is of the essence, equity will not, when a purchaser defaults, prevent a forfeiture.

Conklin v. Davi (1978)

Facts: Conklin's title to a portion of real estate that the Davi (defendant) was to purchase was claimed by adverse possession. The contract of sale required the vendor to convey a "marketable and insurable" title.

Issue: Is a title procured by adverse possession unmarketable?

Rule: A marketable or insurable title is a less-stringent requirement than a title valid of record. Hence, a title resting in adverse possession, if clearly established, is marketable.

Stambovsky v. Ackley (1991)

Facts: The Stambovskys, after contracting to purchase a house, discovered that it was widely reputed as being possessed by poltergeists.

Issue: Does the doctrine of caveat emptor apply in situations where it would be unlikely for the buyer to discover any undisclosed details concerning the home he has contracted to purchase?

Rule: Where a condition which has been created by the seller materially impairs the value of the contract and is undiscoverable by or unlikely to be within the scope of knowledge of a purchaser exercising due care, non-disclosure constitutes a basis for rescission as a matter of equity.

IV. Risk of Loss on Execution of a Contract for Sale: Equitable Conversion

Clapp v. Tower (1903)

Facts: Charlemange Tower (decedent) sold land by executory contract, which was foreclosed subsequent to his death. The executors, claiming Charlemange's interest in the land converted to personalty, sold it to Clapp (plaintiff). The Towers (defendants and Charlemange Tower's heirs) contended that the decedent retained a real property interest and it therefore devolved to his heirs.

Issue: Does realty sold under an executory contract convert the seller's interest in the land to personalty?

Rule: When a vendor sells land under an executory contract, his property, as viewed by equity, is no longer real estate in the land, but personal estate in the price. If he dies before payment, it goes to his administrators, and not to his heirs.

Eddington v. Turner (1944)

Facts: The decedent devised a life estate in certain land to Turner (defendant). He subsequently gave Eddington (plaintiff) an option to buy the same land. Eddington properly exercised the option after the decedent's demise.

Issue: When an option to purchase realty is granted after the execution of a will, will exercise of the option after the death of the optionor operate as an equitable conversion of the property relating back to the date of the option so that the proceeds of sale would pass to the personal representatives rather than to the specific devisee of the land?

Rule: Equitable conversion cannot occur before the exercise of an option, for until then no duty rested on anyone in connection with the land. Consequently, when there has been no conversion of land during a testator's life, the testator did not have a claim for the purchase price transmissible to his personal representatives.

Bleckley v. Langston (1965)

Facts: Before vendee's taking possession, an ice storm substantially destroyed improvements on the land conveyed, decreasing its value. The parties had a valid executory contract and the vendor was able to convey good title.

Issue: If an enforceable contract exists between two parties and the vendor is able to convey good title, which party bears the risk of loss?

Rule: Regardless of which party maintains possession, risk of loss rests with a vendee after the contract is executed, if the vendor is able to convey good title.

Sanford v. Breidenbach (1960)

Facts: Sanford (plaintiff) contracted to sell to Breidenbach certain lands that included a house and outbuildings. Before having met the conditions of the contract of sale, the house was destroyed by fire. Breidenbach (defendant) repudiated the agreement. Sanford sued for specific performance.

Issue: When real property is destroyed before the vendor is able to meet the conditions of the contract for its sale, is the risk of loss borne by the vendee?

Rule: Before fulfilling the conditions of a contract calling for conveyance of good title, a vendor cannot maintain an action for specific performance. Equitable conversion does not occur until a vendor can convey good title and is entitled to specific performance; therefore, the risk of loss remains with the vendor.

Raplee v. Piper (1957)

Facts: The subject matter of a contract was destroyed before the performance date. As required by the contract, the vendee (plaintiff) purchased insurance on the property in the vendor's name.

Issue: Where, pursuant to a contract, a vendee buys fire insurance covering the subject property in the vendor's name and the property is destroyed by fire before the performance date of the contract, is the vendee entitled to have the insurance proceeds applied against the unpaid balance of the purchase price?

Rule: When a contract to purchase land requires the vendee to keep the property insured against fire, insurance recovered by the vendor for a fire that occurred before performance of the contract was completed is to be applied to any remaining balance of the purchase price.

Bean v. Walker (1983)

Facts: Bean contracted to sell Walker a single-family home. The sellers retained legal title to the property, until payment was completed, at which time title was to go to the purchasers. When approximately one-half of the contract was paid off, the Walkers defaulted and the Beans sued for repossession.

Issue: What are the relative rights between a vendor and a defaulting vendee under a land purchase contract?

Rule: A vendee acquires equitable title and a vendor merely holds the legal title in trust for the vendee until such time that the purchase price is paid in accordance with the terms of the contract. Therefore, before a vendor may file an action for repossession, he must first attempt to foreclose the equitable title or bring an action at law for the purchase price.

V. Installment Contracts

Skendzel v. Marshall (1973)

Facts: The Marshalls contracted to purchase land from Burkowski. The sales contract provided for periodic payments, and the vendee's forfeiture of all previous payments and possession if the contract was breached. Before breaching, the Marshalls (defendants) paid $21,000 of the $36,000 purchase price.

Issue: When a liquidated damages clause results in damages being disproportionate to the loss actually suffered, may equity find the clause void as a penalty and require the injured party to seek redress through foreclosure?

Rule: When a liquidated damages clause results in damages disproportionate to the actual loss suffered, equity will hold the clause void as a penalty and compel the injured party to seek foreclosure.

Union Bond & Trust Co. v. Blue Creek Redwood Co. (1955)

Facts: The vendee (plaintiff) willfully defaulted on an installment land sale contract that provided for forfeiture in the event of a breach.

Issue: Does a willfully defaulting buyer have a right to remedy his breach and continue the contract in force?

Rule: A purchaser who willfully defaults on an installment sale may, where there has been substantial part performance or substantial improvements on the property, complete the contract within a specified time by paying the entire purchase price together with the seller's damages resulting from the delay in performance.

Handzel v. Bassi (1951)

Facts: The vendee (plaintiff) entered an installment land sales contract with the defendant, under which the plaintiff could not assign the contract without the defendant's consent. When the plaintiff violated this provision, the defendant proclaimed the contract void and the plaintiff's prior payments forfeited. Despite the plaintiff's tender of full performance, the defendant refused to complete the contract.

Issue: Is a provision prohibiting assignment of an installment land sales contract enforceable when, after the vendee assigns the contract, vendee offers and is able to complete the performance of the contract?

Rule: Because the primary purpose of a provision prohibiting a vendee from assigning an installment land sales contract is to ensure vendee's performance, the vendor cannot forfeit the contract on the grounds that the vendee assigned his interest if the vendee has tendered performance.

Shay v. Penrose (1962)

Facts: Carol Shay entered into separate contracts to sell four parcels of land. Each contract specified that the buyer would pay in installments. Carol Shay died before all the payments were made. She was survived by her husband Arthur Shay (plaintiff), and her sister and heir, Grace Penrose (defendant). Arthur contended the unpaid balance on an installment land sale contract was personalty; Penrose, the decedent's heir, contended the installment was realty.

Issue: When a valid installment land sale contract is executed, does the seller hold a real property interest in the land?

Rule: When one enters into a valid and enforceable contract for the sale of his land, he continues to hold the legal title in trust for the buyer, and the buyer becomes the equitable owner and holds the purchase money in trust for the seller. Therefore, in this case, the plaintiff is entitled to the unpaid balance of the purchase prices.

Moses Brothers v. Johnson (1890)

Facts: Johnson (defendant) purchased forested land from Moses Brothers under an installment contract. By the contract's terms, the land was security for Johnson's payment obligations. When Johnson began cutting trees down, Moses Brothers sought an injunction to prevent waste.

Issue: Can a vendor holding legal title to land sold as security for the purchase money obtain an injunction against a buyer committing waste?

Rule: In an installment sale contract, a vendee committing waste that impairs the security or renders it insufficient can be enjoined from committing further waste.

VI. Mortgages

Bybee v. Hageman (1873)

Facts: Hageman (defendant) held a mortgage on real property. The description of the land in this mortgage was ambiguous as to the land's boundaries. When Hageman sought to foreclose on the mortgage, Bybee (plaintiff), who held a second mortgage on the same land, contended that Hageman's mortgage was not valid due to indefiniteness.

Issue: May a mortgage's latent ambiguities be explained by parol evidence?

Rule: Extrinsic evidence is admissible to explain latent ambiguities in mortgages.

Murphy v. Financial Development Corp. (1985)

Facts: Financial (mortgagee) foreclosed on Murphy's (mortgagor's) property. Financial acted in good faith to arrange a foreclosure sale. A poor showing at that sale resulted in a sales price far below the property's market value.

Issue: Must a mortgagee foreclosing on property exercise due diligence to obtain a fair price for the property, thereby securing the mortgagor's equity?

Rule: A mortgagee must exercise due diligence to obtain a fair price for foreclosed property.

VII. Deeds

French v. French (1825)

Facts: The plaintiff leased land of which he was seized to his father by bargain and sale deed. A statute required deeds to be attested to by two witnesses. Because only one person witnessed this deed, the plaintiff challenged its validity.

Issue: Is every deed not conforming to a statute invalid?

Rule: In passing the statute, the legislature intended to abolish livery of seisin only, not conveyances such as bargain and sale deeds, which need no attestation.

First Nat'l Bank of Oregon v. Townsend (1976)

Facts: Both grantor and grantee were deceased. The plaintiff, the grantee's representative, found a deed among the grantee's effects. The deed was ambiguous regarding the extent of the interest the grantor intended to convey and extrinsic evidence did not resolve the doubt.

Issues: When neither the deed nor extrinsic evidence reveals the extent of the interest a grantor intended to convey, will the grantee be deemed to take the larger interest?

Rule: When there is doubt as to whether the parties intended that a deed transfer a fee simple or a lesser interest in land, that doubt should be resolved in favor of the grantee and the greater estate should pass.

Grayson v. Holloway (1958)

Facts: Holloway and wife (grantors) executed a deed in which the granting clause conflicted with the habendum clause.

Issue: When a granting clause and habendum clause of a deed conflict, does the granting clause control?

Rule: When seeking to determine what estate was conveyed by a deed, the intention of the grantor shall be ascertained if possible by giving to every word of the deed its appropriate meaning, and by enforcing that intention regardless of the formal divisions of the instrument.

Womack v. Stegner (1956)

Facts: Leaving blank the space for the grantee's name, W.B. Womack executed a deed, delivered it to D.R. Womack, and authorized him to fill in his or any name in the blank as grantee.

Issue: When a grantor leaves the grantee's name blank in a deed, but authorizes the grantee to fill in his or any name, does title pass?

Rule: When a deed with the name of the grantee in blank is delivered by the grantor with the intention that title shall vest in the person to whom the deed is delivered, and that person is expressly authorized at the time of delivery to insert his or any other name as grantee, title passes with the delivery.

Walters v. Tucker (1955)

Facts: Despite the clear description of the lot conveyed by the plaintiff's deed, the trial court allowed the defendant to present extrinsic evidence in an attempt to show that the grantor intended to convey less land than the deed described.

Issue: When a description in a deed is clear, definite and unambiguous, both on its face and when applied to the land, may extrinsic evidence be admitted to show that the grantor intended to convey a different sized lot?
Rule: When there is no inconsistency on the face of a deed and, on application of the description to the ground, no inconsistency appears, parol evidence is not admissible to show that the parties intended to convey either less, more or different ground from that described.

Pritchard v. Rebori (1916)

Facts: Rebori (defendant) covenanted to convey unencumbered land. When the grantee (plaintiff) built on the land, he discovered he had infringed on a railroad's easement. The boundary of the easement was unmarked. Both parties believed a retaining wall located inside the easement's outer boundary represented the extent of the easement. In describing the lot conveyed, however, the deed referred to both the wall and the easement.
Issue: When determining the boundaries of conveyed land, is there an absolute hierarchy among natural objects, artificial markers, boundary lines of adjacent owners, and courses and distances?
Rule: The rule that resort is to be had in determining boundaries first to natural objects or landmarks, next to artificial monuments or marks, then to boundary lines of adjacent owners, and finally to courses and distances, is not inflexible or absolute.

Parr v. Worley (1979)

Facts: Parr conveyed to Worley land adjacent to a highway described as "lying to the East of the highway." Parr later purported to convey to a third party the mineral interests under both sides of the highway described as "lying west of the east right-of-way line of" the highway. Worley argued that he owned the eastern half of the highway. Parr (plaintiff) contended that Worley's land's boundary was the eastern edge of the highway.
Issue: When monuments are used as boundary lines, must the presumption that the line runs through the center of the monument be expressly rebutted by language in the deed?
Rule: Absent an expressed contrary intent in a deed, a conveyance of land abutting a road, highway, alley, or other way (i.e., monument), is presumed to take the fee to the center line of the way or monument.

Clevenger v. Moore (1927)

Facts: Clevenger (plaintiff) placed a deed in escrow to be delivered on the occurrence of certain conditions. Although the conditions were not met, the depository delivered the deed to the grantee who conveyed the land to Moore (defendant).

Issue: Is a deed absolutely void when it is placed in escrow and delivered to a grantee without performance of the conditions for delivery and thus ineffective to convey title to either the grantee or the grantee's bona fide purchaser for value?

Rule: A deed placed in escrow to be delivered to a grantee upon the performance of certain conditions will not be valid for any purpose until the condition upon which it is to be delivered to the grantee is met, even though a claimant thereunder was an innocent purchaser for value.

In Re Nols' Estate (1947)

Facts: Prior to and in contemplation of his impending death, the decedent gave Vander Zanden (plaintiff) a parcel and stated, "if I don't come back, you can have it."

Issue: Is a gift causa mortis a testamentary disposition and therefore invalid unless there is compliance with the Statute of Frauds?

Rule: The doctrine of gifts causa mortis is an exception to the rule against testamentary disposition except by will. Thus, a gift conditioned upon the donor's death is valid.

McMahon v. Dorsey (1958)

Facts: Dorsey (defendant) lived and worked on McMahon's farm for many years. After McMahon's death, a deed conveying the farm was found in a safe deposit of which McMahon and the defendant were joint lessees. The decedent's sole heirs sued to have the deed put aside on the grounds that no delivery was made.

Issue: Must manual delivery of a deed be shown for the deed to be a valid conveyance?

Rule: Delivery of a deed is strictly a matter of the intention of the grantor as manifested and evidenced by the words, acts, and circumstances surrounding the transaction. Manual delivery is but one factor evidencing delivery.

Martinez v. Martinez

Facts: The grantor sold land to the grantee, who agreed to assume mortgage payments on it. The grantors gave to the grantees a deed to the land, and orally gave instructions that the grantee take the deed to the bank, where it was to be held in escrow until the mortgage was paid in full. Before delivering the deed into escrow, the grantee recorded the deed. None of the documents mentioned an escrow agreement.

Later, the grantee defaulted on the mortgage payments, but claimed title to the land.

Issue: Is parol evidence admissible to determine the intent of the grantor as to when a deed was to take effect?

Rule: Parol evidence is admissible to determine the intent of the grantor as to when a deed was to take effect. There is no legal delivery, even where a deed has been physically transferred, when the evidence shows that there was no present intent on the part of the grantor to divest himself of title to the land.

Thomas v. Williams (1908)

Facts: Before his death, Lewis conveyed land to Williams (defendant) by deed, contingent on the grantee surviving the grantor. The plaintiff claimed the deed was testamentary in character and therefore void.

Issue: Is a deed unenforceable as a testamentary instrument when the grantor, though grantee's enjoyment is postponed, intends to pass an interest presently vesting?

Rule: If by the terms of the instrument a right or interest passes at once, subject to a contingency over which the grantor has no control, it is a deed and irrevocable even though the enjoyment of the thing granted is postponed until grantor's death.

Smith v. Fay (1940)

Facts: White deeded land to G.E. White, contingent on the grantee surviving the grantor. The grantor left the deed with a third party together with instructions to deliver it to the grantee after the grantor's death.

Issue: Does a grantor's act of leaving a deed with a third party with instructions to deliver it to the grantee after the grantor's death effectuate an absolute delivery?

Rule: Delivery of a deed to a third party, with instructions to deliver it to the grantee on the grantor's death and no reservation of a right to recall the deed, constitutes good delivery with title passing immediately to the grantee subject to the grantor's reserved life estate.

Raim v. Stancel (1983)

Facts: William L. Raim conditionally delivered a deed to Stancel.

Issue: Is an inter vivos gift valid when a conditional delivery is tendered?

Rule: Unless donor has a clear intention to pass all right, title, and dominion over the gift to the donee, an inter vivos gift is invalid. When a deed is delivered to the grantee with intention that it become operative only on the death of the grantor, it will not pass title.

Merry v. County Board of Education of Jefferson County (1956)

Facts: Snedecor negotiated the sale of land with the County Board of Education (defendant) shortly before her death. She left with her lawyer an executed deed with instructions to deliver it when a deal was struck. The proposal was not accepted, nor the deed delivered before her death. The plaintiffs, the executors of the estate, sought cancellation on the grounds that the deed was never delivered.

Issue: Is an escrow revocable if not supported by a contract?

Rule: An escrow is revocable at any time before it is accepted by the grantee, and if not done in the lifetime of the grantor, it is ipso facto revoked on her death.

Meyers v. Meyers (1926)

Facts: Meyers (the donor) while ill and just prior to an operation following which he died, signed and left a deed of assignment with his lawyer. The donor instructed the lawyer to put the deed on record if anything happened to him.

Issue: Is a delivery effectuated when a donor retains the object of a deed of assignment but instructs a third party to deliver the deed upon the donor's death?

Rule: A gift made by delivering a deed with donative intent is a valid symbolic delivery even though the subject does not accompany the deed.

Sechrest v. Safiol (1981)

Facts: Safiol contracted to purchase land from Sechrest. A provision of the sale agreement allowed Safiol to terminate the contract if he was unable to secure approval from the public authorities for the construction he planned. Safiol never submitted building plans to the authorities, nor did he seek any other necessary town approval. Subsequently, Safiol was unable to find a builder and attempted to terminate the contract. Sechrest sought to retain the deposit on the purchase agreement.

Issue: Does a provision in a purchase agreement allowing a buyer to terminate the contract if conditions are not fulfilled obligate the buyer to take action reasonably calculated to satisfy those conditions?

Rule: When a purchase and sale agreement permits a buyer to terminate the contract on the buyer's failure to meet certain conditions, the buyer is obligated to undertake activity reasonably calculated to meet those conditions.

Sweeney, Administratrix v. Sweeney (1940)

Facts: The decedent Maurice Sweeney had two deeds drawn at the same time. The first deed, which was recorded, conveyed a farm to the defendant. The second deed was not recorded because Maurice was afraid he would predecease the defendant. The second deed conveyed the farm back to the decedent. Maurice took home both deeds, which were attested. The plaintiff contended that the farm was part of Maurice's probate estate.

Issue: May a deed delivered to a grantee be held conditional?

Rule: Because conditional delivery must be made to a third party, conditional delivery to a grantee vests the grantee with absolute title.

Johnson v. Johnson (1903)

Facts: The grantor left a deed with a third party and instructed the third party to deliver the deed to the grantor's daughter if the grantor should die. The grantor continued to exercise dominion over the property during her life. On her death, the third party delivered the deed to the daughter.

Issue: To effect a valid delivery of a deed, must a grantor divest himself of any right of future control over the deed?

Rule: To constitute a delivery, the grantor must absolutely part with the possession and control of the deed.

Stone v. Duvall (1875)

Facts: Duvall (plaintiff) deposited a deed in escrow which was to be delivered upon his death to his daughter, Mary Stone. When she died, Duvall sought to abrogate the deed, thereby preventing Mary's husband from inheriting the land.

Issue: Is a deed in escrow abrogated when the grantee dies before the performance of the condition of delivery?

Rule: The death of a grantee prior to the performance of a condition of a deed held in escrow does not abrogate the deed.

Mays v. Shields (1903)

Facts: Shields (plaintiff) deposited a deed in escrow. The deed was subsequently improperly delivered and recorded. Shields did not act to have the record expunged. Mays (defendant), an innocent purchaser for value, had no notice that there had been an escrow or that the deed had been recorded.

Issue: May a grantor who deposited a deed in escrow and knew that it was improperly delivered and recorded be estopped from denying the title of an innocent purchaser when the grantor did not act to prevent the improper recording?

Rule: To avoid being estopped from denying the title of an innocent purchaser buying on the faith of the record, a grantor of an escrow deed who has knowledge of the deed's improper recording must take steps to expunge the record.

Smith v. Hadad (1974)

Facts: Smith and Hadad were owners of adjacent portions of property, both of which were previously owned by Nichols. The deeds from Nichols were ambiguous as to whether Nichols intended to measure their respective lots from the edge or center of an abutting road.

Issue: In the absence of expressed intent by the parties to a transaction, will a measurement given in a deed as commencing on a public way be presumed to begin at the center or at the side line of that way?

Rule: In the absence of a clear showing of contrary intent, a measurement given from a stream or public or private way shall be presumed to begin at the side line of that stream or way.

Bernard v. Nantucket Boys' Club, Inc. (1984)

Facts: Potter owned a lot located directly north of the northernmost of Adams' three adjacent lots. Adams conveyed to the defendant land described in the deed as both bounded to the north by other land of grantor and as being entirely enclosed by fences. At the time of the conveyance, there was a single fence around all of Adams' lots but no fence separating the separate lots. Additional evidence failed to clarify whether the parties intended to include Adams' northernmost lot in the conveyance.

Issue: If a deed contains conflicting descriptions of real property conveyed, which description will govern?

Rule: When a deed contains inconsistent descriptions of the land conveyed, and the parties' intent is unclear, and neither description is more specific, then the grantee is entitled to that interpretation which will be most beneficial to him.

VIII. Covenants of Title/IX. Applicability of Covenants to Future Grantees

Hilliker v. Rueger (1920)

Facts: Rueger (defendant) covenanted that he was "seised of the said premises in fee simple and had good right to convey the same," and conveyed the property to Hilliker. When he tried to sell the same, Hilliker discovered that Rueger did not in fact have title to part of the premises. Hilliker contends that damages should be only nominal because the plaintiff had not actually been evicted.

Issue: May a grantee recover damages for breach of a covenant of seisin if he was not evicted?

Rule: If a covenant of seisin be broken at all, it is at the time of the delivery of the conveyance. If the covenant be broken by the failure of title then an action can be maintained to recover the damages which result directly from the breach. It is not essential in an action to recover damages for the breach of such a covenant that the grantee should be evicted.

Schofield v. Iowa Homestead Co. (1871)

Facts: The plaintiff sold a portion of land, which he had bought from the defendant. The defendant's deed contained a covenant of seisin. The plaintiff subsequently sold the land to another. Later, the plaintiff discovered that the covenant of seisin had been breached, but did not suffer any damages.

Issue: Does a covenant of seisin run with the land?

Rule: A covenant of seisin runs with the land. The first grantee who purchases land under a covenant of seisin and then conveys the land to another is thereafter not entitled to recover for a breach of that covenant. The remote grantee who suffers the injury can maintain an action on the covenant.

Solberg v. Robinson (1914)

Facts: Robinson (defendant) conveyed land to the Smiths, who in turn conveyed the same to Solberg (plaintiff). Robinson's deed contained covenants of seisin and quiet enjoyment. Neither Robinson nor Smith was ever in possession of the premises. The parties later realized that Robinson was not the true owner.

Issue 1: Does a covenant of seisin run with the land?

Rule 1: A covenant of seisin does not run with the land. Therefore, remote grantees cannot recover from the original grantor on this covenant.

Issue 2: Is actual possession necessary for the covenant of a grantor without title to inure to the benefit of his remote grantees?

Rule 2: Constructive possession of a grantee is sufficient to carry a covenant of quiet enjoyment (future covenant) forward. Thus, a grantor without title is estopped by deed from claiming he had no estate in the land attempted to be conveyed, and is therefore liable to remote grantees who are evicted.

Rockafellor v. Gray (1922)

Facts: Connelly purchased Rockafellor's land at a foreclosure sale. He sold the land by warranty deed to Dixon, who sold it by warranty deed to Hansen and Gregory. Subsequently, the court invalidated the foreclosure sale. Hansen and Gregorson, the remote grantees, sued the remote grantor, Connelly, for breach of the warranty of seisin.

Issue: Does a covenant of seisin run with the land even though the original grantor never had actual possession of the land conveyed?

Rule: A remote grantee can maintain an action on a covenant of seisin given by the grantor in the original deed, regardless of whether the original grantor ever had actual possession of the land.

CHAPTER 12

Recording and Title Assurance

I. COMMON LAW

A. First in Time Rule

When two parties have conflicting valid claims to the same parcel of land, the first in time will prevail.

Example: A conveys his home to B. The next day A conveys the same home to C. B will prevail over C.

B. Exceptions

1. Conflicting claims are equitable and the first party is estopped from benefiting under the rule because of his actions.

2. Conflicting claims are equitable and the second purchaser later acquired "legal title" in good faith and for valuable consideration.

3. A holder of a legal interest will always prevail over one who holds an equitable interest if the legal interest was acquired first. The holder of the legal interest will prevail over the holder of the equitable interest even if the legal interest was acquired later in time if the legal holder acquired the title in good faith and for value.

4. A party who conveys land to another before obtaining title, and then obtains title and records first in an attempt to claim superior title, may be estopped from arguing that he did not hold title at the time of the conveyance.

II. RECORDING STATUTES

A. In General

Recording statutes were enacted to provide a buyer with more title assurance than the common law allowed. Recording acts establish how title to property is determined.

B. Effect of a Recording Act

A recording act will determine who obtains title to real property. The act will not affect a contractual or other relationship.

Example: A pays B $100,000 for title to land. A later discovers that he cannot receive title to the land because another purchaser has already recorded his interest. A may sue B for breach of contract.

C. Types of Recording Acts

  1. Pure Notice Acts

    A bona fide purchaser will prevail over an earlier purchaser regardless of who was the first to record.

  2. Pure Race Acts

    A subsequent purchaser, whether bona fide or not, will prevail against an earlier purchaser if he (the second purchaser) recorded first. The second purchaser may prevail even if he had notice of the first purchaser. (The winner of the "race" to record will receive title). This rule is only followed in two states.

  3. Race-Notice Acts

    A subsequent bona fide purchaser will prevail against a previous purchaser if the subsequent purchaser recorded first without notice of the earlier conveyance.

III. MECHANICS OF RECORDING

A. Deposit with County Recorder

The grantee brings the deed to the county recorder who stamps, copies, and files the deed.

B. Indices

The deeds are indexed by grantor and grantee. Some jurisdictions require indexing by tract, the most accurate method to follow a title.

IV. INTERESTS TO BE RECORDED

A. Interests That Must Be Recorded

  1. Instruments that affect title to real property such as deeds, mortgages, powers of attorney, covenants, tax liens, etc.

  2. Instruments that modify title to real property or any interest in the examples above.

B. Interests That Need Not Be Recorded

  1. Adverse Possession

    a. An adverse possessor will prevail over a grantee if the adverse possessor's claim ripened before the grant. This rule is consistent with the rule that the earlier of two legal claims will prevail.

  b. Abandonment of the property by the adverse possessor after his title ripens will not extinguish his priority over a subsequent grantee, because an adverse possessor's title is not extinguished by physical abandonment of his premises.

 2. Short-term leases.

 3. Executory contract of sale.

 4. Easements by implication and necessity.

C. The Bona Fide Purchaser

A bona fide purchaser will be entitled to certain rights. The general requirements are:

 1. Purchaser for value does not have to be fair market value but nominal consideration will not suffice.

 2. Antecedent debt

  a. Cancellation of a debt in return for a conveyance of property will constitute valid consideration.

  b. Courts are split if a mortgagee maintains the same rights of collection.

 3. Persons not considered purchasers for value:

  a. Those who promise to pay at a future date given in exchange for the conveyance.

  b. Donees, heirs, devisees.

  c. Lien creditors (some states will consider lien creditors purchasers for value).

  d. Unsecured creditors.

V. NOTICE

The purchaser must show he did not have notice. There are three kinds of notice: actual, record, and inquiry (good faith) notice.

A. Actual Notice

B. Record Notice

If a deed was recorded and appeared in the chain of title, the purchaser will be charged with notice. The mere fact that a deed was recorded will not confer notice if the recording was outside the chain of title.

 1. Problems in the Chain of Title

A deed that is outside the chain of title is one that would not be discovered by due diligence and therefore would not provide "notice" to a purchaser. A deed may fall outside the chain of title for a number of reasons:

  a. Link was not recorded.

  b. "Wild" deed. A deed given by a grantor whose claim to title came from a source which was not recorded.

      c. Error by county indexer. A deed misindexed by the recorders office will *not* remove the deed from the chain of title (majority rule).

      d. Deed recorded late. Courts are split when a subsequent purchaser records before a previous purchaser of whom he had no notice.

      e. Deed recorded early. A deed recorded before the title actually passed will not be in the chain of title and will not serve as notice. (Minority Rule: The recording in such cases becomes effective when the title actually passes.)

      f. Easements and servitudes on land that is eventually subdivided. Courts are split whether the purchaser of a subdivision is on notice of the easements and servitudes.

  2. Defective Document

  Will not serve as notice — Most states have passed "curative acts" allowing a defective writing to be valid notice if a technical defect is not challenged within a certain amount of time.

  3. Requirements of a Proper Search:

      a. Check grantor, grantee and other applicable indices maintained by the county.

      b. Trace title for the statutorily required period (e.g., 60 years).

      c. Trace mortgages, probate proceedings and other encumbrances discovered.

C. Inquiry (Good Faith) Notice

Notice imputed to a purchaser who had neither record notice nor actual notice, but had information that would cause a "reasonable person" to make further inquiries about the title. A purchaser's obligations include:

  1. Investigate an unrecorded transaction referred to in a recorded document.

  2. Physically examine the premises.

  3. Quitclaim deed — In a majority of states a quitclaim deed in the chain of title will not place the purchaser on notice.

VI. THE TORRENS SYSTEM

A title registration is merely evidence of title to real property. Under the Torrens System, the act of registration provides the title. This system is followed only in a minority of jurisdictions and is only optional in these jurisdictions.

VII. TITLE ASSURANCE

A. Generally

A purchase of real property is usually accompanied by a covenant of title. Very often a buyer may not be able to recover for breach of a covenant because the seller is insolvent, dead, or hiding in Paraguay. To protect himself, a buyer's lawyer will seek assurance of the validity of the title to be conveyed. Because tracing a title is cumbersome and time-consuming, lawyers usually purchase an abstract or title insurance from companies that specialize in these services.

B. Abstract

1. Definition

A summary of the conveyance history of real property.

2. Practical Use

A lawyer will examine an abstract and then render an opinion as to the validity of title.

3. Liability

a. Lawyers are liable for results of their negligence but not for the negligence of the abstract company.

b. Abstract companies are liable for their negligence to the purchaser of the real property even though they never had actual dealings.

c. Third parties relying on an abstract may recover from a negligent abstract company.

C. Title Insurance

1. Definition

Insurance against any loss incurred by a buyer due to an imperfect title.

2. The insurance usually encompasses any covenant extended to a future buyer by the insured.

3. Coverage

May be limited by the policy but usually extends to all risks that would be disclosed by a competent examination of the public records.

4. Defects that an insurer will *not* be liable for if not discovered:

a. Public records relied upon that were incorrect.

b. Encroachment of the insured onto adjacent property and encroachment of adjacent property owners onto the insured's property.

c. Violation of setback rules.

d. Adverse possession claims.

    e. Taxes, assessments and other charges that do not appear as liens.

5. Negligence

The insurer will be held liable for a negligent search even though the purchaser's loss would have been excluded from the policy.

CASE CLIPS

I. Common Law

Stone v. French (1887)

Facts: Although recorded, French's deed was void for lack of delivery. Stone, who was unaware that the deed was void, bought the land from French.
Issue: Does the recording of a void deed validate a transfer of an interest in land represented by the void deed?
Rule: A void deed, although recorded, is still void and a purchaser of realty from a person holding under a void recorded deed, although in fact a bona fide purchaser, cannot obtain a good or valid title.

Earle v. Fiske (1870)

Facts: In 1864, Fiske conveyed her interest in land by deed, which was not recorded until 1867. In 1865, she died and her sole heir by a valid and recorded deed conveyed the same real property to Earle, who lacked actual notice of the prior conveyance.
Issue: Does an unrecorded deed void a subsequent transaction involving the same land when the purchaser lacks actual knowledge of the prior conveyance?
Rule: Although an unrecorded deed is binding upon the grantor, his heirs and devisees, and all persons having actual notice of it, it is not valid and effectual as against any other persons.

II. Recording Statutes

Mugaas v. Smith (1949)

Facts: Mugaas (plaintiff) gained title to land by adverse possession but did not record his title. Smith (defendant), without actual notice of the Mugaas's claim, purchased property by legal description and with record title that included Mugaas's land.
Issues: Under a recording statute, does a conveyance of the record title to a bona fide purchaser extinguish a title acquired by adverse possession?
Rule: Because recording statutes relate exclusively to written titles, a conveyance of the record title to a bona fide purchaser will not extinguish a title acquired by adverse possession.

Mortensen v. Lingo (1951)

Facts: In 1941 McCain conveyed realty to Anglin. The deed was recorded but not indexed. In 1947, McCain conveyed the same land to Lingo (defendant), who conveyed by warranty deed to Mortensen (plaintiff). Mortensen brought suit against Lingo, contending that Anglin threatened to evict him.

Issue: Is a deed properly recorded in the office of the district where the land lies, but not indexed, constructive notice against subsequent innocent purchasers for value?

Rule: The recording of a deed without indexing is insufficient to give constructive notice to a bona fide purchaser for value.

Simmons v. Stum (1882)

Facts: To secure a debt, in 1874 Stum (plaintiff) took a mortgage from McHenry. McHenry conveyed the property to Cochran and Strong, both of whom had actual notice of the mortgage. Stum recorded his mortgage on March 15, 1879. Two days earlier, Cochran and Strong conveyed to the defendant, who did not claim actual notice of the mortgage.

Issue: Under a race-notice statute, must a bona fide purchaser for value without notice prove in a title conflict that she recorded her deed before the recordation of an outstanding mortgage in order to defeat the mortgagee's interest in the land?

Rule: Under a notice-race statute, a bona fide purchaser for value without notice must prove that in a title conflict her deed was recorded before an outstanding mortgage in order to defeat the mortgagee's interest in the land.

Eastwood v. Shedd (1968)

Facts: On December 2, 1958, a donor deeded land to Eastwood (defendant) who recorded on October 16, 1964. On October 15, 1963, the donor conveyed the same land to the plaintiff, who recorded on October 23, 1963. Shedd (plaintiff) had no actual notice of the prior conveyance. Both conveyances were gifts, Shedd brought suit to quiet title.

Issue: In a jurisdiction with a race-notice statute, must a subsequent grantee purchase the conveyed property to be protected by the recording statute?

Rule: Because the legislature deleted the language "purchaser" from the statute, the statute grants priority to a second grantee only if he takes the instrument without notice of the prior conveyance and has his instrument recorded ahead of the prior instrument. (This case represents a minority view.)

Gabel v. Drewrys Limited, U.S.A., Inc. (1953)

Facts: Drewrys Limited, Inc. (plaintiff) received from a debtor a note secured by a mortgage. Concurrently, the parties agreed that Drewrys would forbear collection, but no definite time extension was mentioned. The debtor previously mortgaged the property to secure a debt owed to Gabel (defendant) who recorded his mortgage after Drewrys who, without notice of Gabel's mortgage, recorded theirs.

Issue: When a mortgage is given to secure a preexisting debt, is a mortgagee a purchaser for value and thus protected by the recording statute?

Rule: If a mortgage is taken to secure a preexisting debt and no new contemporaneous consideration passes (either of benefit to the mortgagor or detriment to the mortgagee), then the mortgagee does not thereby become a purchaser.

Wineberg v. Moore (1961)

Facts: Barker sold land to Wineberg (plaintiff), who took possession of the land but failed to record his deed. Subsequently, Barker sold the land to the defendant by a deed, which was recorded. Wineberg brought suit to quiet title.

Issue: When land is patently in the possession of one who is not the record owner, are subsequent grantees who fail to inquire bona fide purchasers in good faith?

Rule: The law imputes to a purchaser all information which would be conveyed to him by an actual view of the premises, and if such inspection reveals possession by another, the purchaser has notice of the possessor's interest in the property. In the absence of such inspection, purchasers are on constructive notice as to all facts that such inspection would have revealed, as well as to facts discoverable by inquiry suggested by such inspection.

Kindred v. Crosby (1959)

Facts: In 1938, Kindred (plaintiff) received a quitclaim deed from Crosby. This deed was not recorded until 1957. In 1953, Crosby executed and recorded a joint tenancy deed of the same interest to himself and his wife. Crosby died soon thereafter. Crosby's wife (defendant) now claims to own an undivided half-interest in the property.

Issue: Does a subsequent purchaser have the burden of proving that he was a subsequent purchaser for valuable consideration without notice?

Rule: One claiming to be a bona fide purchaser as against the holder of a prior unrecorded conveyance or encumbrance has the burden of showing by evidence apart from the deed that he paid a valuable consideration for the conveyance.

Sabo v. Horvath (1976)

Facts: Before title passed to him, Lowery conveyed real estate to Horvath by deed recorded in January 1970. In August 1973, Lowery received title to the land, and in October 1973, he deeded the land to Sabo by a deed recorded in December 1973. After Lowery obtained title, Horvath did not rerecord his deed. Horvath brought suit to quiet title.

Issue: Where a grantor-grantee index is used, does a wild deed (i.e., a deed recorded outside the chain of title) give constructive notice to subsequent innocent purchasers for value?

Rule: Only instruments that are recorded after the grantor obtains title, and therefore are within the chain of title, serve as constructive notice to a subsequent purchaser who duly records.

In Re Walker (1986)

Facts: Debtor filed for bankruptcy in 1985. Mortgagor sold the property to Purchaser in February 1986. Purchaser failed to record the trustee's deed until March 24, 1986. Debtor recorded a notice of the filing of the bankruptcy on March 13, 1986.

Issue: Does a debtor's recording of a bankruptcy filing defeat the rights of a third-party bona fide purchaser with a prior unrecorded deed?

Rule: Under a "race-notice" recording statute, a debtor who recorded notice of the bankruptcy before the purchaser's recordation of the trustee's deed may void the prior purchase.

III. Mechanics of Recording/IV. Interests to Be Recorded

Patterson v. Bryant (1939)

Facts: Bryant (defendant) sold the same timber rights twice, first to the plaintiff who failed to promptly record title, and secondly to another who promptly recorded and thereby defeated title pursuant to the recording statute.

Issue: Is a grantee's failure to promptly record title a defense in a restitutionary action against a grantor?

Rule: Recording statutes only protect subsequent purchasers. Hence, a grantee's failure to promptly record his title is not a defense in a restitutionary action against a grantor who subsequently sells the same property again.

Osin v. Johnson (1957)

Facts: Osin (plaintiff) sold land to Johnson (defendant), who promised but fraudulently failed to properly record a trust on the land. The defendant then executed deeds of trust to others on the land, which were recorded. Still other creditors obtained judgment liens on the land. Osin brought suit for equitable relief.

Issue: Does a constructive trust that is incapable of being recorded have a superior claim to subsequent lienholders who rely on the record title when deciding to extend credit?

Rule: A constructive trust only has priority over lienholders who did not rely on the record title when deciding to extend credit.

Leach v. Gunnarson (1980)

Facts: A property owner gave Leach (defendant) an irrevocable license to construct a well on a piece of land. The well was an obvious physical structure. The owner subsequently conveyed with a covenant against encumbrances to Gunnarson (plaintiff) who was, at the time of the conveyance, cognizant of the well. The original owner told Gunnarson that the defendant had no enforceable right to use the well. Leach filed suit seeking a decree that they owned an easement for drawing water from the well.

Issue: Is an irrevocable license to use a spring on a grantee's land a breach of the grantor's covenant against encumbrances if the license is an open, notorious, and visible physical encumbrance?

Rule: Absent an express exclusion in a deed, a grantor's covenant against encumbrances in a warranty deed protects the grantee against all encumbrances existing at the time of delivery of the deed even if the grantee knew about the encumbrance.

Presbytery of Southeast Iowa v. Harris (1975)

Facts: The Marketable Title Act required holders of future interests in land to file notice of their interest in the land within one year of its enactment. If notice was not filed, their interest was to expire 21 years after the Act's creation. In 1898, Elizabeth Cline conveyed land to the Presbytery of Southeast Iowa (plaintiff) by a deed, which required that a church building be built on the land within two years of the conveyance, or the premises would revert to the grantor. When the plaintiff brought suit to quiet title, the heirs of Mrs. Cline challenged the statute.

Issue: Does a statute requiring future interest holders to record their interest before they may enforce their rights violate substantive Due Process?

Rule: When an act does not abolish or alter any vested right but simply modifies the procedure for effectuation of the remedy by conditionally limiting the time for enforcement of the right, it does not bar a claimant's remedy before he has had an opportunity to assert it, and is therefore not violative of substantive Due Process.

Messersmith v. Smith (1953)

Facts: Messersmith (plaintiff) acquired title to real estate by quitclaim deed, but did not immediately record the deed. In the interim, the same vendor deeded mineral rights in the property to defendant Smith. Smith in turn deeded his interest to defendant Seale. This deed was recorded before plaintiff's deed, but the act of recording was not in conformity with statutory law. A second statute voided unrecorded deeds if an innocent purchaser for value recorded his deed first. Messersmith brought suit to quiet title.

Issue: Must a deed be acknowledged in conformity with the applicable statute to be validly recorded?

Rule: To be validly recorded, an instrument conveying title of real estate must conform to the statutory requirements of the recording laws.

Luthi v. Evans (1978)

Facts: Owens assigned to the defendant "all interest of whatsoever nature in . . . all Oil and Gas leases in Coffey County, Kansas." Owens later assigned to Burris, a third party, a lease known as the Kufahl lease, which was in Coffey County. Defendant claimed superior title.

Issue: Does the recording of a deed that intends to convey real property and describes that property as "all the grantor's property in a certain county" constitute constructive notice to subsequent purchasers?

Rule: The recording of a deed that purports to convey real property and describes that property as "all the grantor's property in a certain county" is not effective as to subsequent purchasers unless they have actual notice of the transfer.

Orr v. Byers (1988)

Facts: Orr received a judgment from Elliott, whose name was misspelled by Orr's attorney and thus, was recorded erroneously. When Elliott later obtained title to property, it became subject to Orr's judgment lien. Elliott then sold the property to Byers, who conducted a title search which failed to disclose the abstract of judgment. This action sought to obtain judicial foreclosure of Orr's judgment lien.

Issue: Does the doctrine of *idem sonans*, that although a person's name has been written inaccurately, the identity of such person will be presumed from the similarity of the sounds between the correct pronunciation and the pronunciation as written, apply to title records as based upon constructive notice?

Rule: In undertaking a title search, where a name is misspelled, an individual does not have constructive notice the error in an abstract of judgment under the doctrine of *idem sonans*, as it would place an undue burden on the transfer of property.

V. Notice

Alexander v. Andrews (1951)

Facts: Alexander sought to obtain quiet title of land conveyed to him and sought to remove a deed, for the same property, held by Andrews.
Issue: When two individuals hold title to the same deed, what are the rights of a subsequent holder of the deed?
Rule: Where there are two holders of a deed, and the subsequent holder of the deed is without notice of the former deed and pays a valuable consideration for its conveyance, relief may be granted only if the transaction is complete on actual or constructive notice, i.e., if full consideration is paid before the former deed is recorded.

VI. The Torrens System

Abrahamson v. Sundman (1928)

Facts: The holder of a good title duly registered under the Torrens Act conveyed the land by warranty deed to S.J. Johnson, who conveyed to Abrahamson (plaintiff). Neither Johnson's nor Abrahamson's deed was noted on the certificate of title. Abrahamson took possession. Glass-Melone Lumber Co., Johnson's lienholder, subsequently foreclosed on the land, obtained a new certificate by court decree, and conveyed the land to the defendant. Abrahamson was not made a party to the lien foreclosure proceeding. Abrahamson claimed superior title.
Issue: Under the Torrens System, can the lienholder who forecloses terminate all rights and interests to the property by limiting the parties to the suit to those whose names appear on the certificate or some memorial or notation thereon?
Rule: Under the Torrens Act, one who takes possession without any notation or memorial of his right on the registration certificate is charged with knowledge that his possession is not notice of any interest in him, and that such possession will never ripen into a right adverse to the registered owner.

Killam v. March (1944)

Facts: Killam (plaintiff) purchased land registered under the Torrens System. Before the purchase, the plaintiff had actual notice that the defendant had a valid, although unregistered, 25-year lease granting the defendant use of the plaintiff's driveway from the plaintiff's predecessor in interest.

Issue: Does one purchasing registered land take the land subject to an unregistered lease if he has actual notice of the lease?

Rule: A subsequent purchaser of registered land does not have an indefeasible title as against interests of which he had actual notice.

United States v. Ryan (1954)

Facts: The United States (plaintiff) had a tax lien against property in Minnesota, a Torrens System state. Pursuant to state law, all lienholders had to obtain a court decree directing the registrar to issue a new certificate of title noting the lien on the property. The plaintiff, who did not comply with the state law, contended that Ryan (defendant) purchased the land subject to the lien.

Issue: In a state using the Torrens System, may the U.S. perfect a lien against real estate even though it does not comply with state registration law?

Rule: The U.S. government is not exempt from state laws affecting title to property. Failure to have a certificate of title altered to reflect a tax lien as required by state law will mean that a tax lien is not perfected.

VII. Title Assurance

First American Title Insurance Co., Inc. v. First Title Service Co. of the Florida Keys, Inc. (1984)

Facts: First Title Service Company (defendant) prepared abstracts for the sellers of two lots. First American Title Insurance Company (plaintiff), relying on the abstracts, issued owners' and mortgagees' title insurance policies to the buyers of the two lots and their lender. The abstracts failed to note the existence of a recorded judgment against a former owner of the lots, and that the holder of the judgment had made demand on the new owners for payment of the judgment. The plaintiff brought suit as a third-party beneficiary of the contract of employment of the abstractor.

Issue: Can an abstracting company be held liable to a landowner's title insurance company for abstracts that were negligently prepared for the landowner?

Rule: If the abstractor knew or reasonably should have known that his customer requested an abstract for purposes of inducing third parties to rely on it as evidence of title, the abstractor is liable to those third parties for damages caused by the negligent production of the abstract.

White v. Western Title Insurance Co. (1985)

Facts: The Whites (plaintiffs) purchased title reports and insurance from the defendant. The defendant failed to mention a water easement on the property either in the reports or the insurance policy. The easement was a matter of public record. The contract between the plaintiffs and the defendant excluded coverage for claims or title to water rights. When the Whites discovered the existence of the easement, they sued for damages.

Issue: Where a title insurance policy excepts from coverage certain easements, is the insurer nonetheless liable in negligence for failure to advise an insured of recorded easements in the subject land?

Rule: A title insurer has a duty to list all matters of public record regarding the subject property, and failure to so do is prima facie negligence from which the insurer cannot, by contract, exculpate itself.

Transamerica Title Insurance Co. v. Johnson (1985)

Facts: Transamerica Title Insurance Co. (plaintiff) issued title insurance to Johnson's vendees. Johnson (defendant) paid the premiums. Johnson contractually agreed to convey unencumbered land. When it was discovered that the land was encumbered, the plaintiff paid the assessments and sued Johnson under its policy subrogation rights. Johnson argued that the plaintiff, who negligently failed to disclose the encumbrances, was liable to the defendant for its failure to disclose, Johnson knew of the encumbrances long before the plaintiff became involved in the transaction.

Issue: Is a title insurance company liable to noninsured vendors who pay title insurance premiums for failure to reveal encumbrances on the land?

Rule: A title insurance company is liable to noninsureds for failure to disclose encumbrances only when the noninsured shows foreseeable reliance on the title search.

Shada v. Title & Trust Co. of Florida (1984)

Facts: Shada (plaintiff), in purchasing property, relied on the defendant title insurers' commitments instead of obtaining an attorney's opinion of title. When the plaintiff later discovered that the title was clouded, the defendant refused to indemnify the plaintiff.

Issue: Does failure to cure or schedule title defects constitute a breach of contract or actionable negligence?

Rule: A title insurer has a duty to exercise reasonable care when it issues a title binder or commitment and its failure to do so may subject it to liability in either contract or tort.

Hebb v. Severson (1948)

Facts: The plaintiffs, a title insurance company, contracted to sell to Severson (defendant), a piece of property, and to insure the title by warranty deed. Severson subsequently discovered the seller's title to be encumbered and unmarketable. The title insurance company sued for specific performance.

Issue: Must a purchaser accept the unmarketable title of a seller when an insurer will nevertheless insure the title?

Rule: A purchaser is not compelled to accept an unmarketable title when an insurance company is willing to insure the title.

Metropolitan Life Insurance Co. v. Union Trust Co. (1940)

Facts: Union Trust (defendant) excepted encumbrances, liens, and charges existing at or before the policy date from its title insurance policy issued to the plaintiff. Before the policy date, local public improvements were completed and paid for by bond. The bond assessment did not take effect until after the policy date.

Issue: Is a title insurer liable for the cost of the assessments to the insured when assessment for local public improvements is levied after a title insurance policy is executed, but improvements are completed before the policy date?

Rule: Title insurance is not prospective in its operation and has no relation to an assessment that is not an actual, fully matured lien at the time the policy is executed.

Harper v. Paradise (1974)

Facts: In 1922, Susan Harper deeded a farm to Maude Harper as life tenant with remainder to her children. The deed was subsequently lost, and later discovered and recorded in 1957. In 1928, Susan's heirs conveyed to Maude by quitclaim their interest in the land with an instrument that referred to the lost deed. In 1933 Maude conveyed the farm to Thornton. The plaintiff Paradise, who had an unbroken chain of title from Thornton, recorded a deed for the property in 1955. Maude Harper's children claim title under the first (lost) deed as remaindermen.

Issue: Does a purchaser have a duty to ascertain the contents of an earlier deed referred to in his chain of title and the interests conveyed therein?

Rule: A deed in the chain of title that is discovered and contains references to other deeds constitutes constructive notice of those other deeds. Any investigator who discovers such deed is obligated to inquire into those deeds to which it refers.

Walker Rogge, Inc. v. Chelsea Title and Guaranty Co. (1989)

Facts: Walker Rogge purchased real estate without conducting a land survey. It instituted this action upon discovering that it had acquired only 12.5 acres of land, 5.5 acres fewer than the 18 acres it paid for and thought it had purchased.

Issue: Is a shortage of acreage an insurable loss under a policy?

Rule: In the absence of a recital of acreage, a title company does not insure the quantity of land. To obtain coverage, an insured should provide the title company with an acceptable survey that recites the quantity of land described or obtain an express guarantee that the quantity of land purchased is insured in the policy.

Lick Mill Creek Apartments v. Chicago Title Ins. Co. (1991)

Facts: Plaintiffs took out three policies from Chicago Title Insurance for three parcels of land. At the time that the policies were issued, however, various agencies had records disclosing the presence of hazardous substances on the lots. Plaintiffs incurred costs for removal and cleanup of the hazardous substances and then sought indemnity from the defendants.

Issue: Where a clause in an insurance policy protects against unmarketability of title, can an insured claim coverage for a property's physical condition?

Rule: Where a clause insures against the unmarketability of title, and the market value of land is not encompassed by the definition of marketable title, a plaintiff cannot claim coverage for the physical condition of his land.

Radovanov v. Land Title Co. of America (1989)

Facts: The Radovanovs brought suit to recover damages incurred by the failure of defendant to disclose the existence of a pending lawsuit concerning building code violations that were supposed to have been resolved by the time of closing, or to obtain the provision of coverage for financial loss that resulted from the lawsuit.

Issue: Does an exclusion clause protect an insurance title company from covering claims that affect the marketability of land when the litigation causing the damages was pending before the title commitment and policy were issued?

Rule: Where a title insurance company contracts to provide coverage for damages resulting from unmarketability of title, an obligation is created to provide coverage for damages rendering a title unmarketable even if they were caused by pending lawsuits which predate the issuance of title commitment and policy.